Postcolonialism

For Jijo and Abena

though for myself alone
I would not be ambitious in my wish
To wish myself much better, yet for you,
I would be trebled twenty times myself.

William Shakespeare

Postcolonialism

Theory, Practice or Process?

Ato Quayson

Polity Press

First published in 2000 by Polity Press in association with Blackwell Publishers Ltd

Reprinted 2005

Polity Press
65 Bridge Street
Cambridge CB2 1UR, UK

Polity Press
350 Main Street
Malden, MA 02148, USA

ISBN 0-7456-1712-3
ISBN 0-7456-1713-1 (pbk)

A catalogue record for this book is available from the British Library and has been applied for from the Library of Congress.

Typeset in 10.5 on 12 pt Times
by Best-set Typesetter Ltd, Hong Kong
Printed and bound in Great Britain by Marston Book Services Limited, Oxford

This book is printed on acid-free paper.

For further information on Polity, visit our website: www.polity.co.uk

Contents

Acknowledgements

The Akans have it that when someone is hacking a path through the bush, they constantly have to turn to those behind them to know whether the path is straight or crooked. It is with this sense of the importance of others in helping to direct the progress of this book that I wish to thank the following: Samuel Amanor Dseagu, an old teacher of mine at Legon for giving me advice on the English novel which I only belatedly recognized as being significant for my ongoing work; Robert Young, Alison Donnell and Raji Sunder Rajan for great help and advice whilst we hammered out postcolonial ideas at several meetings of the editorial board of *Interventions*; James Shapiro, Drew Milne, Ruth Morse, Tim Cribb, Robert Young (again), Tejumola Olaniyan, Kweku Larbi-Korang, John Lonsdale, Joanna Lewis, Tony Hopkins, Simon Jarvis, Neil Lazarus, Julian Murphet, Julia Swindells and Benita Parry for reading and commenting on drafts of various chapters of the book; Nigel Leask for many hours of conversation on numerous topics from Romanticism and empire to contemporary politics; Gavin Williams, Nana Wilson-Tagoe, Susheila Nasta and Kenneth King for the opportunity to share some of my observations at seminars at Oxford, SOAS, Edinburgh and York; participants in the Race, Class and Identity Seminars at Cambridge for providing a perfect forum for debating issues around postcolonialism; Julia Swindells and Brian Ridgers for generously making available to me bibliographic data they had compiled on eighteenth- and nineteenth-century English theatre traditions; Jim Murray, Ralph Dumain, Brett St Louis, Nicole King and Wendy Lee for the stimulating environment they provided me with on my research visit to New York and to the C. L. R. James Institute in the summer of 1997; Cheryl-Ann Michael, Sanjay Reddy, Sunil Agnani, Conrad James and Alissa Trotz for providing companionship and constant discussions of unfolding perspectives over the past seven or so years; the Pembroke College

(Cambridge) Fellows' Research Fund for timely assistance in procuring some books that helped to clarify the arguments of the last chapter; Sarah Irons, librarian of the African Studies Centre at Cambridge, for help in digging out books at very short notice; also Casey Synge, the administrator, for her efficiency and sharp eye for detail. I also want to extend warm thanks to Shafiur Rahman, Alice Owens, Justin Willis, Alicia Fentiman, Mark Chingono and Stephanie Newell, all of the ASC, for regularly sharing their work with me on different aspects of African and postcolonial studies. Shafiur and Alice have to be thanked a second time for their long-suffering patience in answering my many confused questions on computers and IT; Valentina Napolitano for support in a period of great personal and intellectual turmoil; and, finally, Mawuena, Jijo and Abena for being there and for reminding me about the complicated entanglements of life.

Introduction:
Postcolonializing

And Polo said: 'The inferno of the living is not something that will be; if there is one, it is what we form by being together. There are two ways to escape suffering it. The first is easy for many: accept the inferno and become such a part of it that you can no longer see it. The second is risky and demands constant vigilance and apprehension: seek and learn to recognize who and what, in the midst of the inferno, are not inferno, then make them endure, give them space.'

Italo Calvino, *Invisible Cities*

Genealogies and Inflections

Let me start at a basic level and attempt to trace the genealogies of the term 'postcolonialism' and its cognates and the uses to which they have been put. Like postmodernism and poststructuralism, postcolonialism designates critical practice that is highly eclectic and difficult to define. The term itself is sometimes written with a hyphen (post-colonial/post-colonialism) and sometimes is left unhyphenated (postcolonial/postcolonialism), with the two forms being used to designate the same areas of interest by different critics. The hyphenated version was first used by political scientists and economists to denote the period after colonialism, but from about the late seventies it was turned into a more wide-ranging culturalist analysis in the hands of literary critics and others (see Ashcroft, Griffiths and Tiffin, 1998: 186–92). I prefer the unhyphenated version, mainly to distinguish it from its more chronologically inflected progenitor and also to indicate a tendency, marked mainly in conference papers and book titles, that seems to be gaining dominance in the field.

A possible working definition for postcolonialism is that it involves a studied engagement with the experience of colonialism and its past and present effects, both at the local level of ex-colonial societies as well as at the level of more general global developments thought to be the after-effects of empire. Postcolonialism often also involves the discussion of experiences of various kinds, such as those of slavery, migration, suppression and resistance, difference, race, gender, place, and the responses to the discourses of imperial Europe such as history, philosophy, anthropology and linguistics (see Ashcroft, Griffiths and Tiffin, 1995: 1–12). The term is as much about conditions under imperialism and colonialism proper as about conditions coming after the historical end of colonialism. A growing concern among postcolonial critics has also been with racial minorities in the West, embracing native and African Americans in the US, British Asians and African Caribbeans in the UK and Aborigines in Australia among others. Because of these features, postcolonialism allows for a wide range of applications, designating a constant interplay and slippage between the sense of a historical transition, a sociocultural location and an epochal configuration (Slemon, 1994). However the term is construed, a central underlying assumption is that a focus on the discourse and ideology of colonialism is as important as one on the material effects of subjugation under colonialism and after.

Postcolonialism has also involved attempts to formulate non-Western modes of discourse as a viable means of challenging the West. Though this idea is first forcefully spelt out in Ashcroft, Griffiths and Tiffin's *The Empire Writes Back* (1989), it is Bart Moore-Gilbert who provides a more interesting genealogy of this tendency, particularly as he is able to show how some key concepts in contemporary postcolonial theorizing were worked out in the writing and criticism of authors such as Chinua Achebe, Kamau Brathwaite, Wilson Harris, Wole Soyinka and others from the 1960s onwards (Moore-Gilbert, 1997: 152–84). Another inspiration behind postcolonial studies is the theories and processes of decolonization of the 1950s and 1960s. The effects of the discourse of decolonization on later configurations of postcolonial theory are traceable to the writings of Albert Memmi, Frantz Fanon, Kwame Nkrumah, Amilcar Cabral and Mahatma Gandhi, among many others. The centrality of these thinkers and political activists in addition to the increasing attention being paid in postcolonial studies to the work of the Trinidadian Marxist C. L. R. James ensures that the link between the era of decolonization and

contemporary postcolonial concerns is kept alive, even though there
is as yet no steady coherence in how these thinkers have been appropriated.[1] After independence a highly charged and polemical
cadre of writers and critics also emerged in figures like Chinweizu
(*The West and the Rest of Us*, 1975) and Walter Rodney (*How Europe
Underdeveloped Africa*, 1969). On the other hand some critics have
tied the emergence of postcolonial theory more closely to the appearance of Third World intellectuals in the Western academy. The various
concerns of postcolonial theory are then thought to be those of
nomadic Third World intellectuals whose ideas do not always coin-
cide with the concerns of those constituencies in the Third World
proper. This is a theme developed polemically especially by Dirlik
(1994; see also Hall, 1996 and Rajan, 1997).

It should be acknowledged, however, that whatever the developments were that led to the formation of the field of postcolonial
studies, it has to be seen more in terms of a long *process* rather than
a series of events, with the central impulses of this process coming
from a variety of sources, sometimes outside any concern with colonialism. These may be traced in a variety of directions such as in the
changing face of global politics with the emergence of newly independent states; in the wide-ranging re-evaluation begun in the 1980s
of the exclusionary forms of Western reason and in the perception of
their complicity with imperial expansion and colonialist rule;[2] in the
debates that raged about empiricism and culturalism in the social
sciences from the 1960s;[3] in the challenges to dominant discourses
of representation from feminist, gay, lesbian and ethnic studies in the
1970s and 1980s;[4] and, finally, in what has been described as the 'linguistic turn' in contemporary theory largely attributable to Ferdinand
de Saussure at the start of the twentieth century and elaborated and
taken in different directions by Lévi-Strauss, Barthes, Derrida, Lacan
and others.[5]

Ever since Robert Young's excellent introduction to postcolonial
theory in *White Mythologies* (1990) postcolonialism has been linked
predominantly to Edward Said, Gayatri Spivak and Homi Bhabha,
and it is Said's work that helps bring together the various interwoven
strands of the field. Born in Palestine but brought up in Egypt and
the United States, he represents to a certain degree the hybrid nature
of the postcolonial critic that serves to feed postcolonialism itself. It
is generally agreed that the single most influential work to define the
purview of the term was Said's *Orientalism*, published in 1978.
Drawing on the work of Michel Foucault, Said's main thesis was that

the Western academic discipline of Orientalism was a means
by which the Orient was produced as a figment of the Western
imagination for consumption in the West, and also as a means of subserving imperial domination. The criticisms against *Orientalism* range
from pointing out that Said did not fully acknowledge his debt to
Marxism, that he created an overly monolithic image of both the West
and the Orient, and that he ignored the mutually entangled factors
of the resistance and complicity of the colonized peoples with the
forms of knowledge that were being produced concerning them.
Said's *Orientalism* marked a move from the description of the material factors governing empire (economic, bureaucratic) to an analysis of representation and the links these have with the ultimate
constitution of imperial and colonial power. But in doing this it was
both extending the practices of imperial historiography as well as
instituting a crucial paradigm shift. Non-economic considerations
were discussed quite prominently before the publication of *Orientalism*, especially in relation to missiology, education and the ideology of race, but Said's distinctive contribution was to have made a
clear connection between knowledge and power, thereby inserting a
poststructuralist problematic into the study of colonialism that was
becoming central to concerns being developed in other discourses.
With the texts that followed, such as *The World, the Text, and the Critic*
(1983), *Culture and Imperialism* (1993) and *Covering Islam: How the
Media and the Experts Determine how we see the Rest of the World*
(1997), he further elaborated the central ideas in *Orientalism* in
various political, sociological and literary/cultural directions. Said's
work helped establish what was later to be known as colonial discourse analysis, a vastly expanding field of research that analyses a
broad range of disciplines from economics right through to mathematics. We shall turn more fully to colonial discourse analysis and
Said's place in it in chapter 2.

Said's work has impacted so widely on both individuals and disciplines that it can even be seen as having taken its place as a 'cultural'
product, spawning not just interdisciplinary appropriations but also
a familiar usage in popular culture. The words 'orientalism' and
'orientalist' are now standard ways of designating any attitude of
knowing the Third World which is actually meant to serve Western
interests. These terms are often carelessly used as forms of censure
especially in academic contexts concerned with otherness. But consider a half-serious, half-humorous appropriation of Said's theory of
Orientalism posted on several Internet listserves in the winter of
1995/6:

CLINTON DEPLOYS VOWELS TO BOSNIA
CITIES OF SJLBVDNZV, GRZNY TO BE FIRST RECIPIENTS

Before an emergency joint session of Congress yesterday, President Clinton announced US plans to deploy over 75,000 vowels to the war-torn region of Bosnia. The deployment, the largest of its kind in American history, will provide the region with the critically needed letters A, E, I, O and U, and is hoped to render countless Bosnian names more pronounceable. 'For six years, we have stood by while names like Ygrjvslhv and Tzlynhr and Glrm have been horribly butchered by millions around the world,' Clinton said. 'Today, the United States must finally stand up and say "Enough." It is time the people of Bosnia finally had some vowels in their incomprehensible words. The US is proud to lead the crusade in this noble endeavour.' The deployment, dubbed Operation Vowel Storm by the State Department, is set for early next week, with the Adriatic port cities of Sjlbvdnzv and Grzny slated to be the first recipients. Two C-130 transport planes, each carrying over 500 24-count boxes of 'E's,' will fly from Andrews Air Force Base across the Atlantic and airdrop the letters over the cities. Citizens of Grzny and Sjlbvdnzv eagerly await the arrival of the vowels. 'My God, I do not think we can last another day,' Trszg Grzdnjkln, 44, said. 'I have six children and none of them has a name that is understandable to me or to anyone else. Mr. Clinton, please send my poor, wretched family just one E. Please.' Said Sjlbvdnzv resident Grg Hmphrs, 67: 'With just a few key letters, I could be George Humphries. This is my dream.' The airdrop represents the largest deployment of any letter to a foreign country since 1984. During the summer of that year, the US shipped 92,000 consonants to Ethiopia, providing cities like Ouaouoaua, Eaoiiuae, and Aao with vital, life-giving supplies of L's, S's and T's. The consonant-relief effort failed, however, when vast quantities of the letters were intercepted and hoarded by violent, gun-toting warlords.[6]

The link between knowledge (the distribution of vowels) and power (Operation Vowel Storm) seems to have been inspired directly by Said's work. Significantly also, the implied rationalization provided by the recipients of the 'humanitarian' assistance goes to show how the imperial logic tries to find justification from the ranks of the 'other'; the Bosnian Grg Hmphrs wants to become George Humphries, presumably fulfilling an 'American dream'. The passage also attempts to expose the ideological drive behind humanitarian assistance. To justify itself, any propaganda supporting such assistance has to historicize itself especially in relation to the 'barbarian' impulses of some of the darker places in the world, figured here in the hijacking of the earlier consonant-relief effort to Ethiopia by 'gun-toting warlords'. This history is essentially a form of imperial history, and is one in which the propaganda machine feels compelled to manufacture the acquiescence of the beneficiaries of this thinly veiled form of American imperialism in their own subjugation. All this is conveyed in a language that mimes the propagandist discourse of Western journalism in times of such crises. By rendering these manoeuvres in such a half-serious light, however, the passage succeeds in exposing the ideologically laden interests of such assistance whilst at the same unravelling its central logic by the sheer force of the ridiculousness of its expression.

What is most fascinating about this piece is its nonchalant combination of discourse analysis *à la* Said with what we could take as a parodying of 'serious' media and diplomatic discourse. This puts us in mind of Bakhtin's notion of the carnivalesque, in which the dominant categories by which reality is perceived are taken as the focal point for subversion by a demotic laughter. But more to the point is that the piece helps put into perspective what I shall argue has to be one of the central tenets of any project of postcolonialism. This, to echo Slavoj Žižek (1991) is the ability to 'look awry' at the phenomenon under analysis, but in such a way as to disclose its complex expression of the interrelationship between postcolonialism and other domains of contemporary experience. To do this whilst keeping in focus the complexities of contemporary existence, however, postcolonialism has to take account of two seemingly contradictory emphases. On the one hand, there is the pull towards discourse analysis. On the other, there is the need to attend to the material, social and economic factors within which any discourse is framed, and which, given the fraught nature of the postcolonial referent in the real world, always require urgent attention. To grasp the mutual interdependency and antagonism of these two pulls, let us turn to a contrasting pair of models of engaging with social reality, starting with Italo Calvino's *Invisible Cities*.

Postcolonialism as Process

A striking feature of Italo Calvino's *Invisible Cities*, from which the epigraph to this chapter is taken, is the constant oscillation between sensory description and enigmatic promise. The descriptions that Marco Polo gives to Kublai Khan of the numerous cities he visits constantly hover between a series of tactile, visual, and auditory evocations that give the cities a powerful and almost sensuous quality. At the same time this sensuous quality is repeatedly undermined by being relayed in a language which is designed to baffle more than to enlighten, or to enlighten only by way of proliferating a bewildering set of paradoxes and contradictions. It is the language of parable and allegory, but transposed onto a thoroughly secular sensibility, that tries to make sense of the world by instituting a form of alienation from it. And though there is a frequent promise of the disclosure of the rationale for this parabolic form, it is only at the very end that the true motivation for the form is made apparent. It is, in one reading of the epigraph to this chapter, a means by which to encourage a 'constant vigilance and apprehension' about the things of positive value in the world that need to be identified and helped to flourish. But the vigilance is necessary precisely because the discovery of what is of value is ultimately an immanent rather than a transcendent process. All of us, good or bad, are as much caught up in the inferno; indeed, in the idiom of postmodernism, it is a factor of the very language by which we declaim our innocence or our freedom. The parabolic form of *Invisible Cities* grounds this problematic firmly in a sense of space and time, by enforcing the feeling, routed through Kublai Khan's bewildered responses, that the cities he hears about are as much those of the mind as of reality, and that reality is dialectically constituted between the real and the imagined.

It could well be argued by someone sceptical of this kind of interpretation that the struggle for the discovery of the things of value in the world is best pursued through an idiom of material rather than imagistic struggle, that the density of reality which postmodernist writing such as Calvino's suggests is nothing but the ruse of advanced capitalism to force a retreat from reality into a theatre of the mind's phantasms. To such a sceptic the brutal facts of existence in the world today are increasingly those of injustice, inequality and exploitation, all of which cannot be tackled except through a rigorous and direct engagement with the capitalist social and economic forces that have shaped and continue to shape the world. And this, the sceptic might add, should be the supreme task of any responsible postcolonial critique.

I raise these two contrasting positions to point out one of the problems I recognized in writing this book. At every turn in the field of postcolonial studies there seems to be an undecidability between an activist engagement with contradictions in the real world and a more distanced participation via analyses of texts, images and discourses. Furthermore, there is a constant reluctance to take radical ethical standpoints. This is perhaps due to a widespread postmodernist nervousness about predictable accusations of totalization or the explicit or implicit disregard for the perspective of others. Thus postcolonial theory and criticism have increasingly become riven by a contradiction: the social referents in the postcolonial world call for urgent and clear solutions, but because speaking positions in a postmodernist world are thought to be always already immanently contaminated by being part of a compromised world, postcolonial critics often resort to a sophisticated form of rhetoric whose main aim seems to be to rivet attention permanently on the warps and loops of discourse. In a sense, these sets of contradictory impulses are not mutually exclusive. It is very stimulating to be able to attend to both discourse and materiality, to speak and yet to indicate an existential tentativeness in whatever has been spoken. It is, however, in the strategic configuration of these contrasting modes of analysis and understanding that the problem for responsible postcolonial studies makes itself felt. What should the ultimate objectives of a responsible postcolonial discourse be? What, for instance, is the use of a discursive analysis of the language of the IMF's economic recovery packages when this does not address the terrible economic and social disjunctures produced on developing countries by the application of IMF policies and those of other international monetary agencies? Or what is the use of talking heatedly about the language of multiculturalism and racism if this does not signal ways in which to address the blatant inequalities of the dynamics of the global labour market, the gradual disappearance of middle-level opportunities for migrant labour, and the sense that this produces that the labour market is increasingly being shaped for them like an hourglass rather than a pyramid, with greater obstacles in the way of gaining higher administrative and managerial positons?[7] What, to follow E. San Juan's anguished queries to postcolonial critics, is the use of undermining discourses of power when 'we never encounter any specific scenario of injustice, domination, or actual resistance from which we may gather intimations of the passage through the postcolonial ordeal' (San Juan, 1998: 2)? What, to put it bluntly and even simplistically, do academic postcolonial studies contribute to the *experience* of postcolonialism in the world today?

   This book is devoted to answering these and many other similar questions. I propose to do this through a mixture of careful contextualization of key debates in the field with explicit assertions of directions in which these debates could be fruitfully taken in order that postcolonial studies might be moved into a more lively engagement with specific problems in the real world. Consequently, the book is envisaged as a cross between a critical introduction to postcolonial studies and an agenda-setting work. If I take this rather slippery and controversial track, I do it not in the hope of claiming a monopoly over current wisdom in the field, but rather in the expectation that a debate can be generated about enabling models of postcolonial critiques, ones that should be useful not only for academics but for activists, non-governmental organizations and all those concerned with the problems of a world shaped by colonialism and empire. I draw inspiration for this kind of approach from Terry Eagleton's inimitable *Literary Theory: An Introduction*, where he notes that 'since there is in my opinion no "neutral", value-free way of presenting it' he will argue throughout a particular *case* in the hope that it adds to his book's interest (1996: ix). Being Marxist, he argues eloquently in chapter after chapter for a perception of the social and political function of literary criticism in the full implications of its role in class struggle. Eagleton sets up the case via what he describes as a popular style, a style that relates the most complicated philosophical ideas in literary theory to mundane everyday reality. It is, to my mind, the work of a writer committed to establishing the philosophical principles behind literary criticism in tandem with a rigorous engagement with problems in the real world. The two areas of the equation make themselves felt at various levels of Eagleton's text, making it a real masterpiece of *engaged* academic discourse without sacrificing its rigour.

Without attempting to directly parallel Eagleton's achievement, I would for my part also like to argue for a particular case. Put formulaically, it is that postcolonialism has to be perceived as a *process of postcolonializing*. To understand this process, it is necessary to disentangle the term 'postcolonial' from its implicit dimension of chronological supersession, that aspect of its prefix which suggests that the colonial stage has been surpassed and left behind. It is important to highlight instead a notion of the term as a process of coming-into-being and of struggle *against* colonialism and its after-effects. In this respect the prefix would be fused with the sense invoked by 'anti'. Peter Childs and Patrick Williams gesture towards this sense of postcolonialism in their recent critical introduction to the field when they write: 'We could, however, argue for postcolonialism as an anticipatory discourse, recognizing that the condition which it names does not yet exist, but working nevertheless to bring that about' (Childs and Williams, 1997: 7). This fascinating viewpoint, arrived at after a discussion of problems with the term, is however never allowed to inform the structure of their work. There is no attempt by them to define what it might mean to think of postcolonialism as an anticipatory discourse, and their observation remains at the level of tantalizing definition.

To think of postcolonialism as a process of postcolonializing would allow us first of all to affirm what many critics have already noted about the problematics of any precise dating of the postcolonial phenomenon (see, for instance Shohat, 1993; McClintock, 1994; Mishra and Hodge, 1991). The resistance against colonialism during the high point of the colonial era was itself part of the process of the postcolonial since it is this long process that arguably led to the decolonization struggles that served to topple the institutional structures of colonialism. But colonial resistance cannot be seen as homogeneous across time. There were numerous inflections which themselves have had to be accounted for both in space and time. As we noted earlier, the term is currently used to designate a variety of quite disparate discourses. One of the less satisfactory elements of its use is in the implicit equation of different forms of postcolonialism (in the chronological sense). Brazil can be said to be postcolonial but in a very different way from that of Nigeria; and Japan has postcolonial elements which are quite different from any perceivable postcolonial realities in Britain or France. The implicit elision of radical differences under the rubric of the postcolonial may however be interpreted in a more positive light. In my view, what has served to energize the term is the desire to perceive cognate or parallel realities within seemingly disparate contexts and to draw on a notion of the centrality of colonialism for understanding the formation of the contemporary world.

In a sense we are obliged to react with some scepticism to Ashcroft, Griffiths and Tiffin in *The Empire Writes Back* when they argue that the term can be extended to cover any place that has ever had an experience of colonialism, including the United States, simply because it was once colonized by the British. This is too simplistically chronological and quite ignores America's own imperial status in the world today. However, looked at another way, the social and cultural configurations of the United States today do bear comparison with situations in real postcolonial societies. Think of the mutually illuminating comparisons that can be established between sociocultural conditions affecting both majority and minority populations in the United States, South Africa, Australia and Canada. Or consider what insightful work could be achieved if the condition of micro-minority 'tribals' in India were compared not to their aborigine counterparts in Australia, but to the conditions of native

Americans in the United States itself, or to that of other micro-minorities in Africa and Latin America. Factors like multiculturalism, ethnicity, diaspora and transnationalism as they apply in the West can only be fully understood if seen in tandem with the realities of struggles in real postcolonial societies, precisely because some of these factors are actually the effects of global population and cultural flows after colonialism. The argument, then, is to see postcolonialism not merely as a chronological marker but as an epistemological one; it focalizes a constellation of issues integral to the formation of a global order after empire. And this, it has to be noted, is not merely a sensibility reserved for the formerly colonized. As will be shown in chapters 5 and 6 and at various other points in the course of this book, there is an inextricable relationship of epistemological dependency between the West and its formerly colonized Others that makes itself felt at the most subtle points in the West's perception of itself. Postcolonialism has to be seen as a viable way not just of interpreting events and phenomena that pertain directly to the 'postcolonial' parts of the world, but, more extensively, as a means by which to understand a world thoroughly shaped at various interconnecting levels by what, following Leela Gandhi, we might describe as 'the inheritance of the colonial aftermath' (1998: x). The process of post-colonializing, then, would mean the critical process by which to relate modern-day phenomena to their explicit, implicit or even potential relations to this fraught heritage.

If, as we noted earlier, it is the case that postcolonialism bears a resemblance to an ensemble of discourses emerging from the late 1960s that all aimed at challenging central Western philosophical ideas, then it is important to bear in view the overlapping nature of problems that postcolonialism and these other discourses attend to. This recognition brings with it the need to forge wide-ranging links between postcolonialism and these other discourses in a larger project of addressing injustice and inequality anywhere they may show themselves in the world. In other words, to my mind a 'postcolonial' project has to be alert to imbalances and injustices wherever these may be found in East and West, North and South, and whether they are to do with racism or child pornography, women's labour or micro-minority rights, political authoritarianism or the degradation of the environment. The point is that postcolonialism must be seen as a project to correct imbalances in the world, and not merely to do with specific 'postcolonial' constituencies. The justification for postcolonialism and postcolonializing must not be sought solely in the explicit forms of injustice that are often thought to be visited upon the hapless and the oppressed in and from formerly colonized societies. To take just one example among many others that come to mind, it is the necessity for exploring the varied and *intersubjective* relations that arise out of responses to crime from both crime fighters and racial minority victims that call for a more sensitive version of postcolonialism. Thus, for example, until racial minorities in the West feel it reasonable not to reach automatically for explanations of racism when they are confronted by police brutality, but are able to identify the failures of the police as systemic failures, postcolonialism will be relevant to understanding the conditions of such minorities. Even the reflex actions that the oppressed see as relevant to negotiating their condition of being oppressed should be subject to investigation. On the other hand, until police forces everywhere feel it unhelpful to turn to stereotypes (whether of racial, class, gender or other provenance) as a primary means of responding to crime, a wide-ranging postcolnializing discourse sensitive to injustice everywhere will always be useful.

Something of such an overlapping project will be explored in chapter 5, focusing on postmodernism and postcolonialism. However, in the wider context of the case being made in this book, I would like to clarify a number of methodological procedures that help define what the precise means of conjoining postcolonialism with other progressive discourses might be. The first point I wish to make, somewhat polemically, is that unlike most postcolonial commentators I do not think it is possible or desirable completely to debunk Western-inspired theories. The case has often been made, and sometimes rightly, that postcolonial theory is oversaturated with ideas and concepts from Western thought (especially French high theory), and that this defines it as the West's re-colonizing of the thought patterns of others. I think this line of reasoning is quite spurious and does not stand up to any close examination. It is undeniably the case, of course, that discourses manufactured in the West have regularly been used as tools for marginalizing others. And yet at the same time these same tools, in the hands of both Westerners and others have also been used in serious struggles for liberation, not just from the West but from constrictive patterns of thought. There is no question, for instance, of the efficacy of Marxism in providing progressive ways by which non-Western nations have grasped the processes of globalization and helping them to position themselves strategically with regard to these processes. In fact, there is no question that, without Marxism, some of the best ideas that postcolonialism has produced, from Fanon through to C. L. R. James and Gayatri Spivak, would have been much less interesting than they have turned out to be. And this despite the fact that they have all reconstellated Marxism in various ways. Like them, I wish to clearly align my own project of postcolonializing to Marxism as a broad discourse of continuing significance to understanding the condition of the world today. Marxism provides a particular constellation of concepts to account for facts in the sociocultural configurations of the postcolonial world order, with plenty of room for internal development and debate. This becomes evident even when we take a glance at the work of Marxists such as Aijaz Ahmad, Arif Dirlik and E. San Juan, who are completely sceptical about the objectives of postcolonial studies and have not hesitated to say so quite strongly. In my view what they achieve in doing this is to force a more rigorous engagement of postcolonialism with the legacy of Marxism in ways that are highly illuminating and fruitful for future work. Thus Ahmad's debate with Jameson about Third World literature and 'national allegory' provides a very useful way of framing debates about the relationship between postcolonial literature and politics (Ahmad, 1992: 95–122). And in San Juan's *Beyond Postcolonial Theory*, we see the coupling of a classical Marxist analysis of commodity fetishism with an astounding focus on tropes and textuality which would be the envy of dyed-in-the-wool poststructuralists. To take just one example from this fascinating work: after a discussion of a picture in *Newsweek* of 11 May 1992 used to frame the Los Angeles riots, he concludes with all the standard formulas of deconstruction:

> This formation is situated within an interdiscourse, a structured totality of various discursive formations, that is inscribed within a complex of ideological formations – in particular, the jurisprudence of individual rights (right of ownership, self defense, etc.), its grammar and lexicon. It is this ideological formation, whose function in generating the image-text is 'forgotten' by the reader or viewer, that needs to be recalled by the analyst. This is part of the reification process: by repressing or occluding the process whereby a discursive sequence linked to its ideological context is produced, the photograph creates the illusion that the subject precedes discourse and lies at the origin of meaning. Whereas it is the subject that is 'always already produced' by that which is 'preconstructed' (the forgotten sociohistorical determinants of Los Angeles' political economy, Korean immigration and global politics of the Pacific Rim, deindustrialization and its impact on African Americans, demographics of the Latino community, and so on) in the sequence.
>
> (San Juan, 1998: 132)

Admittedly his concerns are with how the 'image-text' he is discussing parallels the workings of wage form and the processes of
reification, but his idiom is thoroughly informed by both Marxist
discourse and those normally associated with postmodernists and
poststructuralists. The heavy saturation of psychoanlytical language
and the detailing of the chimerical centrality of the individual in
determining the social significance of the image-text are all traceable
to poststructuralist theories from Lacan, Derrida and Foucault as well
as Althusser. The point I want to make here is that from the point of
view of postcolonialism, there is no need to perceive Marxist and
poststructuralist discourses as mutually incompatible. The crucial
index for evaluating any particular configuration of ideas is whether
it provides ways of getting out of confusing habits of thought.
This is not to call for the gratuitous simplification of complicated
concepts. But it does mean that complexity serves an end other
than itself. Something of the merits of Marxist and poststructuralist
ideas informing postcolonial theory will be touched on in chapter 1,
where the discussion is centred on the relative strengths and
weaknesses of various configurations of interdisciplinarity in postcolonial studies.

That said, however, it is also important to take note of some of
the limitations of classical Marxism and the tragic obsfuscations
that Marxist rhetoric has produced in the postcolonial world. At one
level, the limitations of Marxism might be thought to lie in an overly
deterministic mode of analysis that views transformations strictly
in terms of the move from economic feudalism to capitalism. Ali
Rattansi puts the problem succintly in a recent review of the state of
postcolonial studies:

> Now, it is quite clear that viewed in *this* light, the imperial and colo-
> nial projects cannot be reductively analysed simply by reference to a
> decisive economic logic which narrates the formation of colonial cul-
> tures and politics as just another version of the familiar transition from
> feudalism to capitalism, except this time imposed from above by the
> metropolitan powers, and in which class formation, class interests and
> class conflicts remain the main engines of transformation. A properly
> 'postcolonialist' analysis, on the contrary, requires the acknowledge-
> ment of a set of processes in which cultural formation is dispersed
> along a number of axes of potentially *commensurate* importance –
> class, certainly, but also sexuality and gender, racism, familial relations,
> religious discourses, conceptions of childhood and child-bearing prac-
> tices, and requiring therefore also an understanding of underlying
> processes of psychic development and 'deformation'. The societies that

came into being through colonial encounters can no longer be discursively appropriated through a grid which reads them as re-runs of an oft-told linear narrative of the transition from one mode of production to another, whether in Marxist or Weberian vocabulary, and certainly not as an equally straightforward story of 'modernization' as functionalist, mostly American sociology would have it.

(Rattansi, 1997: 482–3)

I will return a little later to what Rattansi points to here about dispersed axes of commensurate importance. For now, suffice it to note with him that any unifocal interpretation that foregrounds a single modality (the economic) is bound to be inadequate to the analysis of postcolonial realities.

The other level at which Marxism has had unhappy consequences has to do with the pragmatic choices made after decolonization about which sectors of the newly freed societies would bear the mantle of social transformation. Marxism did provide a prime anti-hegemonic discourse by which to contest the West. However, within the dynamics of certain newly independent states that opted to turn to Marxism to mobilize the ordinary people for the business of building viable post-independence societies, the rhetoric hardly ever matched with the practice, partly because this derivative ideology had to take shape within contexts that were riddled with their exarcerbated cultural contradictions. Thus, in practice, the mobilization of the masses actually entailed the concentration of power in the hands of a radical elite who turned out not to be very different from the Western bourgeoisie they so vehemently criticized. In the hands of certain postcolonial nationalists, this mass mobilization impulse was conjoined to the consolidation of a cult of the leader which was projected as the primary embodiment of the welfare and aspirations of the people. In Africa in particular, the cult of the leader as culture hero entailed a series of tragic distortions in social arrangements, with an entire cohort of sycophants growing around the nationalist leader to prop up his self-image and to project him (they were invariably men) as the representative of the nation. The odd thing, which will have to be analysed on its own terms by future researchers, is that this process of culture heroism, though propped up in socialist African countries by an explicitly Marxist rhetoric, could also be interpreted as the reproduction of tendencies which even non-Marxist and quite capitalist-oriented leaders were also espousing. Thus we are forced to note the strange fact that from different parts of the continent, both Kwame Nkrumah of Ghana and Kamuzu Banda of Malawi carefully cultivated a personality cult from different ideological positions, the first being ardently Marxist and the other an unflinching capitalist. These could be multiplied across the entire gamut of post-colonial African politics. This had to do with local cultural factors as well as straightforward economic and political ones; the key distinction to be drawn between the two types of politicians of post-independence Africa was that the cult of the culture hero in the hands of the Marxists was part and parcel of the effort towards collective mobilization.

Explaining this phenomenon in a complex model that pays attention to the cultural factors underpinning this peculiar process calls for a more culturally sensitive form of Marxism. If we focus on the phenomenon in terms of what Raymond Williams discusses in *Marxism and Literature* (1977) as the dialectic of 'residuality' and 'emergence', a different perspective is brought to bear. In Williams's discussions of the terms, residuality is not to be taken as synonymous with the 'dying', or the emergent with the 'being born' in social phenomena. On the contrary the two terms are to be seen in the light of historical configurations that gradually bring new values to the foreground whilst marginalizing others. But the relation between the two is not to be seen as a cycle, but rather as a dialectical mutation in which a variety of 'old' and 'new' ideas are sometimes reconstellated to produce new perspectives and realities. This has a recognizable Kuhnian sense to it, but with the difference that, unlike what happens in the scientific community where entire laboratory apparatuses are eventually changed to accommodate the paradigm shift in response to new scientific problematics, in the sense elaborated by Williams the old and the new often persist side by side in language, in theoretical discourse and even in the disposition of the various social attitudes. Thus, going back to the parallel impulses behind the personality cults created by Nkrumah and Banda, what we discern is a relationship of residuality and emergence between a traditional notion of culture heroism and more modern ideas of state formation, but in such a way that the traditional notions of culture heroism are conflated with the imagining of the modern state itself. This process of conflation is itself partly governed by the degree to which the modern nation-state is conceived of as a market, a field where political ideologies compete as in a marketplace, sometimes skewed via a state-dominated monopoly capitalism manifested within a totalitarian structure or, at other times, mediated through a 'free market' system of democracy. More importantly, the transfer of quasitraditional ideas of culture heroism into a postcolonial political domain is part of a desire to define modes of authenticity which have as much to do with traditional values as with understandings of modern ideas about social agency. And often the tropes from the traditional domain mutate across a range of seemingly disparate fields from literature right through to politics. We shall have more to say on these matters of culture heroism and African politics and literature in chapter 3.

Arjun Appadurai provides a way by which to extend Williams's ideas about residuality and emergence from a nuanced and multi-focused Marxian perspective. In a fascinating essay entitled 'Disjuncture and Difference in the Global Cultural Economy' (1994) he elaborates a set of terms – ethnoscape, technoscape, financescape, mediascape and ideoscape – by which to try and grasp the varying degrees of overlap between ethnicity, technology, financial flows, media images and ideology in a world where primordial mechanisms of affiliation such as the family and the nation are constantly being constituted in relation to a global arena of perception. The key thing to remember is the degree to which, with vastly expanding possibilities of association and communication across cultures and spaces, the individual becomes the locus of a perspectival set of landscapes, landscapes 'eventually navigated by agents who both experience and constitute larger formations, in part by their own sense of what these landscapes offer' (p. 329). Thus, as he points out, '[T]he imagination has become an organized field of social practices, a form of work (both in the sense of labor and of culturally organized practice) and a form of negotiation between sites of agency ('individuals') and globally defined fields of possibility' (p. 327). Critically, the way in which to understand these complex interactions between the global and the local is not to see them in mechanical terms of hard-and-fast polarities, but rather in terms of overlaps. And even the overlaps themselves have to be complexly grasped:

> What I would like to propose is that we begin to think of the configuration of cultural forms in today's world as fundamentally fractal, that is, as possessing no Euclidean boundaries, structures or regularities. Second, I would suggest that these cultural forms, which we should strive to represent as fully fractal, are also overlapping, in ways that have been discussed only in pure mathematics (in set theory for example) and in biology (in the language of polythetic classifications). Thus we need to combine a fractal metaphor for the shape of cultures (in the plural) with a polythetic account of their overlaps and resemblances.
>
> (p. 337)

What Appadurai seeks to achieve in his evocation of the dual metaphors of the fractal and the polythetic (the one pointing to the irregular boundaries between cultural phenomena and the other hinting at simultaneous disjunctures and overlaps) is to pinpoint the extent to which each phenomenon under discussion is consistently affected by the changes occurring within the other phenomena with which it is placed in a dialectical relationship. Thus, as he points out, ethnic identities in the Third World are constantly being shaped by the images of identity shifts brought back by Third World migrants to the West, and, concomitantly, by the degrees of changes in the political ideologies governing the nation-state, the financial shifts in global markets and so forth. Appadurai sets up a useful means by which to analyse various configurations of residuality and emergence across a range of phenomena (ethnic, technological etc.) at the same time. For him, the imperative for this is drawn from a Marxian concern with dialectical relationships, perceived as ramifying at various interconnected levels from the very basic one of subjectivity right up to the global flows of capitalism. Appadurai's formulations allow us to recall Rattansi's point about 'dispersed axes of commensurate importance'. It is a purview germane to our concerns in this book.

If as postcolonial critics we have come to question classical Marxism's overly determinsitic grid as somehow disenabling a naunced understanding of the multiple commensurate axes of significance governing postcolonial phenomena, we have to concede at the same time that no serious Marxian analysis can do without the concept of the dialectic. It is the rigorous practice of dialectical thinking that makes Marxism so appealing, whether from an entirely economistic perspective or from a more multi-focused standpoint. The elaboration of dialectical thinking perfected by countless people inspired by Marx makes it evident that any dialectic we might try to adduce for the phenomena we engage with has to attend to the epistemological verities that govern the phenomena under analysis. Thus, the analysis of labour relations would have to find a different epistemological ground from the analysis of an unequal relation between men and women or between traditionalism and modernity. The postcolonializing critical method being elaborated here then requires not just an engagement with the major narratives of bondage and freedom in all the empirical detail that can be marshalled, but also with the cognitive poetics of colonial and 'postcolonial' culture itself.[8]

At this stage, it is useful to clarify a number of methodological procedures which will recur regularly in this book. These are (1) the isolation of individual phenomena for a detailed examination of their internal dynamics; (2) the related move of linking the phenomena, no matter how apparently discrete, to wider social, political and cultural flows germane to a postcolonial analysis; (3) the careful elaboration of the various levels of connection within and between phenomena as part of a process of transition in which disjunctures and continuities are marked as defining the historical realities of change. Concepts such as 'configuration', 'conjuncture', 'intersection' and 'overlap' will constantly be invoked in these pages to try to centre upon a continuing dialectical analysis of transition in the postcolonial world. These three methodological procedures will be combined with an attempt to look beyond the determinants of the phenomena under consideration to spell out directions for future thinking, research, and action. It is always important, following Marxian practice, to try to discern the features of each moment which harbour signs of the future and to commit oneself rigorously to highlighting these signs. It is this imperative that would enable Calvino's idealism in *Invisible Cities* to be conjoined to a reconstellated but clear-eyed Marxian analysis. Arguably, of course, any such future is only putative and hoped for. Though I pursue wide-ranging interdisciplinary references, because of my own background as a literary and cultural critic, my Marxian analyses will have a culturalist tinge to them. But at all times cultural products will be read as a means of grasping social, political and economic realities. This will be done not in order to prioritize the literary, but to indicate ways in which, starting from the literary, its boundaries can be broken to bring it into a dialectical relationship to other discourses and socio-cultural phenomena.

Plan of the Book

Each chapter of the book is devoted to a specific set of issues. Some of these will readily be recognized by scholars working in the field, others will not. As a rule, I eschew the habit of extended discussions of the work of Said, Spivak and Bhabha, except in so far as they help me to focus on the set of issues I am concerned with. Consequently, the book will not be an elaborate introduction to the work of these three. For such a critical introduction it is best to turn to the excellent books by Robert Young (1990), Bart Moore-Gilbert

(1997), Peter Childs and Patrick Williams (1997), Ania Loomba (1998) and Leela Gandhi (1998). At various points I refer readers to parts of these texts for further discussions about the 'big three' of postcolonial theory.

On the whole the book is pitched at the level of the advanced undergraduate student or the graduate student who has some familiarity with key debates in the field. However, I always try to give brief and accessible synopses of various concepts and debates in order to guide the way for people completely new to the field. It is my hope that specialists and teachers may also find something useful in these pages for teaching the subject. Ultimately, it is my wish that activists and workers 'in the field' (NGOs, women's agencies etc.) will find some illumination in these pages for thinking about their own work.

The chapters are perfectly intelligible as individual pieces, but there is a line of argument running through about the practice of postcolonializing that will not be evident until at least two chapters are read. With this in mind, I have roughly paired the chapters and introduced a number of overlaps and echoes to reinforce the arguments. Thus, chapter 1, though concerned mainly with postcolonialism and interdisciplinarity, ends with a discussion of Homi Bhabha's colonial discourse analysis and prepares for the discussion of the appropriations of history for present-day uses in chapter 2. Chapter 3 on postcolonialism as a politically symbolic act is partly devoted to elaborating the trope of culture heroism in African literature and politics. Chapter 4, on postcolonialism, feminism and the contradictory orders of marriage in modernity, contrasts with the previous chapter not only in its focus on women but in shifting from the analysis of the public political sphere to an examination of the conditions governing women's positions in nuclear conjugal relationships and the conflicts that are set up between these and extended family systems. Chapter 5, 'Postcolonialism and Postmodernism', is about the overlap between the two 'posts' and how we might conceive of reading postmodernism *as* postcolonialism and vice versa. This chapter also contains a discussion of diaspora and multiculturalism and prepares the way for chapter 6, which though ostensibly about Shakespeare and the canon is actually an attempt to read *The Merchant of Venice* as a secular parable by which to resituate issues of race, class, multiculturalism and diaspora in the West today. In each chapter I take up issues that I believe to be pertinent not just for the field of postcolonial studies, but for defining an attitude to the world from the informing purview of concepts and ideas elaborated from within postcolonial studies.

At all times my aim is to give a steady methodological grounding to what I describe as postcolonializing discourse. Though deriving essentially from current debates in the field of postcolonial theory, postcolonializing is meant to suggest creative ways of viewing a variety of cultural, political and social realities both in the West and elsewhere via a postcolonial prism of interpretation. As I will try to demonstrate in the chapters that follow, there are a variety of ways in which this can be pursued. Sometimes this involves a rigorous analysis of existing theoretical paradigms to show up potential aporias that require explanation for a progressive leap to be achieved (chapter 1). In other instances it requires a careful analysis of the disjunctive conditions governing particular subject positions in the modern world (chapter 4). At other times it calls for an interdisciplinary reading of different discursive phenomena such as the cultural and the political via a commonly shared if conflictual ground of imaginative understanding (chapters 3 and 5). At others the emphasis is on looking awry at specific canonical texts, and pressing to find creative ways beyond the dominant modalities of analysing particular social issues (chapter 6). This attitude of looking beyond may be thought by some to be deluded, especially in a postmodernist world where any assumed position is always open to accusations of conscious or unconscious exclusion of other positions. But it seems to me that the habit of optimism is a necessary one, especially in the field of postcolonial studies, which in direct and indirect ways purports to be concerned with problems in real-life situations.

The sense I have of postcolonialism (and postcolonializing) being a continuing project and an anticipatory discourse is captured in part by an apocryphal anecdote about Gandhi's response to a question on modern civilization:

> Journalistic legend has it that once, when in England, Gandhi was asked the following question by an earnest young reporter: 'Mr Gandhi, what do you think of modern civilisation?' In some versions of the story Gandhi laughed heartily, in others, became very serious, before replying: 'I think it would be a good idea.'
>
> (Gandhi, 1998: 22)

Both of Gandhi's reported responses capture the sense that he perceives 'civilization' as an enigma. But his laughter in the first may be linked directly to his answer in the second. If he laughs at this question, it is perhaps to suggest that the question is preposterous in assuming that civilization has already been achieved. The second response then shows up the contradiction by suggesting that, in his view, civilization would be a good idea if it could be hoped and worked for. That, in a sense, is the view I take of postcolonialism. I also think it 'would be a good idea'.

1
Instrumental and Synoptic Dimensions of Interdisciplinarity

Interdisciplinarity is a buzzword in academic circles. A sample of titles from the 1997 MLA meeting in Toronto easily attests to this:

- 'The Architextual Structures of James Joyce's Ulysses: Colonised Homes, Hegemonic Schools, National Taverns, and Heterotopic Brothels' – Robert Bennett, University of California, Santa Barbara.
- 'Post-World War II Westerns, the Cold War, and the Politics of Asexual Reproduction' – Stanley J. Corkin, University of Cincinnati.
- 'Metaphors We Live by in Academe; or, Why is a University Like a Box of Chocolates?' – Evelyn J. Hinz, University of Manitoba.
- 'Reconstructing the Bible Belt or, How I Stopped Worrying and Learned to Love Rednecks' – Harriet Andreadis, Texas A&M University, from the programme *Voices in the Wilderness: Teaching Queer Studies in Strange Places.*
- 'Limit of the Nation: The Hymen and Griselda's Smock' – Kathleen Davis, Bucknell University, from a programme on *Chaucer's Queer Nation.*

The tendency amongst critics to conjure wilfully strange titles for essays and papers may be intended to signal a desire to disrupt normal boundaries in the quest for an interdisciplinary perspective. In addition to these scattered titles, there was also an entire forum on *Interdisciplinarity: Art, Literature, and Music*, chaired by the 1997 president, Herbert Linden, and with contributions from Edward Said on *Così fan tutte* and *Fidelio*, and from Linda and Michael Hutcheon arguing how the figure of Salome appeared in Wilde's writing, Moreau's painting and Strauss's opera.[1]

In its wide usage, the term 'interdisciplinary' itself proliferates a number of confusions which turn on the issue of what exactly such work in the arts and sciences entails. In her book entitled *Interdisciplinarity: History, Theory, Practice* (1990), Julie Thompson Klein provides a useful means of thinking round this problem. For her, interdisciplinarity designates a whole range of activities such as:

1   engaging in collaborative problem-solving (e.g. when a health-care team of university researchers, clinicians, corporate officials, agency staff and citizens come together to tackle a particular health issue);

2   bridge-building between disciplines that remain discrete (e.g. in the C. P. Snow and F. R. Leavis 'two cultures' controversy and the subsequent attempts to make connections between science and literature);

3   developing synthetic theories that operate across disciplines (e.g. Marxism, structuralism, post-structuralism, general systems theory);

4   constituting new fields from overlapping areas of separate disciplines (e.g. psycholinguistics, criminology, Egyptology, urban studies among others);

5   borrowing metaphors and procedures across disciplines (such as is the case when literary scholars turn to the history of science for an examination of the persistence and mutations of scientific ideas).

The first category can be designated as instrumental interdisciplinarity, designed to intervene directly in specific problems in the world outside academia, while the others (2–4), which collate ideas either for the constitution of different disciplines or in the application of a synthetic theory across disciplines may be described as 'synoptic interdisciplinarity', which is when a synoptic overview leads to the collocation of ideas, methods and procedures either for the constitution of different disciplines as in 4 or in the application of a synthetic theory across disciplines as in 3. The peculiarity of category 5 is that it appears to be predominantly geared towards addressing concerns in its 'home' discipline even when borrowing liberally from others. This is perhaps most acute when a particular interdisciplinary model is thought to be new and untested. In relation to the history of science, for instance, this was the case with books such as Gillian Beer's *Darwin's Plots* (1983), which attempted to trace Darwin's ideas of evolution within literary texts of the nineteenth century. Originally thought of as a work on literature, it is now regarded as a major contribution to the history of science. So too the theories of Bakhtin, Foucault or Edward Said are not reducible to any single discipline and have impacted on many fields. Some literary writers such as Jorge Luis Borges are notorious for being interdisciplinary in their creative writing, and the same boundary transgressions define books as different as C. L. R. James's *Beyond a Boundary* (1963) (cricket history, biography, cultural studies, epic), Amitav Ghosh's *In an Antique Land* (1992) (ethnography, biography, travel narrative, Egyptology and epic) and Charles Van Onselen's monumental *The Seed is Mine: The Life of Kas Maine* (1996) (history, political science, anthropology, biography, epic).[2] There are, however, wide areas of overlap between the instrumental and the synoptic definitions for the obvious reason that both require a constant structure of dialogue between the disciplines that have been brought together (see Klein, 1990: 41–4, 55–73). Furthermore, both types of interdisciplinarity are ultimately concerned with intervening in the constitution of reality, even when this proceeds from a primary engagement with texts and concepts rather than with the real world itself.

But how are these considerations of instrumental and synoptic interdisciplinarity to be applied to postcolonial studies? And how are we to trace the implications of the interdisciplinary paradigm for a field whose social referent is a peculiarly anguished domain that is post*colonial* in the sense of coming problematically after colonialism and *post*colonial in the sense of struggling to transcend the effects of colonialism through an engaged and situated practice? Postcolonial studies have been highly interdisciplinary in the synoptic sense, borrowing freely from a wide range of fields in a desire both to challenge received assumptions as well as to shed light on the configurations of the present and the future. And postcolonial critique has taken on, and has in turn influenced, a range of disciplines. The Igbos have a saying that when the world is dancing, it is impossible to see it in proper perspective by standing still. Postcolonial critique is often thought to have to move across boundaries in order to adduce adequate criteria for understanding what are complex relations secreted both during the processes of colonialism and in its aftermath. At the end of his insightful essay 'Blurred Genres: The Refiguration of Social Thought,' the anthropologist Clifford Geertz

(1983) makes the point that if the 'social technologist notion of what a social scientist is is brought into question' by all the common concern with sense and signification, then 'even more so is the cultural watchdog notion of what a humanist is.' I take Geertz to mean here that the blurring of genres in interdisciplinary studies also produces a blurring of the roles that are normally seen to apply to scientists and cultural critics in their different pursuits. In this respect, his point that clarity is necessary as a means of gauging the forms of action to be derived from interdisciplinarity is one that gains added significance in postcolonial studies, where the social referents press for instrumental solutions and not merely for imaginative recastings of old problems.

This chapter, then, will attempt to look more carefully at the assumptions about interdisciplinarity in postcolonial studies. My main aim will be to explore whether interdsciplinarity offers or forecloses possibilities for defining an engaged attitude to the world of postcolonial relations outside the academy to which postcolonial studies so persistently gesture. As a means to unpacking certain potentialities and weaknesses in postcolonial interdisciplinarity, I want to proceed by a somewhat circuitous set of situated readings of two interdisciplinary theoretical texts. These are: Achille Mbembe's 'Provisional Notes on the African Postcolony' (1992c) and Homi Bhabha's 'Signs Taken for Wonders: Questions of Ambivalence and Authority under a Tree outside Delhi, May 1817' (1994: 102–22), both of which achieve what might be described as the defamiliarization of constituted disciplinary boundaries. However, to focus the discussion more fully, I wish to read them first and foremost as the defamiliarization of the 'everyday'. In the case of Mbembe, it is the everyday of the riddled political existence of people under the domination of tyrannical regimes in postcolonial Africa, while for Bhabha it is in the constitution of an everyday object, the book, which in the context of colonialism becomes a surrogate of much more than itself. To help us in evaluating the strengths and weaknesses of their two different approaches and to evaluate their methodologies for thinking about the implications of interdisciplinarity for postcolonial studies, I will begin with an analysis of two short passages from Theodor Adorno's *Minima Moralia* (1978) where everyday phenomena and concepts are negated in such a way as to open them out to a process of defamiliarization that is ultimately instrumental rather than merely synoptic. All three critics recognize that the multi-textured phenomena of the everyday are not reducible to a single explanatory system, but they each proceed from distinctive epistemological foundations, which we shall highlight in the course of the discussion.

The passages from Adorno manifest his procedure of consolidating aphorisms through an exploration of the quotidian, a practice which, I shall argue, is reproduced in different guises and to different effects in the other texts we will be discussing. Adorno is also particularly fruitful for this exercise because much of his work, and that of the Frankfurt School of which he was a key figure, was written to meet the need for a vigorous analysis of the peculiar development of totally administered societies, the negative potential of which could be seen in the fascism of Nazi Germany, whose true genealogy they traced back to Enlightenment philosophy. The critical theory they espoused preceded the victory of Nazism and had continually addressed the loss of the momentum for a historical socialist project in Germany and Europe since the 1930s; their work also addressed the condition of the working class, thought to have slid into chauvinism, racism and reaction in the period. In this regard Adorno's work becomes pertinent as an example of a conjunctural theory whose referent is a disillusioned social, cultural and political sphere, albeit in a Western Europe arguably very different from anything we might discern in the contemporary postcolonial world. His writing shows the critical value of clarity and rigour in dissociating one's thinking from the constitutive paradigms of established systems of thought. The parallels with postcolonial studies, though seemingly tenuous, are currently being fruitfully explored in the writings of various postcolonial critics.[3]

Adorno and the Negations of the Everyday

It is not possible, in the space available here, to give a full account of the development of Adorno's thought and of the critical theory of the Frankfurt School more generally.[4] I am deliberately going to read the passages from *Minima Moralia* out of context, as it were, and will gradually filter into view those other aspects of Adorno's life and work that help us grasp the nature of his aphoristic thinking. He grants in the preface to the book that 'dialectical theory, abhorring anything isolated, cannot admit aphorisms as such', but then goes on to add that 'if today the subject is vanishing, aphorisms take upon themselves the duty "to consider the evanescent itself as essential"' (p. 16). And this is precisely what he pursues. But in his practice, the 'essential' is not to be confused with the observed phenomenon which often forms the trigger for his reflections. The essential is what makes itself manifest only after the phenomenon is explored in terms of its antinomic structure, something that it does not seem to possess on a cursory encounter.[5]

The passages entitled 'Refuge for the Homeless' (no. 18) and 'Do not Knock' (no. 19) in *Minima Moralia* help in clarifying these issues. 'Refuge for the Homeless' proceeds from an examination of the problematic status of human dwelling: 'Dwelling, in the proper sense, is now impossible.' The first point of disturbance is the fact that somehow each trait of comfort is a musty pact of family interests and paid for 'with a betrayal of knowledge'. Adorno leaves this curious point unclarified. Instead, without allowing us to dwell too long on what this might be, he moves on to suggest that the functional modern habitation (centrally planned housing) is nothing but the intrusion of mechanical reproduction into the sphere of modern living. It is, in his words, much like 'factory sites that have strayed into the consumption sphere'. Not only does this suggest the degree to which a centrally planned economy saturates the everyday; more importantly, it also points to the fact that dwelling is 'devoid of all relation to the occupant'. But Adorno does not stop here. Once again, without allowing us fully to unpack the rich implications of what he has just said, he turns his attention to the organization of sleeping space. He observes that people seem to require beds close to the ground, so close that the threshold between waking and dreaming seems to have been abolished. But this has sinister implications, for, as he reads it, the apparent abolition of the threshold between sleeping and waking is precisely to allow the worker to be on call at any hour 'alert and unconscious at once'. And these disjunctures do not impact solely on the working classes. There is a sense in which even the attempt to 'evade responsibility for one's own residence by moving into a hotel or furnished rooms' is nothing but a rehearsal of 'enforced conditions of emigration'. (Here one senses that his own alienation from his native Germany because of anti-Semitic persecutions is being globalized into an existential condition *par excellence*.)

It is after this that Adorno delivers what I think is the logic of these series of antinomies. He points out that, as always, the people that suffer most are those who have no or little choice. 'They live, if not in slums, in bungalows that by tomorrow may be leaf-huts, trailers, cars, camps, or the open air. The house is past. The bombings of European cities, as well as the labour and concentration camps, merely proceed as executors, with what the immanent development of technology had long decided was to be the fate of houses.' Taking the first part of this statement on its own, it is interesting to note how it maps out an inverse evolution from the urban habitation into the homelessness of the open air. And the stages are significant in themselves. There is a move from stable houses through mobile ones (trailers and cars) and through a more communally shaped form of habitation (camps) to an ill-defined and empty space of the open air. This carefully defines a process from the implicit contours of the nuclear family unit, whether this be in the decrepitude of the slums or in the relative comfort of the bourgeois bungalow, and into a more tragic individuation and aloneness in the homelessness of the open air. This inverse evolutionary topos is not taken to be natural, but is explained as the ultimate logic of the effects of technology. And it is a technology that is transmogrified, as it were, into weapons of mass destruction. In this it has found a means by which to speed up the processes of the inversion of social and personal evolution. It is at this point that we get a grasp of the effect of the Adornian procedures. His focus on an everyday concept in the form of the dwelling is meant, through a series of startling disjunctures, to open out into revealing the abiding logic of late capitalism and its scientific surrogate, technology. The immanent development of technology decides the fate of dwelling, but this is simultaneously paralleled in the campaign of bombings which are themselves a product of that immanent development. Here one senses a recurrent concern of Adorno's which is taken up and elaborated more fully in *Dialectic of Enlightenment* on which he collaborates with Max Horkheimer. In *Dialectic of Enlightenment* there is a larger attack on the rabid universalizing tendency of Enlightenment rationality whose effect was thought by them to be the subsumption of specificities in a totalizing logic that ultimately undergirded totally administered societies. We shall return briefly to Adorno's own attitude to totality later in the course of this discussion.

If we ignore for the time being the formulations for existence he proposes for living under such conditions at the end of the passage and move on to the next meditation in 'Do not Knock', we see the extension of the ideas he has expressed with respect to the distortions imposed by technology on the individual's relationship to objective reality, but this time pursued more intently in terms of the automatization of human gestures within the domestic sphere. Once again Adorno opens by focusing on simple mundane phenomena, this time in the area of how people relate to objects such as doors and the interior of houses. 'Technology is making gestures precise and brutal, and with them men', he writes. 'It expels from movements all hesitation, deliberation, civility.' People seem to have lost the ability to close a door quietly and discreetly. Those of cars and refrigerators are often slammed. Some have the tendency to shut of their own accord. For him, then, the thing to understand is that the seeming freedom that technology makes possible in allowing people not to pay direct attention to their mundane surroundings, marked here by doors, is that by the law of pure functionality 'things assume a form that limits contact with them to a mere operation'. Crucially, however, this is a form of unfreedom, because things now have no surplus, nothing which would survive in the core of experience outside their own functionality. The objective functionality of the everyday, then, is entirely consumed in the moment of action, so as to institute in the sphere of the everyday the mechanical reflexes of capitalist production. As he puts it, the direct and tragic implication of this is that 'The new human type cannot be properly understood without awareness of what he is continuously exposed to from the world of things about him, even in his most secret innervations.' Here Adorno expresses in his peculiar way the inextricable existential relation between human subjectivity and the objects with which it is surrounded on the outside. This brings to mind a common theme of Disney cartoons of the 1920s and 1930s where characters like Donald Duck were constantly confounded by the technology of domestic appliances. As C. L. R. James astutely observes in another context, 'In an age when machinery was crushing man, he [Disney] gave life to machinery; successions of fantastic brooms, teapots, staircases, etc. became alive and tormented innocent bystanders. Donald Duck voiced a perpetual exasperation with the never-ending irritations of modern existence' (1993: 135). The difference here, of course, is that for Adorno the automatization of everyday life is no mere irritation but represents the complete dominance of a technological totality.

It might be stated, and with some justification, that Adorno is ignoring the positive aspects of technology for the sake of making a polemical philosophical point. But that would actually to be missing the point about the ultimate effect of technology when it is aligned to a consolidation of the petrified state systems of capitalism or fascism. Joseph Rothschild argues in his highly illuminating book *Ethnopolitics* that ethnicity takes a political intensity in the modern world precisely because it is sometimes thought to be a bulwark against a subsuming technology:

ethnicity can be honed to that trenchant political cutting edge because it also fulfils other, nonpolitical, prepolitical, or only incipiently political, human needs – emotional, cultural, moral needs. *Among these, ironically, is a need for some psychological distance and social autonomy from the technocratic rationality that fuels the scientific modernization process, catalyzes its contradictions and conflicts, and thereby prompts the politicization of ethnicity.*
(Rothschild, 1981: 5; emphasis added)

Even though, in *Minima Moralia*, the problems Adorno focuses upon seem to pertain mainly to individual subjectivity, he is really interested in the class dimensions of the individual, or the individual as a product of a specific class. The point to note is that Adorno's exposure of the effects of technology on individual subjectivity proceeds from an intense focus on everyday material and cultural phenomena as they manifest class relations so that when he proceeds to read these phenomena as containing a series of negations within their forms, he is ultimately aiming at liberating the phenomena from their dominant ideological and class articulations. An antinomic structure is brought into view. But this antinomic structure is ultimately part and parcel of a larger process of history, here aligned rigorously to the processes of technology under capitalism. When Adorno triggers an aphorism, therefore, the aphorism is launched not as a means of consolidating the clichéd view of existence which it might be thought to attest to in ordinary discourse. On the contrary, it is to help focus intensely on the quotidian in order that, by a process of rapid and frenetic discursive negations, it is defamiliarized in the service of a larger critique of society. In this way a rigorous dialectical reasoning is allied to an exploration of the everyday in such a way that the everyday is simultaneously recognized and apprehended as not at one with itself. It is seen to be disturbed. This applies both in terms of the phenomenon or concept in and of itself and also with regard to how the subject, thinking dialectically, relates to the object. For Adorno, of course, this is a project undergirding his philosophy which he repeats in different forms in his works.

Even though his procedures might seem to make themselves amenable to absorption into a postmodernist antisystemic rationality, it is important to note that Adorno is not necessarily opposed to totality as a concept. Totality and universals are concepts that are central to his procedures. And yet there is always an uneasy dialectical oscillation between totality and particularities, but in such a way as to leave neither the same. There is, as Jameson notes, a relation between a presupposed totality (normally construed as late capitalism or the totally administered society) and the phenomenon (cultural, conceptual or otherwise) in which the focus on the phenomenon, 'unexpectedly, addresses that totality itself and modifies it, not the particular that was its pretext'. This proceeds in direct relation to its inalienable flipside where the thematization of totality 'that drew in this or that isolated historical particular as a mere example or illustration proves itself to have been a subterfuge for the striking modification, the interpretation by way of shock and novelty, of the putative example itself' (Jameson, 1990: 33). In *Minima Moralia*, because of the aphoristic structure of the discourse, there is frequently a priority given to the particular in the scheme of dialectical investigation, but in such a way as to destabilize its priority and to demonstrate its ground of being in the presumed totality. The crucial impact of Adorno's method is the rapid oscillation that he institutes between the two poles of the particular and the totality, but in such a way as to transform 'the putative universal without warning into the particular, unmasking the alleged particular as a universal in true sheep's clothing' (ibid.).

The idea of 'suddenness' that Jameson invokes in explicating Adorno's rhetorical method is particularly interesting because it can also be conjoined to an idea of logical defamiliarization where prior terms are grasped both in their priority and non-priority and destabilized in order that they can be superseded. But the supersession is not a straightforward transcendent supersession. The immanent logic Adorno practises has to be carried along even beyond the boundaries of the first bringing-to-the-foreground of the antinomic structures of the phenomenon. Thus his aphorisitc method, and the antinomic exposure of the phenomenon, is ultimately aligned to a critique of capitalist society. The price of freedom, Adorno would seem to be saying, is eternal vigilance, but it is a vigilance that has to be vigilant even about itself. Furthermore, it is impossible to attain any freedom from unclear thinking without aligning this to a rigorous analysis of the forms of social organization themselves which arguably produce that unclear thinking in the first place. He implies this everywhere in his work, often aphoristically, as in the 'Finale' of *Minima Moralia* when he asserts: 'The only philosophy which can be responsibly practised in face of despair is the attempt to contemplate all things as they would present themselves from the standpoint of redemption.' It is useful to gloss redemption here as social emancipation and to note that in this formulation we get an echo of Marx's view that there is no individual emancipation without that of society. In *Negative Dialectics* this essential methodological premise is glossed more fully:

> The dialectical mediation of the universal and the particular does not allow a theory that opts for the particular to treat the universal overzealously as a soap bubble. If it did that, theory would be incapable of registering the pernicious supremacy of the universal in the current state of things in which the universal would find itself stripped of its bad particularity insofar as individuals were restored to what rightly belonged to them. Nor are on the other hand conceptions of a transcendental subject acceptable, *a subject without society and without those individuals whom for good or ill it integrates.*
>
> (Adorno, 1973: 199–200; emphasis added)

How do we conceptualize instrumental and synoptic interdisciplinarity in the light of Adorno's distinctive methodologies and conceptual presuppositions? Like the other critics we are going to discuss, Adorno considers everyday reality to be too multifarious and complex to be addressed from a single perspective. But his methodology is not interdisciplinary in the straightforward sense of the integration of different disciplines. It is such rather in terms of the manner in which concepts are shifted rapidly between universalized and particularized perspectives in such a way as not to make them amenable to easy appropriation by any single disciplinary perspective without recourse to the simultaneous undoing of such a perspective – what, in another context, might be described as the shift between identity and non-identity in his thought. Crucially, however, and this is particularly true of *Minima Moralia* as we have seen, the exploration of concepts is first of all grounded in everyday reality. Thus it is that Adorno's interdisciplinary methodology is on the one hand synoptic in forcing a multifocal (one is almost tempted to say here dialectically kaleidoscopic) perception, and instrumental in that it forces a perception of abstract concepts in their concrete and particular phenomenal and cultural articulations. Within this perception and by means of the 'suddenness' of his methodological shifts he simultaneously allows an aligment of perception to critique, so that perception is not merely the recognition of a datum of lived experience, but is thoroughly evaluative as well, and not merely evaluative, but evaluative in terms of a more critical engagement with the forms of capitalist social organization.

Achille Mbembe: The Banalities of Power

With Achille Mbembe's essay, 'Provisional Notes on the African Postcolony', some of the themes we discerned in Adorno could be said to come into effect in a fertile interdisciplinary account applied to postcolonial Africa. This is by no means to suggest that Mbembe is influenced by Adorno. Rather, it is to hint at certain similarities that may be adduced in the studied disruption of everydayness. This is done from entirely different parameters in Mbembe's essay. For one thing, unlike Adorno, Mbembe does not proceed aphoristically. Secondly, he is focusing in his essay not so much on individual phenomena and abstract concepts as on the presumed lived experience of ordinary Africans as their subjectivity is enacted in the public sphere. Thirdly, Adorno's notion of what Neil Lazarus (1987: 135) describes as 'the implacable hegemony of the total administration' is here dissolved into a play of the simultaneous assertion and disruption of state authority in the lives of ordinary Africans. Mbembe is also keen to expose the antinomic structure of the everyday, but this time not in the service of a higher critique of political economy but as a means of dissolving the dichotomies between state and civil society in the constitution of political subjectivity.

Mbembe brings an innovative note to the study of postcolonial African politics in his combination of Foucault and Bakhtin, and behind them of Gramsci, Bataille and Habermas. The central focus of the essay is on what he describes as the banality of power. Banality, in his terms, does not mean merely the ways in which bureaucratic formalities are routinized. Rather, he refers directly to those elements of the obscene and the grotesque which in Bakhtin's formulations are located in 'non-official' cultures 'but which in fact are intrinsic to all systems of domination' (1992c: 3). Mbembe also has a wider interest in how such systems are confirmed or deconstructed.

His identification of the obscene and the grotesque as being intrinsic to specific systems of domination might be thought to be exorbitant, but he highlights this collocation to significant effect when he proceeds to trace the various ways in which postcolonial African leaders regularly focus on the hedonistic satiation of the body as a means of foregrounding their power. This satiation of the body is governed by a specific dynamic of public rituals, seen most effectively in 'the rounds of administrative authorities, their discursive performances, ceremonies and banquets, official visits of foreign dignitaries, national holidays, presentations of medals, radio and press communications, tax collection; ordinary interactions between citizens, the police and bureaucracy, school teachers and pupils, husbands and wives, church leaders and their flock'.[6] Critically, however, the body and all its functions also provides metaphors by which the popular imagination attempts to subvert the discourses of power. Here, however, the Gramscian notion of hegemony is being located in a peculiarly new way. Consent and coercion go hand in hand in the totalitarian African postcolony but in such a way as to appear quite unstable and difficult completely to identify solely with the politically dominant authorities. Mbembe grounds this particular instability in two main ways. Firstly, he elaborates the degree to which ordinary people discompose serious political slogans or ideas into metaphors of sexual and bodily functions. This is done by various linguistic devices involving puns, innuendoes and direct misinterpretations of official discourses. He draws examples of this from various African countries but focuses mainly on his own country, Cameroon.

The other way in which he consolidates his notion of the unstable relation between coercion and consent lies at a more complex level of his discussion and marks the specific configuration of his interdisciplinary model. In attempting to describe the special features of the African postcolony, he notes that it is 'a specific system of signs, a particular way of fabricating simulacra or re-forming stereotypes' (p. 3). The influence of poststructuralist theories of the implicit links between images, stereotypes and power is very much in evidence. This would place Mbembe squarely among those who conflate the power-laden effects of real-life events with the devices and import of textuality, rendering the real world graspable in essentially textual terms. But Mbembe adds another dimension to his definition of the African postcolony that serves both to undermine this textualized and sign-oriented definition and to put it on a more secure footing. The African postcolony is not 'just an economy of signs in which power is mirrored and *imagined* self-reflectively'. It is characterized further by 'a distinctive style of political improvisation, by a tendency towards excess and a lack of proportion as well as by a distinctive style in which identities are multiplied, transformed and put into circulation'. 'What distinguishes the postcolony from other regimes of violence and domination', he writes, 'is not only the luxuriousness of style and the down-to-earth realism that characterise its power, or even the fact that it is particularly raw power that it prefers to exercise; peculiar also to the postcolony is the way the relationship between rulers and ruled is forged by means of a specific practice: simulacrum (*le simu-lacre*) (p. 10). And yet, as he states earlier,

> the signs, vocabulary and narratives that it produces are not meant merely to be symbols; they are officially invested with a surplus of meanings which are not negotiable and which one is officially forbidden to depart from or challenge. So as to ensure that no such challenge takes place, the champions of state power invent entire constellations of ideas; they adopt a distinct set of cultural repertoires and powerfully evocative concepts; but they also have resort, if necessary, to the systematic application of pain.
>
> (p. 4)

We see in such a formulation the uneasy recognition that the means of force requisition consent by being kept in the background but with the threat of being used at any time. Thus the seeming symbolic nexus of gaining consent always has a potential for being short-circuited by the intrusion of force. This configuration of items ensures that the means of subversion, of the banalization of the discourses of authority in the hands of the ordinary people, has to take an especially subtle edge. And that is why the discourses of power are subverted from within their own symbols and repertoires and not from without.

In what ways is Mbembe here being interdisciplinary and what is to be extrapolated from his specific interdisciplinary configuration? The first thing to note is that he very carefully avoids centring his discussion solely on either the separate domains of excessive actions of political authorities or on the subtle activities of subversion generated by ordinary people themselves. As he points out early in the essay, he is keen to avoid simple binary categories used in standard interpretations of domination such as resistance v. passivity, autonomy v. subjection and so forth. However, really to sidestep these binarisms, he is also obliged to suggest a certain equivalence in the production and circulation of signs between the political authorities and the ordinary people. This is suggested in his argument that though it is those in power who frequently engender the symbols and rituals of authorization, these are quite quickly wrested from them and rendered 'commonplace' through the active participation of the populace in proliferating and subsequently transforming them. But his production of equivalence can be seen as operating at another level. He also sets up equivalence between the domain of the aesthetic or literary (at least in its broad potential) and the political, and reads both domains through the interdisciplinary theoretical model he has devised by crossing Gramsci, Foucault and Bakhtin. It is not insignificant that the version of his paper published in the United States is entitled 'The Banality of Power and the Aesthetics of Vulgarity in the Postcolony'. It is also significant that he frequently refers to Sony Labou Tansi's novel *La Vie et demie* for examples about the corruption of the political elites which he puts on a par with the examples he has taken from national newspapers in Cameroon.[7] In other words, fiction and fact are put on the same footing in discussing the realities of consent and coercion. They both, as he notes elsewhere, contribute to the 'configuration of reality'. This then allows a simultaneous reading of the literary/aesthetic as political and the political as literary/ aesthetic.

One of Mbembe's key analytic innovations is to have deployed a cultural studies approach for the elaboration of political subjectivity in the African postcolony. In this process he avoids the normal development-orientated discourses of the discipline of political science and encourages an engagement with ideas and realities that can only be fully joined via a comparative and interdisciplinary methodology. Nevertheless, it is precisely in his innovative reformulation of political theory in the light of cultural studies that his interdisciplinary model founders. For, even though his methodology is clearly synoptic and allows the analysis of political issues in interdsciplinary ways that have not seemed obvious before, it is still the case that his method of analysis ends up foreclosing the possibility of imagining a means of transcending the problems of civil society he is laying out. This must not be mistaken as a call for a critic's responsibility to proffer solutions to problems that are clearly intractable, but the case still remains that what he describes sidesteps issues of antagonism and places the discussion of the relation between the dominated and their oppressors in an idiom that ends up obscuring the sources of effective political power and how they might be appropriated for more beneficial material uses. Even though he notes the constant presence of a potential for state violence and gives some examples of contexts in which it comes into effect, the idea of violence and its effect on people's responses to the state is not integrated into the discussion. Subversion is constantly caught in his model within the regulative parameters allowed by the state, but this is not shown by him to be expressed in any form of political struggle or antagonism. As Tejumola Olaniyan rightly points out, the more violent and organized challenge of the dominated is completely peripheralized by Mbembe:

Thus the emphasis should be not only on the stated logics as Mbembe recommends, but also on the equally important logics of how that epistemological field is the site and stake of most often agonistic and unequal struggles among different groups over its definition, structure, and character; how it is perpetually, with varying degrees of failure or success by unsteady alliances, restructured, realigned, re-visioned, consolidated, etc.

(1992: 51)

By rendering a series of equivalences both in terms of the subject matter and in the method by which he describes the postcolony, Mbembe precludes the discussion of the postcolony as a terrain of life-and-death struggles. For standard commentaries on Africa, life-and-death struggle is figured in relation to famines, disease, civil wars and refugees. These make for headline political science studies. Mbembe is obviously not interested in this kind of analysis and it is useful that he helps us focus on seemingly peaceful but persistent modes of subversion. Yet if the insights of his interdisciplinary model are to be further elaborated, they would have to be joined to an analysis of such life-and-death struggles for reconstituting the postcolony. For ordinary Africans, like any other people under totalitarian oppression anywhere, desire alleviation of their suffering and a freedom to fulfil their deepest aspirations. Thus, it is how the special dynamics Mbembe speaks of might lead to positive change that should be of greatest concern. And this should not be as a supplement to his fertile kind of synoptic interdisciplinarity but as an integral part of it.

The second weakness in Mbembe's model is the fact that in discussing African politics in a scatological register, he does not trace the history of how this scatological register was developed and deployed in the West as a stereotype of African politics. It would be interesting to unearth the ways in which images of African politics and politicians in the West have replayed this stereotype, the mode of formation of the scatological register and the changes and intensities it has undergone from the 1960s till now, and how it has played across documentaries, news bulletins and general opinions about Africa beamed across the world. This is critical also because even as Western governments were criticizing the likes of Mobutu, Bokassa, Amin and others, they were keen to prop them up both financially and militarily in the service of Cold War strategic planning. The scatological register has a genealogy whose implications ramify well beyond the area delimited by Mbembe. Finally, it might also be useful to investigate what directions such a register has for the analysis of the nation-state in Africa and its potential futures.

Homi Bhabha: Interdisciplinarity as Catachresis

If Adorno and Mbembe allow us to glimpse the fractious nature of the everyday, and by their various interdisciplinary processes of defamiliarization allow us also to view the everyday either as not at one with itself or as part of a fractious simultaneity of domination and subversion, in Bhabha's work the defamiliarizing work is not merely applied to the object(s) of discussion itself, but is part of a constant process of the deconstructive dissolution and re-aggregation of the conceptual categories brought to bear on the objects of discussion in the first place. As was noted earlier, in Adorno's hands aphoristic thought becomes the conduit for disrupting clichéd modes of thought for the antinomic structure of the everyday phenomenon or idea to shed light on a larger movement in history. For Mbembe, the everyday of political existence becomes the site for a series of mutualities between the *commandement* and the ordinary people in such a way that the everyday becomes the simultaneous assertion and disaffirmation of the discourses of power. With Bhabha, something different takes place. In his writing, an apparent aphoristic structure generates what I would like to describe as 'quotationality'. But I use this somewhat clumsy neologism to distinguish his aphoristic structure from that of Adorno. For, whereas in Adorno the aphorisms can be quoted out of context (and in fact, they frequently are), they are so well grounded within a studied movement of thought that they can be put back into the contexts from which they were taken and make perfect sense as aspects of a coherent flow of thought. In Bhabha's case quotationality is meant to mark something entirely different. His aphoristic structure serializes seeming aphorisms without allowing them to be properly grounded in the observation of the everyday as in Adorno. This, in its turn, is part of a larger feature of his interdisciplinary model, which oscillates so rapidly between different disciplinary boundaries as to blur these boundaries and also to refuse completely the possibility of any coherent totality that might be thought to be implied by the energy with which he excavates the configurations of the object. His writing, especially in that to do with the colonial encounter, implies sentiments of considerable ethical intensity without allowing for the possibility of consolidating a precise location for that intensity. This is a key issue that will be elaborated more fully in the conclusion.

'Signs Taken for Wonders' (1994) provides a good example of such manoeuvres. Bhabha opens this essay with a setting that prepares for a tropological reading of power. He opens with a telling type of scene-setting:

> There is a scene in the cultural writings of English colonialism which repeats so insistently after the early nineteenth century – and, through that repetition, so triumphantly inaugurates a literature of empire – that I am bound to repeat it once more. It is a scenario played out in the wild and wordless wastes of colonial Africa, the Caribbean, of the sudden, fortuitous discovery of the English book. It is like all myths of origin, memorable for its balance between epiphany and enunciation. The discovery of the book is, at once, a moment of originality and authority. It is, as well, a process of displacement that, paradoxically, makes the presence of the book wondrous to the extent to which it is repeated, translated, misread, displaced. It is with the emblem of the English book – 'signs taken for wonders' – as an insignia of colonial authority and a signifier of colonial desire and discipline, that I want to begin this chapter.
>
> (p. 102)

Note certain key words and phrases: 'scene', 'cultural writings of English colonialism', 'repeats insistently', 'so triumphantly inaugurates a literature of empire', 'scenario', 'fortuitous discovery of the English book', 'myths of origin', 'epiphany and enunciation', 'originality and authority', 'presence of the book', 'emblem of the English book', 'signs taken for wonders', 'insignia of colonial authority', 'signifier of colonial desire and discipline'. Note also the idea of a 'primal scene' which he reiterates first in relation to an Indian catechist Anund Messeh in 1817 and his attempts to convince a group of Indians that when read in a Brahminical light, the Bible was the Word of God; second in Marlow's discovery of Towson (or Towser's) *Inquiry into Some Points of Seamanship* in Conrad's *Heart of Darkness*, and third in V. S. Naipaul's encounter with the same passage from Conrad and his reflections on it. These three encounters are read as enunciatory of significations beyond their immediate contexts, the implication being that 'The discovery of the book institutes the sign of appropriate representation: the word of God, truth, art, creates the conditions for beginning, a practice of history and narrative' (p. 105). So far the implications Bhabha abstracts seem to do with questions of narrative, these three instances of the book's discovery being the epiphanic moments that trigger particular narrativizations of selfhood as it is linked to the past as well as the imagined putative future that could be grasped from that past in its relation to the moment of the book's discovery.

But Bhabha is not content to let matters rest at that, and he makes a startling assertion lower down on the same page: 'For despite the accident of discovery, the repetition of the emergence of the book, represents important moments in the historical transformation and the discursive configuration of the colonial text and context.' For, as he tries to show later on in the essay, the discovery of the book exposes the discourse of civil address, and, in doing this, reveals a particular entailment of books and their discovery with the wider processes of colonialism. Thus, with respect to Anund Messeh, his 'lifeless repetition of chapter and verse, his artless technique of translation, participate in one of the most artful technologies of colonial power' (p. 106). In the case of Marlow, the book he discovers 'is the book of work that turns delirium into the discourse of civil address'. For Naipaul, his attempt to translate Conrad from Africa to the Caribbean is 'in order to transform the despair of postcolonial history into an appeal for the autonomy of art' (p. 107).

Bhabha then proceeds to do what he has barely hinted at in the multiplicitous and shifting nature of his first paragraph, and that is now continually to shift 'the book' from its ordinary material parameters into the domain of colonialist discourse more properly. In doing this, he interprets the book as having material effects in establishing and helping to maintain colonialism. The book is an *embodiment*, almost a colonial body in itself, and sometimes is described as if, by its mere existence, it acquires a specific form of agency tied to the colonial enterprise. This is never stated explicitly but is allowed to gather implication incrementally by being associated with the colonial encounter. Thus he writes:

> If these scenes, as I have narrated them, suggest the triumph of the writ of colonialist power, then it must be conceded that the wily letter of the law inscribes a much more ambivalent text of authority. For it is in-between the edict of Englishness and the assault of the dark unruly spaces of the earth, through an act of repetition, that the colonial text emerges uncertainly.
>
> (p. 107)

Now, we might pause to ask how 'the discovery of the book' turned into the 'triumph of the writ', 'the wily letter of the law' and 'the ambivalent text of authority'. What Bhabha has done by this stage is to foreground what was always implicit in his accounts of the book's discovery, that is, that it is somehow at one with colonial authority itself. After this, the rest of the essay is devoted to deconstructing the nature of colonial authority and showing how its authoritarian discourse always harbours essential contradictions that undermine it both from within itself and from the context of the colonial encounter.

If the processes of unpacking this essay prove frustrating, it is the precise effect that he seems to desire out of this mode of interdisciplinarity. The difficulties in the way of arriving at any easy interpretation of Bhabha derive from the fact that, as in this particular case, he focuses on a putatively concrete object, the book, but dematerializes it and discusses it in terms of an abstraction. At the same time, and quite contradictorily, he is interested in retaining the materiality of the book in order to attack the logocentrism of colonialist authority deconstructively. He almost gives his intentions away when he opens the paragraph after the discussion of the 'wily writ of the law' with these words: 'Consequently, the colonial presence is always ambivalent, split between its appearance as original and authoritative and its articulation as repetition and difference' (p. 107). And yet he has at no time in the essay attempted to discuss instances of colonial authority in terms of colonial persons and authority figures. They, as it were, are present by their proxy, which is the book.

The implications of Bhabha's writing have been criticized by many commentators, but perhaps nowhere more perceptively than in Bart Moore-Gilbert's account.[8] For Moore-Gilbert, the problems with Bhabha's kind of analysis do not lie merely in the fact that he conflates psychology with politics or that he reads the symbolic as the political as such; for Moore-Gilbert, the problems proliferate when one takes account of the fact that Bhabha does not bother to question the apparent Eurocentric biases of some of the Freudian and Lacanian psychoanalytic paradigms he uses. And when it comes to Bhabha's use of Fanon, Moore-Gilbert shows how much Homi Bhabha disavows a key methodological move in Fanon involving the careful historicization of the psychological phenomena to be examined: 'What sometimes seems to get lost in Bhabha's homogenizing and transhistorical model of the mutual (mis)recognitions of all cultures is Fanon's insistence that the psychic economy of colonialism mediates material, historically grounded, relations of power' (1997: 147). He poses a number of questions that Bhabha's methodology seems unable to answer:

Even at the level at which Bhabha customarily works, his method would be unable to explain the varied patterns and expressions of affective structures like ambivalence in diachronic terms, thus registering the fact that certain stereotypes emerged in particular periods and locations, and often in response to specific socio-political developments. To take just one example: why did the Anglo-Indian vision of the educated Indian in the relatively positive terms of the 'pundit' or 'munshi' prior to 1857 give way by the 1880s to the stereotype of the 'babu', who, characteristically, malapropistically misappropriates the discourse of the colonizer? Why is there no real equivalent to the stereotype of the 'babu' in fiction in Africa? Such questions can indeed be answered, but only by a differential engagement with the complex histories and material processes of which imperialism is made up.

(1997: 151)

Considering these trenchant criticisms, then, what value is to be gained from Bhabha's form of interdisciplinarity? Crossing Derrida, Lacan and Foucault, he seeks to address several audiences simultaneously, but in such a way as not to be recognizably tied to any single discipline. Thus his work seems to be aimed at literary theory in the fertile way in which he reads tropes; to psychoanalysis in the febrile 'nervous conditions' of the encounter between the colonizer and the colonized he attempts to formulate; and to historians in his postulation of these encounters as being between subjects situated in a putative history whose lineaments are recognizably those of the colonial era in India and elsewhere. In this sometimes productive, sometimes obfuscating interdisciplinary loop, the writing becomes self-referential and calls for judgement on its own terms. Bhabha produces a kind of catachrestic discourse in which the various ideas he puts together deliberately generate a 'misfit', as it were, a deliberately non-integrated and continually mobile series of positions and ideas that are meant to mime the very labile processes he is at pains to describe. Furthermore, Bhabha's discourse resolutely resists assimilation into a holistic picture. His language, though seemingly aphoristic, has the restless quality of proliferating a series of discrete observations which resolutely refuse to cohere into a perspectival totality. This is not to say that we do not get the general drift of his arguments, but that his writing sows permanent doubt as to whether it has all been fully understood.

In Mbembe's interdisciplinary model, a radical perspective is produced but is not aligned directly to an ethical domain. This is despite the fact that his examples are frequently to do with violence and brutality. Because he situates the dominated and the dominating within the same epistemological domain and shows them to be entrapped in certain mutualities of subjectivity, the shock and anger that might have attended his model are short-circuited. There is clearly a scale of power, but this is simultaneously dissipated by the model of analysis deployed. Thus, equivalence sheds light, but arguably dissipates anger. It is not at all clear whether the recognition of the degree of subjective proximity between the *commandement* and the people is meant for us to laugh angrily at the oppressors or to retain an objective distance and to perceive the disposition of mutualities as a series of proliferating simulacra. In other words, there is a dramaturgical intensity in Mbembe's model which locates us as spectators almost ready to applaud the cleverness of the people rather than to be agitated by the subliminal violence to which they have continually to respond. If the dramaturgical recognition yields fruit, it yields it in the measure to which it keeps the co-dependent relation between the *commandement* and the people simultaneously in view, so that any form of response or reaction has to take account of the one *and* the other at the same time.

With Bhabha, something decidedly different takes place. As was noted earlier, there is a vigorous retreat from any totalization whatsoever and every category gets discomposed through his energetic and almost delirious deconstructive strategy. With him, we seem to be encouraged simultaneously to contemplate the fact of colonial epistemic violence but not to be able to stabilize it easily in relation to an idea (the book), to a specific materiality (the book again) or to the discursive relations between colonizer and colonized. Thus it is that we are placed within a theoretical loop: there is a lot of sound and fury, but we are not sure whether we can ever fully grasp what it signifies or whether it signifies anything at all.

This somewhat despairing account of Bhabha's interdisciplinary model has to be counterbalanced by a more positive perspective, drawn not so much from his better-known pieces exemplifying colonial discourse analysis as from his reflections on the place of theory in contexts of political interpretation. Homi Bhabha's own sense of the political implications of reading the past is conveyed in 'The Commitment to Theory', where he outlines what can be said to be his manifesto of what it is to read historical and other texts 'theoretically' for present-day uses (1994: 19–39). More importantly, he notes that 'the dynamics of writing and texuality require us to rethink the logics of causality and determinacy through which we recognize the "political" as a form of calculation and strategic action dedicated to social transformation' (p. 24). For him, political action is no simple business that can be defined in terms of binaristic polarities, for 'the fragmentation of class and cultural consensus' frequently represents 'both the historical experience of contemporary social divisions, and a structure of heterogeneity upon which to construct a theoretical and politcal alternative' (p. 28). Thus, history 'happens' for him, even in the pages of theory, where the language of critique 'properly alienates our political expectations, and changes, as it must, the very forms of our recognition of the moment of politics'. He continues: 'The challenge lies in conceiving of the time of political action and understanding as opening up a space that can accept and regulate the differential structure of the moment of intervention without rushing to produce a unity of social antagonism' (p. 25). In other words, any form of political intervention needs to take account of the mutual implicatedness of opposed political positions, something which, in liberal political discourse is subsumed under the binary modalities of good and bad. This is of course a very significant point, except that sometimes when faced with real-life struggles, people find themselves obliged to move through phases of engagement with reality, sometimes starting from simple binarisms and only opening up into more complicated visions in the unfolding processes of struggle. This cannot be theorized into irrelevance.

This brings us to an issue of critical significance: what does interdisciplinarity provide both for our understanding of postcolonial relations and, more importantly, for the ways in which we may address *post*colonial questions (simultaneously as a project and as an engagement with theories, paradigms and inflections)? How does interdisciplinarity allow us to postcolonialize?[9] It could seem pretentious in this phase of postmodernist *Angst* to raise this question at all. What right, a cynic might ask, do postcolonial intellectuals working in Western universities have to intervene in the real-life crises of the postcolony? And on whose behalf would they be doing this, their paymasters' or the postcolonials' themselves? And if these questions are not resolvable, why be concerned with the implications of postcolonial interdisciplinarity? It is by no means possible to give a full answer to all these questions. However, it has to be noted that the project of postcolonialism, if indeed there is thought to be one, is always entangled with ethical questions. In other words, it seems to me almost impossible to talk about the negative effects of colonialism past and present without implicitly or explicitly being tied into discussions of the ethical value of the knowledge that is produced. And, in the context of postcolonial studies, this would seem to be a much more anguished and pressing question than, say, in the study of Milton, for the simple reason that the postcolony is almost a palpable affect wherever we find ourselves, recurrently recycled on television, newspapers, the Internet and various other media. What, for instance, is one to make of the fact of the hanging of Ken Saro-Wiwa when teaching his novel *Sozaboy* or his TV series *Basi and Co.*? How does one relate Fanon's *The Wretched of the Earth* to the context of the brutalities in present-day Algeria? To my mind, the two domains of pain and discourse seem impossible to separate completely and any move to do so can only create a reified form of knowledge divorced from the realities of the world and indulged in for its own sake.

Thus, the interdisciplinary model has ultimately to answer to the ways in which it shapes an ethical attitude to reality, in this case to postcolonial reality. In this, Adorno's defamiliarization of the everyday becomes pertinent. For it is arguable that when Adorno launches his defamiliarization, it is meant to raise our consciousness of the degree to which everyday phenomena are overdetermined by world-historical processes not readily perceivable via the usual forms of philosophizing. Everything is implicated in a reverse procedure that threatens an atrophying of spirit under the violence of capitalism and the totally administered state. Even though Adorno's pessimism never allows him to specify a project, at least his methodology alerts us to the pitfalls of complacency in our engagement with seemingly innocent everyday concepts. There is always an implicit ethical dimension to which he gestures in his polemical defamiliarizations of the phenomena he focuses upon. Thus, Adorno fufils what Gramsci describes as a pessimism of the intellect and an optimism of the will, something which seems to me to be absolutely necessary for any responsible postcolonializing critique.

If I identify Adorno's method of critique as preferable to those of Mbembe and Bhabha, it is not to privilege a critical practice developed under the peculiar constraints of a fascist Germany as the paradigm for a postcolonializing practice, or even to suggest that Mbembe's and Bhabha's models are irrelevant to our current postcolonial concerns. What I do want to say, however, is that interdisciplinarity has to be placed in the service of something much larger than the interdisciplinary model itself. There is often a sense, sometimes produced quite in spite of the good intentions of the critics deploying interdisciplinary models, of a frenetic celebration of theory in and for itself. It is almost as if we are being invited to contemplate the critical model as a coherent and self-contained field amenable to various degrees of separation from the problems that are being accounted for or discussed. In certain cases this is not necessarily a bad thing, as the alienation effect engendered by the critical discourse can sometimes force a fresh view of the object under discussion. However, in some cases, such as is quite common in postcolonial studies, especially in its sometimes careless engagement with post-stucturalism, the critical discourse captures us in a loop, where there doesn't seem to be any way out of its parameters for a contemplation of the problems that are being discussed in the material world. The interdisciplinary model should provide ways out of itself and into the real world. This is not to be done in any simplistic way, as Bhabha notes in 'A Commitment to Theory', but it is still the case that ultimately we need clear tools by which to understand and struggle against injustice, oppression and even obfuscation.

It is by no means possible or even desirable to legislate what models of interdisciplinary configurations should be deployed in postcolonial studies. But one thing remains clear, that for the synoptic perspective to be simultaneously of some instrumental value in a context of continuing anguish and confusion, we have to be extremely rigorous and self-conscious about how we configure our interdisciplinary studies. Nicholas Thomas provides an apposite conclusion to this discussion:

> If there is something basically enabling and positive in the undoing of disciplinary boundaries, authoritative privileges and canonical sources and modes of presentation, it may nevertheless be too easy to celebrate this new fluidity, this new scope for exhilarating trespasses. It would be a pity if the spectacle of intellectual plurality fostered a relativist permissiveness, that acknowledged the fertility of diverse agendas and refused to discriminate among them. It remains important to argue about the effectiveness of different disciplinary technologies; about the politics of analytical strategies; about the appropriateness of particular theoretical languages.
>
> (1994: 19)

2
Postcolonial Historiography and the Problem of Local Knowledge

I ask for a history that deliberately makes visible, within the very structure of its narrative forms, its own repressive strategies and practices, the part it plays in collusion with the narratives of citizenships in assimilating to the projects of the modern state all other possibilities of human solidarity.

> Dipesh Chakrabarty, 'Postcoloniality and the Artifice of History'

Students of colonialism have constantly taken different issues to be at the centre of the colonial enterprise and in the past four decades have brought a variety of methodologies to bear on the issue.[1] In the area of postcolonial studies, the view of the past is arguably so much tied to present-day understandings of what it is to be in a postcolonial world that imperial and colonial history are among the most widely discussed and contested areas. The comments we made in the previous chapter regarding Homi Bhabha's catachrestic use of the past for defining a mode of social being in the present can be resituated and discussed in terms of what I would like to term 'subjunctive historiographies'. A subjunctive historiography may be described simply as that which, even though seeming to be steadfastly engaging with the past, is actually providing models of agency for the present. In this chapter, I would like to take up this idea with respect to the work of the Subaltern Studies group. I shall also expand the discussion further by relating their mode of historiography to what passes under the general label of colonial discourse analysis associated broadly with Edward Said, Homi Bhabha himself and many other people working in postcolonial studies. The discussion of Homi Bhabha's interdisciplinarity in the previous chapter provides a useful background for the discussion of colonial discourse analysis especially in the various mutations that have taken place in it following Said's *Orientalism*. A larger question that I address in the last section of the chapter is to what extent these subjunctive historiographies allow us to imagine the condition of the colonized that takes account of both its indigenousness and its modernity without subsuming one category under the other. To overemphasize indigenity is to lapse into a febrile essentialism, while to write solely from the point of view of modernity is to swallow up indigenous perspectives under implicit evolutionary or developmental theoretical models that end up completely marginalizing the indigenous sense of history and how these might be thought to provide ways of relating to present-day postcolonial concerns. I shall situate this part of the discussion in the debate between Marshall Sahlins and Gananath Obeyesekere and their mutually contradictory interpretations of Captain Cook's 'apotheosis' before moving to conclude with remarks on the Revd Samuel Johnson's *The History of the Yorubas*. The Sahlins–Obeyesekere debate allows us to raise important questions about the history of the native (in this case, Hawaiian) when such a history can only be gleaned with difficulty from what has been said about them from the logbooks and journals of Western navigators; with Johnson I want to highlight indigenous historiography at the conjuncture of orality and literacy and of a traditional world-view in the face of new historical realities. Any subjunctive historiography in the terms in which I describe it here would have to take account of all these issues to be fully alive to the use of the colonial past for the postcolonial present.

On Professional History

In the training of historians, a number of qualities are prized above all others. First is the intimate knowledge of sources.[2] This, in practice, requires the steady immersion in the documentary archive for long periods of time to enable a careful understanding of their location in the historical context. Second is the quality of informed interpretation. This often involves the ability to distinguish usable evidence from suspect sources. The method of establishing the usability of sources requires an implicit comparative framework in which each item is set alongside others to expose the degree to which different documents reinforce or contradict each other. Third, there is a steady focus on the rules of debate inherent in each document or fragment, the degree to which a diary entry, for example, allows a form of knowledge that is different from that in a parliamentary minute. Additionally, the historian is always encouraged to catch wider meanings or patterns between different documents in the effort to understand the significance of different documents or fragments of documents. The central thing to note is the degree to which historians are trained to adjudicate between documents in an informed and rigorously negotiated way. The historian rarely, if ever, makes bold to declare that the significance of a historical epoch is contained or embodied in a single document. If such a historical embodiment is allowed, it is abstracted from the mutually reinforcing or contradictory relations between various documents and sources in the documentary archive. There is also a firm focus on locating events and incidents in their proper chronological sequence even if, in practice, these are not narrativized with equal significance or in the precise temporal sequence in which they occurred. Finally, it is generally accepted by historians that the opinions of historical agents are important in understanding a historical epoch. This is thought to be especially important if the opinions are captured as close as possible to the events in question. In other words, traditional historians take the expressed ideas of historical agents as significant sources for understanding the past.

It is also taken as axiomatic that one of the key problems of history writing is how to write about the facts and data of history in such a way as to show them to have an internal consistency and coherence reflective of a coherence that lies outside the historiographic narrative and in the past itself. In other words, historical analysis is ultimately responsible to a notion of the real world of events which is thought to have existed independently of the processes of writing about it. This general attitude ramifies at various levels, and it is not always possible completely to disentangle the historian from the history. One area of complication is that the historian's perspective lends history a subjectivity quotient which it is impossible to ignore completely. It is this idea that triggers the debate between Rosalind O'Hanlon and David Washbrook (1992) on the one hand and Gyan Prakash on the other on the role of the historian in the face of historical documents. O'Hanlon and Washbrook argue in 'After Orientalism: Culture, Criticism, and Politics in the Third World' that 'the past, including its historical subjects, comes to the historian through fragmentary and fractured empirical sources, which possess no inherent themes in and of themselves and no unequivocal voices' (1992: 149). In their view, these sources in and of themselves represent 'just noise' which it is the historian's task to turn into a sense of coherent voices through which 'the past may give the present intelligible answers'. To this Gyan Prakash, whose essay entitled 'Writing Post-Orientalist Histories of the Third World' (1990) O'Hanlon and Washbrook are reviewing, answers in the same issue of *Comparative Studies in Society and History* by pointing out that this is nothing short of the staging of a primeval scene, an original encounter, but one which places an omnipotent interpreter in front of the void of history. He writes:

> Let us attend to the noise first. Is it the case that the past comes to us through empirical sources with no inherent themes, as noise? Evoked here is a primeval scene, an original encounter before history when the historian faces fragmentary and fractured empirical sources and seeks to give it voice. This staging of interpretation as the first encounter between the all-powerful interpreter and the lifeless evidence is blind to the history of its own enactment: hidden from its view are the stories told in the very presence of particular sources and in the processes by which the historian gets placed as a sovereign interpreter who turns noise into voice. Gone are the traces of the history of the archives, the monumentalization of history in documents, and erased are the marks of the historian's conditioning in the dramatization of interpretation as the first discovery.
>
> (1990: 173)

What Prakash points out here is the implicatedness of the historian's subject position (which could be read as including ideological, institutional and other such biases) in the very processes of interrogating the past. Also significant in this account is the degree of 'framing' in which the fragmentary documents of the past are always already involved in their very archival state, and which often needs to be attended to in extracting a meaningful history from them. It has to be noted in passing, though, that O'Hanlon and Washbrook's position is not one of a naive and passive acceptance of the historical archive. What they want to contest is the apparently random and irresponsible modes of interpretation that privilege the historian above the archive to be examined, and which they thought was partly reflected in Prakash's own earlier calls for a post-orientalist historiography. In this debate a whole lengthy tradition of disagreements in history departments is reproduced in which the quarrel is often on the terms by which a historian, given his or her personal or ideological predilections, can claim to know the past.[3] We shall highlight another dimension of the discursive embeddedness of the historian when we come to the work of the Revd Samuel Johnson, but to draw out quite different conclusions from Prakash and even O'Hanlon and Washbrook.

Another direction in which the historicism of the historian is taken is in the idea that because much of history writing has been carried out by the West, and in pursuit of its own interests, 'History' is a thoroughly Eurocentric enterprise that requires steady critique and subversion. The *Cambridge Modern History* planned by Lord Acton at the end of the nineteenth century was conceived as a study of universal historical factors, yet he took it for granted that this history would be European and that it was in Europe and its colonies that world history was to be found.[4] This Eurocentrism is thought to be the case even with respect to Marxist historiography. Robert Young pursues this line of critique in his insightful book *White Mythologies: Writing History and the West* (1990). He points out that it has always been critical for any historiography to appropriate the Other as a 'form of knowledge within a totalizing system. For orthodox Marxism, however, there can only be one Other, that of the working class, within which so-called minorities must be subsumed' (1990: 4). Ultimately, since history is perceived as inalienably Eurocentric, a 'relentless anatomization of the collusive forms of European knowledge' is one of the more viable ways to challenge unacknowledged Eurocentric assumptions (p. 9). Young shows in his book how this has always been an implicit problematic for Marxist philosophy of history in the work of Sartre, Althusser, Foucault, Jameson and others. He makes the additional point, seen as much in the structuring of his study as in any explicit thing he writes, that history's implicit Eurocentrism has been vigorously challenged by Edward Said, Gayatri Spivak and Homi Bhabha from a postcolonial perspective. To rectify any false impression that it was this 'triumvirate' that posed the most rigorous challenge to Eurocentric models of historiography, we might also like to recall the work of people such as Andre Gunder Frank, Samir Amin, Walter Rodney and others and their elaboration of the thesis of dependency. Coming from different parts of the Third World, these writers provided another perspective on global (economic) history which could be said to have also provided a 'postcolonial' model for people working in the fields of economics and sociology, even if this did not seem then to have had anything to do with the postcolonial paradigm as we know it today.[5] In addition, and in countering any unproblematic conception of (Marxist) historiography as essentially Eurocentric, it is useful to highlight a chance remark by the Trinidadian Marxist C. L. R. James to the effect that 'E. P. Thompson's *The Rise of the English Working Class* is the best

book of black history ever written.'⁶ For people like James, Marxism
was the only viable way of contesting hegemony, whether it was
European or otherwise, and he saw a family affinity with a work that
had nothing to do with race. At issue in these two apparently opposed
attitudes to Marxist historiographies (and it has to be noted that
Robert Young is not dismissing Marxist historiography as essentially
useless, but exposing some of its subtler contradictions that would
undermine its claims to be speaking for the 'oppressed' as a universal category) are contrasting attitudes to race and class. For James,
race is subsumed in class, whereas for Young this is thought not
always to have been the case, at least in the traditions he is exploring. Furthermore, the point for James is that Marxist theory makes
available certain analytical categories which could be used to invig-
orate the discussion of the condition of all oppressed people, including blacks. We shall turn more fully to the relation between race, class
and identity in chapters 5 and 6. For now, let us just note that the
question of Western theoretical categories and their applicability or
otherwise to conditions in the non-Western world is a highly problematic one to which we will be returning regularly in the course of
this book.

The Historiography of the Subaltern Studies Group

The historiography of the Subaltern Studies group, though at one
level quite radical in its mix of Gramscian Marxism and Foucaultian
frameworks, is at a very fundamental level inspired by the methodology of traditional historiography, as we outlined earlier. And yet
at the same time, Subaltern Studies historiography overlaps somewhat with colonial discourse analysis. One thing shared by both is
the desire to identify a form of historical agency in the colonized
sphere. For the Subaltern Studies historians this informs their emphasis on a 'history from below' and the identifying of forms of resistance
in the colonial archive; colonial discourse analysis has similar interests except that the pursuit of resistance is done from a much more
literary/psychoanalytical perspective that to traditional historians
does not seem to yield any historical knowledge at all. In both
cases the different images of individual and social agency that are
produced are really conceptualizations of agency for a specifically
*post*colonial arena of social relations. In this regard, the truth-value
of the various contents of the examples I shall be drawing from is
not of primary concern here. What is significant is how these contents

are shaped and what ideas of historical agency they carry by the narrative formulations that are given to the relevant 'historical' contents.

The work of the Subaltern Studies group was primarily designed to challenge the dominant modes of retelling India's past. In the words of Ranajit Guha, co-editor of *Subaltern Studies* from the early eighties, the historiography of Indian nationalism has been dominated by a colonialist as well as a bourgeois-nationalist elitism. In *Selected Subaltern Studies* (1988), a collection of some of the best work of this group, he points out that the key effect of this elitism, in his view, is that the development of national consciousness is a process attributed exclusively or predominantly to the elites. The central modality common to this kind of historiography, whether done from a colonialist, nationalist or even Marxist perspective, is that Indian nationalism was a sort of 'learning process' through which the native elite became involved in politics by trying to negotiate the maze of institutions and the corresponding cultural complex introduced by the colonial authorities in order to govern them (1988: 38). The objective of Guha and his collaborators was to write the subaltern back into history, to write history from below that would show that the villagers, peasants and workers were indeed agents of consciousness and that their agency often went in different directions from the ones mapped out by the nationalist elite politicians. The term 'subaltern', borrowed from Gramsci, was used to mark out the nature of non-elitist agency and the manifest forms that this took in the formation of Indian history more generally. As such, Subaltern Studies historians sought to extend the 'peasant studies' historiography that came into fashion in the 1970s, but in a more politically oriented fashion.

The major challenge to nationalist historiography, however, is done with a thoroughly traditional methodology. To take one example: in Shahid Amin's superb essay entitled 'Gandhi as Mahatma', it is shown how in the district of Gorakhpur in the early 1920s the idea of Gandhi is appropriated by the peasants to validate their own means of addressing local problems (1988). Thus, in the build-up to Gandhi's visit to the district on 8 February 1921 and well after that, stories circulated about him that were designed to consolidate the locals' sense of dealing with pertinent local issues. 'Though deriving their legitimacy from the supposed orders of Gandhi, peasant actions in such cases were framed in terms of what was popularly regarded to be just, fair, and possible' (p. 341). This conclusion is arrived at by Amin after a careful delineation of the politics and mood of the district in the period. The key items he uses for this are local and national newspaper reports on magical stories about Gandhi, editorials, extracts from the tour diary of Gandhi's secretary, the minutes of meetings of social and cultural groups such as the Gaurakshin Sabha (Cow Protection Leagues), as well as references to books and other documents pertaining to the period. But perhaps most important for our purposes is his treatment of dates and the care he takes to synchronize events in an implicit chronological pattern. To take an extract at random:

> Hindi was officially adopted as the language of the courts of law in UP in 1900. Soon after, the *Nagri pracharini* (Hindi propagation) movement began to pick up momentum in Gorakhpur as well. In 1913 the local branch of the sabha agitated successfully for judicial forms to be printed in Hindi, and in September 1914 *Gyan Shakti*, a literary journal devoted to 'Hindi and Hindu *dharma prachar*', was published by a pro-government Sanskrit scholar with financial support from the rajas of Padruana, Tamkuhi and Majhauli, as well as some from the prominent Rausa of Gorakhpur. In the following year, gauri Shankar Misra, who was later to be an important figure in the UP Kisan Sabha, brought out a new monthly – *Prabhakar* – from Gorakphur. Its object was to 'serve the cause (*sewa*) of Hindi, Hindu and Hindustan'. However, the journal ceased publication within a year; only *Gyan Shakti* remained, and even this closed down between August 1916 and June 1917. The full impact of Hindi journalism was not felt in Gorakphur until 1919. In April of that year two important papers – the weekly *Swadesh* and the monthly *Kavi* – made their appearance. These, especially Dasrath Dwivedi's *Swadesh*, were to exercise an important influence in spreading the message of Gandhi over the region.
>
> (Amin, 1988: 296–7)

What emerges from a passage such as this one is an array of related events in their proper temporal relation. The density of specification in the necessary proliferation of names of newspapers and personalities all come together to generate a sense of the dense activity of the historical process itself. This density of specification is varied according to the needs of the historical account, so that when Amin describes Gandhi's actual visit, the variety of items referred to are meant to convey a sense of the people's reactions to this momentous visit and the energies and ideas that were generated during the visit. All the events described in the extract relate to the significance of local cultural journalistic media in spreading the message about Gandhi, and, by implication, in making him available to the popular imagination in relation to other concerns rooted in the local context.

A number of things are to be noted with respect to the efforts of the Subaltern Studies group generally. As pointed out by Rosalind O'Hanlon (1988) in her thoughtful review essay on the work of the group, it would be a mistake to perceive them as espousing a unified project, even though they display generally held principles that could be identified as integrative were one interested in studying them as a unified body of work. More importantly, O'Hanlon notes that their work espouses an implicit assumption of the 'self-originating, self-determining individual, who is at once a subject in his possession of sovereign consciousness whose defining quality is reason, and an agent in his power of freedom' (1988: 191). She sees this as partly deriving from Enlightenment notions of selfhood, ideals that the contestatory work of the group shared with other liberal traditions of historiography, and suggests that 'the problem of experience, separated from that of agency, might be more fruitfully thought without the notion of universal human subjectivities'. The historians of the Subaltern Studies group seem to have got entangled in an almost inescapable conundrum: in identifying processes of unilinear change in the consciousness and practice of those studied, they inadvertently excluded some resistances thought to be backward and primitive from the historian's purview. What is perhaps most significant from the perspective of agency is that the group located history predominantly in the public sphere, a sphere that allows for a delineation of a specific type of heroic agency for the subalterns and thus constitutes them as the equals of the subjects of bourgeois-elite historiography. Even though O'Hanlon's criticisms about the implicit form of Enlightenment selfhood that the Subaltern Studies historians used to describe subaltern agency have to be taken seriously, it is possible to state a fundamental disagreement. In my view, this mode of delineating subaltern consciousness follows precisely the trajectory and form proposed in the historiography of Subaltern Studies because they are interested in specifying a relation between subaltern consciousness and other sites of consciousness as they interactively constituted the public sphere, the sphere which, ultimately, is the ground of major contestation in the formation of ideas about the nation of India. And the boundaries between public and private are not so easily demarcated, since at certain points, especially during the heyday of nationalist struggle, ideas circulate quite readily between the so-called private and public in such a way as frequently to conflate the two. (Indeed, an excellent account of this process is provided in Raja Rao's *Kanthapura* (1938). Rao's novel gives a fascinating fictionalization of some of the processes that Shahid

Amin speaks of in the essay we discussed. The essay and the novel could be fruitfully read together to focus on definitions of 'private' and 'public' and their problematic boundaries during the decolonization struggle in India.) Contrary, then, to what O'Hanlon asserts, the production of a so-called Enlightenment model of agency to describe subaltern consciousness is in perfect accord with the Subaltern Studies project. In fact, it is historically necessary as a means of countering the absence of the subaltern from the historical archive in the first place.[7]

But how, we might ask, do we derive significant conceptions from the methodology of these historians that would define their delineation of the evolution of subaltern consciousness? The first thing to note is the degree to which diachrony implicitly governs synchrony. In Shahid Amin's account, the plethora of details and names of people, places and organizations is correlated to a general sense of a particularly textured milieu. This, to appropriate Raymond Williams, gives us the sense of a 'structure of feeling', something which Amin is later to expound as determinative of the social and political consciousness of the peasant communities he is interested in. But even as this structure of feeling is produced, we also gain the sense of everything being correlated along a diachronic and temporal axis. This is gained from the careful delineation of times and dates and their relation to each other, always chronologically, and not in terms of images, metaphors or tropes. In this way, we could argue that the historiographical account is designed to give us a sense of forward motion in time, thus indirectly rehearsing the idea that the subalterns' consciousness was an agency that moved through history in an identifiable direction.

The second point, and deriving from the first, is that the plethora of details involved in the historical account are not meant to convey a sense of fragmentation or of not being integrated into a larger and coherent picture. Again, this may ultimately be related to the form of subaltern consciousness. No matter how fragmentary their social existence might appear, to the historian all elements were integrated into a particular mode of intervention in history. In the particular case that Shahid Amin explores, the various apocryphal stories that circulate about Gandhi are turned to addressing specific local needs to do with justice and morality that have a manifestly public and historically graspable mode of manifestation.

As has already been noted, the work of the Subaltern Studies group is devoted mainly to writing a 'history from below' and to giving voice to a hitherto historically silent subaltern agency. To do this properly, they attend to non-conventional sources of historiography since the established documentary accounts are noted to be completely contaminated by the perspectives of the elite classes in whose interests the history of India had predominantly been written. In this they face the same magnitude of problems that professional historians working on African sources face in recovering a usable past from a colonial archive that marginalized certain voices in favour of the official sources. All historians interested in recovering lost voices tie their historiography to the necessary (re)discovery and (re)adjudication of sources in ways that are intended to make these sources *recognizable* to traditional historians as well as to the elites or privileged groups from whose perspective history has always been written. In this respect, the work of the Subaltern historians sets up a necessary dialectical relationship with traditional historiography, as it were weaving questions of historical methodology into the very fabric of challenging the dominant accounts. The point to be noted in concluding this section, then, is that the methodology of traditional historians is not necessarily bad in and of itself; serious questions are constantly posed whenever new sources are being brought to the foreground. The matter becomes even more acute when history is not merely indicative and constrained to illustrate conditions in the past but subjunctive and designed for present uses. If, following the historiographic methodology of the Subaltern Studies group, the peasants did contribute significantly to the formation of Indian history, the implied question is what prevents them from contributing actively to its direction now? And if, because of the inherent biases of the historical archive, their efforts were not properly accounted for, is this not to suggest that there is a pressing necessity to document history from below in the very contemporary moment of its unfoldment? In other words, does the work of Subaltern Studies historiography not indirectly spell out a praxis for the present about how to view the silenced majority *in* history, past, present and future? These and many other such questions would have to be attended to in expanding the implications of Subaltern Studies history for thinking about a postcolonializing historiography for the present time.

Colonial Discourse Analysis and the Issue of Interpretation

The historiographic protocols of colonial discourse analysis seem to be radically different from those of traditional historiography, even in that which shares an affinity of intent in trying to rewrite the history of resistance. For traditional historians, on the other hand, such postcolonial analyses of history are nothing short of irresponsible language games. John Mackenzie's criticism of such theorizing is couched in terms of serious reservations about the methodological implications of colonial discourse analysis. Its worst excesses, he writes 'are at odds with fundamental tenets of historical procedures'. He continues:

> The historian is necessarily concerned with explaining change over time, with the interrelationship of ideas and events, with the social, economic and intellectual milieu in which sources are produced. The historian seeks to tie analysis to a firm empirical base, to specific episodes, particular individuals and territories, definable socio-economic contexts in the historical record...Moreover, the historian trades in the ironic and the unwitting, what has sometimes been dubbed 'incidental causality'. To take some examples derived from the Indian Empire, historical interpretation has been full of the unanticipated: education policies designed to produce collaborators turning out resisters instead ...Paradox has long been the stock-in-trade of the historian whose discipline breeds a certain cynicism.
>
> (MacKenzie, 1995: 37–8)

On the face of it this does not establish a clear difference between traditional historiography and colonial discourse analysis. Colonial discourse analysis is also concerned with many of the central themes outlined here. What does mark a critical difference, however, is that between the two modes of interpreting colonialism there sits a difference in attitude towards the archive from which conclusions are drawn about colonial history. In other words, the difference is not so much that postcolonial theory is not interested in the questions that traditional historians such as the Subaltern Studies group pose about the past, but that radically different methodologies are brought to bear on the entire business of adjudicating between sources and deriving significant conclusions from them. In what is perhaps a more balanced view, Dane Kennedy outlines the differences between colonial discourse analysis and imperial historiography while arguing for a studied engagement with the more productive potential of colonial discourse analysis. His typology of the central features of colonial discourse analysis is worth noting in some detail, particularly as he relates these to specific texts in postcolonial theory. He notes, among other things, its 'theoretical promiscuity', a certain disabling deference to the idea of theory, and a consequent obscurantism. He also notes the indiscriminate use of highly specialized

and often obscure words such as heteroglossy, alterity, aporia, synec-
doche, aleatory, metaphoricity, facticity, narrativity and originary, and
the new and often surprising inflections given to ordinary words such
as gaze, gesture, site, space, efface, erase and interrogate. He observes,
additionally, that postcolonial theory often makes a strong link
between language and liberation. Since this link is seen as crucial,
post-colonial theorists often devote a lot of time to 'deconstructing
representative texts and exposing the discursive designs that under-
lie their surface narrative' (1996: 349–50). What Kennedy perceives,
with understandable frustration, as the predilection of postcolonial
theory to decentre both the history writing process as well as the individual texts to be studied is actually a pointer to the differences in
notions of historical agency and how they are to be described. The
bone of contention that has to be dealt with in any comparison
between colonial discourse analysis and traditional historiography
would always have to centre around deceptively simple questions
asked by any student of history: What is the best attitude to adopt to
contradictory sources? What count as historical facts and how are
these to be interpreted and narrativized into a recognizable coherence? How does this historical narrativization relate to understandings about the past and, possibly, about the present?

Colonial discourse analysis ranges from the Foucaultian sweep of
Said's unmasking of the disciplinary modalities of Orientalism right
through to the Lacanian pyschoanalytic methodologies applied by
Homi Bhabha devolving on a specifically narrow historical context.
However, between these two positions – the broad historical sweep
and the narrowly focused local interpretation – a number of common
ideas continually seem to reproduce themselves. The first of these,
and in many respects the least contentious, is that representations are
always overdetermined by questions of power. This is essentially
Edward Said's well thought-out position, one which he declares early
in *Orientalism* when he states that Orientalism is the Western style
for 'dominating, restructuring, and having authority over the Orient'
(1978: 3). Secondly, colonial discourse analysis is deliberately wide-
ranging and eclectic, crossing disciplinary boundaries with impudence
to show how the issue of colonial authority is established as an
ensemble manifesting itself both at the material domain as well as in
the area of ideas, images, assumptions and discursive representations.
Like the New Historicism, which, as noted by Aram Veeser, 'has given
scholars new opportunities to cross the boundaries separating history, anthropology, art, politics, literature, and economics' (1989: ix),
postcolonial theory is intent on crossing disciplinary boundaries in

the quest for the significance(s) of colonial history. And, like the New Historicism, the belief is that this is necessary to help show that 'every expressive act is embedded in a network of material practices' (p. xi). The next idea, which gets expressed in different configurations from one critic to the other, is that history is first and foremost a mode of textuality. Being primarily textual, it is thought to make itself amenable to the procedures of close reading that literary critics are particularly well positioned to do. This in itself would not make colonial discourse analysis very different from traditional historiography, since, as has already been pointed out, professional historians are themselves taught to read closely. What is more contentious is the view that not only is history essentially textual but every textual fragment of the historical archive allows a similar insight into the significance of historical processes through the inherent *textuality* of the fragment. The historical is thus situated in a deliberately heteronymous domain in which every fragment of the archive, no matter how unrelated or seemingly innocent, can be read for signs of tropes, metaphors and discourses that can be brought into a relationship of equivalence with the major historical documents of the archive such as parliamentary minutes, political speeches, official diaries etc.

In practice this last idea has a number of methodological implications. As textual aspects of a historical documentary archive, documents or fragments are seen to embody contradictions. The contradictions in individual texts are taken as significant in and of themselves. When these texts are set alongside others, it is not just the ways in which they contradict each other that matter as much as the fact that they produce contradictions within themselves as such. If matters were left at that this could be interpreted as a clever if seemingly pointless exercise in literary criticism. However, a much bolder claim is made when the internally contradictory nature of such texts is identified and linked to the nature of the structure of feeling of the wider historical domain. Thus individual documents are seen to be significant embodiments of a larger logic of historical epochs. This, as will readily be recalled, is a very different approach to the historical archive from that which traditional historians are trained to employ.

Now, if this appears on first encounter as a type of Hegelian grasp of the dialectic, it has to be pointed out immediately that the contradictions are rarely if ever synthesized and explained away in the movement of a dialectic of history. Rather, the contradictions are left to reproduce themselves and become the means by which the mentality (as opposed to the consciousness) of the historical epoch is thought through. As part of this move to centralize contradictions and to leave them unintegrated, colonial discourse analysis zeroes in on metaphors, turns of language and discursive tropes as embodiments of the inherent contradictions within texts and from which a dominant logic of the historical moment might be read. It has to be noted that in the hands of some colonial discourse analysts, tropes are rendered the epistemological equivalents of historical documents and almost, even, of events themselves. Thus they are given a determinative status linked directly to other items of a non-linguistic nature and read off as encapsulating the logic of historical processes more generally.

As has been noted by several commentators, Homi Bhabha's work is an important qualification of the type of analysis exemplified in Said's *Orientalism*.[8] Though Said's work was seen to be seminal in unmasking the links between knowledge and power in disciplines such as Orientalism and thus pointed the way forward for numerous other studies with the same impulse, it was noted early that he set up the encounter between the West and the Orient as one essentially between two monads, monolithic entities which were not differentiated within themselves.[9] Secondly, there did not seem to be any clear sense in *Orientalism* of an oppositional voice in the Orient to which the disciplinary modalities of the West might have had to respond to or negotiate. The notions of oppositionality came up in Said's later elaborations of the issues he had raised in *Orientalism*. The most important thing with respect to the direction that Bhabha was to take, however, was the essentially homogeneous nature of both the Orient and the West, something that did not allow for an exploration of the contradictions that could be said to lie within both the Orient and the West itself.

Put schematically, there are three main things that Bhabha attempts to do in extending the implications of Said's work. The first is to press the implications of what Said suggested was the fantastic nature of Orientalist discourse in its often implicit quest to produce the Orient as a fantasy or a figment of the West's representational imagination in the ultimate service of Western domination. Bhabha settles on this notion of the inherent fantasy of representations of the colonized Other and, with the help of Lacanian pyschoanalytic categories, rewrites the colonial encounter as essentially one of deep-seated anxiety for the colonizer. The second thing that Bhabha does is to suggest that resistance is always already enfolded into the moment of the colonial encounter. He suggests that to stabilize a sense of power the colonizers had insistently to confront the frustrating slippages of nomenclature and categorization that they applied to the colonized. For the colonized, it was by way of mimicry that the self-perception of the colonizer was reflected back to them, both as a threat to the source of power and as a form of problematic agency for the colonized. Thus, within a colonial encounter whose ambiguities cut several ways,

> mimicry emerges as the representation of a difference that is itself a process of disavowal. Mimicry is thus the sign of a double articulation; a complex strategy of reform, regulation and discipline, which 'appropriates' the Other as it visualizes power. Mimicry is also the sign of the inappropriate, however, a difference or recalcitrance which coheres the dominant strategic function of colonial power, intensifies surveillance, and poses an immanent threat to both 'normalized' knowledges and disciplinary powers.
>
> (Bhabha, 1994: 86)

For Bhabha then, the colonial encounter is read as a series of tropes of ambiguity, the most prominent of which is that of mimicry. The colonial encounter is historicized for him via images of anxiety-laden power and the various refractions of subversiveness contained within the colonial encounter itself. By centring on tropes, he tries to abstract general principles about the logic of colonial history more generally. As we saw in the previous chapter, he establishes this by way of a subtle and sometimes confusing shifting of ideas across both abstract and concrete categories.

Apart from the difficulty in convincingly establishing the contours of colonial anxiety through a psychoanalytical as opposed to an empiricist reading of the historical archive, perhaps the most problematic dimension of colonial discourse analysis is the interest in interpreting tropes and metaphors and the insistence that these yield a knowledge about the essence of colonialism. A quite startling example of this can be seen in the first section of Anne McClintock's *Imperial Leather* (1995), a study of the links between colonialism, domestic arrangements and sexual labour in South Africa and elsewhere during the nineteenth century. She opens with an astounding reading of the map in H. Rider Haggard's *King Solomon's Mines*. McClintock argues that if the map is inverted, it looks like the form of a woman's body, the coveted mines to which the journeying men are heading being suddenly shown to be located in the pubic area of this tropological map/woman. She goes on to make the surprising assertion that 'Haggard's map thereby hints at a hidden order underlying industrial modernity: the conquest of the sexual and labor power of colonized women' (p. 3). With this, she not only reads the map as inherently gendered, but, pursuing the implicitly inverted and perverse logic concealed in this trope, goes on to extrapolate meanings about the sexual labor of women in real-life historical contexts. This would have been hilarious if it had not been advanced as a serious mode of historical interpretation. What if, following her lead, the map is read not as the image of a woman's body but the skeletal image of a bird with wings spread out in full flight? Could we not then say that the three mounds mark the scavenging bird's beak and represent the concealed desire to rip open the gold mines and to take what is concealed there? This type of interpretation could itself be open to the accusation of labouring within the same potentially tropological reading, since this bird could be read as masculine and trying to rip up a female gendered gold mine. The purpose of my reading, however, is to point out the complete tendentiousness of any such interpretation, since, if we settled on the image of the bird, we would then be hard put to show that birds had something to do with sexual labour, or indeed with environmental degradation in colonial South Africa for that matter.

This focus on tropes and the psychoanalysis of the historical archive allows us to raise an important question: in what ways are such readings merely revealing the imaginative agility of the critic as opposed to historical information about the past itself? More contentiously: how do such readings relate to modes of knowing history that have no relation whatsoever to an indigenous domain? How, for example, would McClintock's cartographic expertise be augmented or challenged by being related to an indigenous understanding of maps and other such things? And how might such a reference to an indigenous domain ultimately help us gain an insight *out of* as opposed to *into* the nightmare of colonial history? Finally, is it ever possible to write about the colonial encounter without somehow distorting the specificity of different historical imaginations as they size each other up in the fraught terrain of colonialism?

History and Local Knowledge: The Sahlins–Obeyesekere Debate

Mudimbe's *The Invention of Africa: Gnosis, Philosophy and the Order of Knowledge* (1988) might be thought to provide a good way of contextualizing the problems of indigenous 'gnosis' and its relationship to historiography, whether Western or local. His argument, resembling in many ways Said's own work but drawing directly on Foucault, is that African studies are perpetually caught within the grasp of

a Western knowledge base, to the extent that both Western interpreters as well as African analysts could be said to have been using
categories and conceptual systems which depend entirely on a
Western epistemological order. This leads him to pose an important
question with what seems to be a measure of exasperation: 'Does
this mean that African *Weltanschauungen* and African traditional
systems of thought are unthinkable and cannot be made explicit
within the framework of their own rationality?' (p. x). Perhaps
the question to be raised, following Mudimbe's line of inquiry, is not
the one that he asks, but a quite different one, namely, whether
an episteme is capable of retaining its essential contours even in
continuing encounters with a radical alterity. Does an epistemic
encounter between Western categories of thought and non-Western
cultural contents permit the retention of a specific mode of
understanding even in the face of the shifting boundaries of both
the West and its 'others' in the world? Does the flow of historical
events not have anything to contribute towards the constitution of
subject positions *between* cultures? Also, what are the issues to be
addressed in trying to adduce a non-Western gnosis when any such
system of thought is always caught within matrices of global historical formations dating from the earliest moment of the colonial
encounter?

The question of whether current postcolonial historiographic
methods may or may not be distorting native voices can be pursued
by following the implications of the debate between Marshall Sahlins
and Gananath Obeyesekere on the 'apotheosis' of Captain Cook.
The key question for the two anthropologists is whether or not
Captain Cook was taken by one of the islands of Hawaii as being
the fertility god Lono and treated as a god on his appearance. A
preliminary sketch of Captain Cook's apotheosis is in order. In
January 1779, Captain Cook's ships *Resolution* and *Discovery* came
accidentally upon the islands of Hawaii. Cook's voyage at this
time (his third) was aimed at ascertaining whether there was a
navigable North-West Passage which would make it easier for
English and European vessels to get to China instead of having to
go round the Cape of Good Hope. For some unaccountable reason,
Cook could not make up his mind whether to land on the islands
or not, and instead circled round them for seven weeks. At the end
of this period, on Sunday 17 January, he decided to land in
Kealekukua Bay. Coincidentally, as it turned out, the people were
at a crucial point in the celebration of their Makahiki festival, a
central piece of which was the ritual return of Lono, god of fertility.

Part of the belief around the god's coming was that he circled the island in a clockwise direction in a boat for a period of time before landing. Cook's ships had also been going in a clockwise direction before landing. On seeing Cook and his shipmates, the islanders took him to be Lono and treated him like the incarnated god. The rituals that followed are given contradictory interpretations by Sahlins and Obeyesekere, the first seeing them as rituals accorded the deity and the second interpreting them as some sort of installation ritual for chiefs. After three days of a great show of respect consonant with Cook's being taken to be a very important cosmological deity or/and chiefly figure, he and his team depart to continue on their journey. Unfortunately, one of the ships develops severe problems with its foremasts, and Cook has to turn back to the island to get wood for repairs, sailing into the bay on 11 February. On his return, all hell breaks loose. There is a taboo on the bay and the people no longer show the same signs of respect or appreciation; in fact they are positively hostile. After a number of incidents of stealing and altercations between the sailors and the islanders, things come to a head when Cook attempts to take one of their chiefs hostage as a way of getting back an important item stolen from the ship. This proves to be a major miscalculation. Tempers fly, confusion breaks out, bullets and missiles are fired in both directions and Cook is stabbed by one of the islanders. His killing, however, is no ordinary killing; he is ritually dismembered and sacrificed in the final step of his apotheosis. In returning to the island, Cook has reproduced a menacing cosmological return of the god Lono which was thought to bode great evil for the people. He has disrupted the ritual cycle and by doing this has also brought to the foreground a series of mythopolitical tensions and ambivalences in the social organization of the people. This is Sahlins's interpretation (1995: 79–84); Obeyesekere's is insistently political and he suggests that Cook was no longer welcome because he had refused to assist the local chief in a war against his enemies. His return and the subsequent incidents made *him* the enemy of the chief. In Obeyesekere's view, having already been made a chief on his first visit, it was now only a short ritual step to transform him properly into a deity by his death and dismemberment, a process applicable to any Hawaiian chief in the process of apotheosization (Obeyesekere 1992: 87–91).

This summary does not do justice to the complexity of the events that unfolded, or, indeed, to the arguments of either Sahlins or Obeyesekere. I give this summary only to help frame our own concerns regarding historiography and indigenous knowledge. A number of things need to be highlighted in the Sahlins–Obeyesekere debate. First is that the initial source of the disagreement was about the relevance of 'Western' paradigms of interpretation of local situations. To Obeyesekere, Sahlins is just going along with an old Western myth-making line in which explorers and suchlike are turned into gods in the Western imagination (pp. 8–15). He contests the view that the islanders must have taken Cook to be a god by trying to adduce more pragmatic reasonings. In doing this, he is charged by Sahlins with himself also producing a largely Western bourgeois Enlightenment view of human rationality and applying it without adequate respect for facts to the Hawaiians (Sahlins, 1995: 5–15). More to the point, Obeyesekere is Sri Lankan, and though proceeding from the view that his familiarity with a traditional ritual universe justifies his suspicions of the implied naive view attributed to the islanders, he is in no better position to judge the event than is Sahlins himself. He is as much an outsider as the Western anthropologist. In a certain important sense, they are both victims of the interpretative paradigms they deploy.

This leads us to the second problem. Both scholars have to have recourse to the existing historical materials. Unfortunately, and this is something that they both acknowledge, almost everything that is known about the Hawaiians from that period is actually what Cook and his shipmates write about them. The Hawaiian voices are refracted through the narrative positions of the shipmen themselves. To get at what happened then requires a careful and rigorous comparative procedure in which various accounts are squared against each other and against a later compilation of accounts of the Makahiki festival brought together in the 1830s by the Revd Sheldon Dibble. Thus both scholars stand on what might be thought to be slippery ground. The voices of the Hawaiians are conveyed strictly by the narrative perspectives of the shipmates, thus requiring a careful process of interpretation for them to be disentangled. This issue of an inextricable relationship between a Western narrative perspective and the secretion of an internal indigenous or native voice is one we shall pick up later with respect to the Revd Samuel Johnson. For now, let us just note that the nature of the inextricable entanglement makes it clear that no point-by-point certainty can be achieved for *every single event* that takes place during Cook's fateful visit to the island. Because of this feature of the historical archive to do with Cook's apotheosis, both interpreters are obliged perforce to apply external paradigms in a dialogical relationship

with what might be thought to be the relevant belief stystems pertaining to the Makahiki festival and the place of Lono in it. I point
this out because, in the effort to strengthen their mutually opposed
positions, both Marshall and Sahlins try to explain *every* possible
incident according to their interpretative schemes. For Sahlins, the
scheme is attributable directly to the Hawaiians themselves; all the
incidents pertaining to Cook's first and second landings are uncannily synchronous with the unfolding processes of the Makahiki ceremonies. Obeyesekere grants that coincidences abound, but disputes
that the Makahiki ceremony could have been taking place at that
time, and, even if it were, adduces a different set of reasons to account
for the coincidences.

The third point to note is that, as a consequence of the fact that
the Hawaiian voices are refracted through the narratives of the shipmates, their oral discursive modes, critical in accounting for an indigenous gnosis, are never fully brought into view. To put it in another
way: if the Hawaiians themselves had been able to describe these
events, they would most probably have done so with different narrative and symbolic categories from those used by the Western sailors.
We can assume that their discourse (here meaning the totality of
expression from words and images to specific dialogical locations
within the expression) may have been quite different. This does not
mean that the same conclusions could not have been reached supporting either the Sahlins or Obeyesekere interpretations, but that
the emphases suggested by formulaic expressions, local metaphors
and other linguistic features could have provided a different set of
clues to be pursued.

Finally, we need to note some of the problems with any ethnohistoriography. Even though I have suggested that the Hawaiian discursive modes were perforce only refracted through the existing
archive, it is by no means the case that any ethnohistory that they
might have produced would not have been open to some doubt and
contradictory interpretations. For it is a key feature of any ethnohistory that it is itself saturated with various political and cultural interests, so that the metaphors and other discursive modes of orality may
themselves have to be historicized and their social and political trajectories properly identified to prevent distortions to the historical
record. Furthermore, and perhaps more problematically, once ethnohistory is set down in writing, it frequently rehearses some of the
codes and paradigms of cultures whose models of writing the local
people are deploying. This could be Western, Arabic, Persian, Chinese
or for that matter any form of writing that has had a long tradition

of written historiography. And this, though leading to some inescapable distortions, is not necessarily a bad thing. Mary Louise Pratt describes the same problem but in the light of what she terms 'autoethnography'. Autoethnographic texts are those that natives construct in response to or in dialogue with metropolitan representations (Pratt, 1992: 7–9). The point is not so much that written ethnohistory is dialogically engaging with colonial representations, as that the very act of taking on a literary mode of self-representation as opposed or in tandem with an oral one produces a series of boundary crossings between the oral and the literary, which makes the ethnohistorical account itself a liminal genre in need of critical historicization.

I should like to point out at this stage that I am not trying to adjudicate between the two rationalizations provided by Sahlins and Obeyesekere. I think it would be impossible to pass any secure judgement without first engaging thoroughly with all the available material. From a layman's point of view, both accounts seem at certain points quite convincing and at others somehow exorbitant and hard to believe. And this is in spite of the fact that they are both scrupulously attending to the sources and to interpretations of the Makahiki festival cycle. In my view, it is not the validity or invalidity of the two accounts that is at issue, but the fact that they are deploying radically different interpretative paradigms to negotiate the same set of events for which the available accounts are themselves inadequate. At any rate, I do not subscribe to the view implied in the debate about whether or not a Westerner is indisputably disqualified from producing any reliable knowledge on others. This is quite an erroneous impression, which, in these days of multiculturalism and ethnic studies is bandied about with great energy and little reflection. It does not stand up to any serious scrutiny. There is no doubt that historically the West has produced all kinds of fictitious knowledge about 'others'. But it is by no means the case that every single piece of knowledge produced in and by the West was necessarily contaminated with fiction or malicious motivations. In our own times, it is easy to show how people from well beyond native spaces have helped to produce and sustain very useful knowledge about local peoples. In the area of Yoruba studies, which I would like to revert to because of the context of the Revd Samuel Johnson's work, one needs only to look at the work of the likes of Ulli Beier, William Bascom and Karin Barber among others to see how a Yoruba self-understanding has been generated dialogically with the rigorous work of Westerners.

History and Local Knowledge: The Revd Samuel Johnson

And now to the Revd Samuel Johnson and his *History of the Yorubas*. I have written more fully elsewhere about Johnson's seminal work.[10] Completed in 1897 but not published till 1920, the *History* attempts to project a pan-Yoruba identity by focusing on the rise of Oyo (or 'Yoruba proper', as Johnson calls its people), its growth in status among Yoruba states and its gradual eclipse due to the rise of other military and metropolitan centres such as Ilorin and Ibadan. It also relates the circumstances that led to the establishment of the British Protectorate in 1893. So broad is the scope of the work and so beautiful its composition that it has been praised by scholars as the principal glory of Yoruba historiography (see Law, 1976; Peel, 1989). The *History* combines an overview of the processes of the formation and later fragmentation of the 'nation' of the Yoruba through a careful interweaving of oral and literary sources. When writing about it in my earlier work, I turned to the *History* as providing a multi-layered dimension to traditional historiography, a rich interface between orality and writing that has not yet been fully grasped by scholars of Nigerian history. I did this to establish its significance to what I saw as a gradually unfolding tradition of Yoruba writing in which an indigenous matrix of discursive modes, proverbs, metaphors and other indigenous oral resources was drawn upon to give the writing in English a peculiar 'indigenous' dimension and feel. Johnson's book was written at a period of cultural transition, just as the traditional boundaries of a 'Yoruba' culture were being formed in the face of wider historical processes that were to integrate it into a larger nation that was to become Nigeria.

The question to be tackled here is not so much whether Johnson, a freed slave from Sierra Leone and a churchman, was actually a person whose history of the Yorubas could be said to have been a true historical account of the Yoruba from the late eighteenth century to the end of the nineteenth. At any rate, the *History* was objective at least in terms of how he sought to relate his historiography as closely as possible to the indigenous narrative forms he collected. But it was far from a disinterested account, trying to construct an Oyo and Ibadan-centred history for a people whose allegiances were predominantly to local structures, and placing a series of Christian and quasi-Christian interpretations on the indigenous arena. The point, rather, is that *The History of the Yorubas* is far richer than what the word 'History' in the title had led historians to believe. It is more in the line of a cultural work, a rich recalling of the past as cultural product with a specific discursive texture and intent. It is ethnohistory in the fullest imaginable sense of the word. This is borne out by the fact that unlike most histories of the Yorubas, Johnson's has 173 pages of ethnographic materials as the introduction to the life and culture of the people. This vast introduction has everything, from Yoruba naming ceremonies to diagrams on Yoruba facial marks. But more important is that the *History* reproduces the mode of recalling the past inherent in indigenous Yoruba historiographic discourses. Yoruba historical accounts are often careful interweavings of *oríkì* (praise names and epithets), songs, etymologies, proverbs and even riddles. They have an essentially performative inflection which relates to the fact that history in traditional culture is part of an active social arena in which people are encouraged to participate imaginatively in the historical account as a means of engaging with the relevance of the past to the present. The extent and mode of Johnson's reliance on the traditional mode of Yoruba historiography is so extensive that his work reads almost like a series of cultural quotations. On a broader discursive level, the past in Johnson's work is recalled as a *cultural production*, whereas at the micro-narrative level it operates as a series of what might be termed 'cultural teloi'. These cultural teloi are themselves loaded with other significations and can be likened to the menu icons on an Apple Mac computer screen: inno-cent at first, they reveal a dense hinterland when isolated and 'opened'.[11] Johnson's work turns out to be an archive of cultural materials at the same time as it is a 'history' in the ordinary sense of the word.

Further implications of Johnson's work lie in the relationships it establishes with the cultural nationalism of late nineteenth-century Yorubaland. Various other collections of Yoruba materials were published in the same period, ranging from collections of proverbs to commentaries on Ifa divination. From this perspective, Johnson's work was significant for being a compendium of all such cultural resources put in the service of mapping out a pan-Yoruba ethos. Johnson's was part of a general move to assert the viability of tradi-tional culture. Even though these attempts were often incoherent and frequently replicated Western analogues of nationhood and of cultural development, their significance can only be seen when read together as part of an interconnected discursive field.

The peculiar historiographic discourse of the *History* allows us to see more clearly how the problem of historiography and local know-ledge manifests itself in postcolonial historiographies, both of the Subaltern Studies kind and of the colonial discourse analysis variety. For one thing, Johnson's work is positioned delicately between an oral discursive domain of meaning-making and an exclusively literary and Western one. He negotiates this balance by writing the *History* as if he is directly rendering the indigenous historiographic mode of the Yorubas themselves. But there is a point when this breaks down. It is the period when Western writing and things written become important for negotiating the politics of the British administration, which grew slowly from the 1880s and was fully established in 1893. It is signalled in this section of the work by frequent references to writing as a means by which the characters set down their positions in relation to political issues to be discussed. There is an early casual reference in chapter 26 to one Mr A. F. Foster, 'by whom the letter to Mr. Olubi was written for the king' (p. 462) but the reference to writing and its importance in negotiations becomes pronounced at a meeting with the governor. We are told that the governor had several interviews with the *Aláàfin*'s messenger in order to learn from him particulars about the state of affairs inland. He also held meetings with the representatives of the Oyos and Ijeshas in Lagos, but these fell to undermining each other's positions to gain favour for their respective tribes. The reported reaction of the governor is fascinating as it reveals the foregrounding of writing as a necessary first step towards future action:

> Under the circumstances the governor asked the messenger to put down in writing his opinion of the situation, the exact state of things, and his reasons for believing that the people wanted peace and that the Lagos Government's interference would be acceptable. And this he did in a letter addressed to His Excellency on the 28th of November, 1881.
>
> (p. 466)

The question of the significance of writing is given centrality again, but with an ironic emphasis when we are told that to a request by a member of the Oke Igbo delegation to Lagos that the *Aláàfin*'s (King of Ife's) messenger divulge the purpose of the king's message, the retort of the members of the Oyo delegation is that since a messenger is not allowed to know the contents of a sealed letter, they are incapable of divulging its contents (p. 469). Though orality is clearly a dominant mode of interaction, writing seems to become the new focus for the construction and negotiation of various discursive positions in relation to politics.

The consciousness of writing and of dealing with written documents is what alters the quality of the report of events in this part of the *History*. Johnson seems to wish to allow the various documents to speak for themselves. But, because these documents have been set down in writing, they establish boundaries between their content and that of the rest of the narrated events. Unlike the narratives in earlier parts of the work, these documents contain no accounts amenable to imaginative entry and embellishment in the oral discursive mode. Johnson is forced by the boundaries inherent in these documents to surrender the freedom he exercised when acting as a narrator of oral traditions. In a sense, he is forced by the nature of the events he is describing at this stage to go as close to a Western mode of historical reconstruction as possible. This mode is modulated for him by the nature of the written sources he is working with. This relates not only to the fact that documents were available for this period, but also to the fact that he has now entered a historical zone in which the Western culture is itself a dominant player.

But this Western mode of historical construction based on documents has certain implications. They do not allow the same blurred interaction between mythology and history proper. In earlier sections of the *History*, Johnson frequently described personages and characters in quasi-mythical terms, the most significant being *Başorun* Gaha, chief officer of the King of Oyo in the late eighteenth century:

> Gaha was famous for his 'charms'; he was credited with the power of being able to convert himself into a leopard or an elephant and on this account was much feared. He lived to a good old age and wielded power mercilessly. He was noted for having raised five kings to the throne, of which he murdered four and was himself murdered by the fifth.

> (p. 178)

It is clear here that Johnson speaks about Gaha in the same quasi-mythical terms that gods and other deities are spoken of. As he proceeds to his own times and turns to written documents, however, this quasi-mythical interpretation is absent from his account. Furthermore, he does not accord the characters he speaks of any special *oríkì*, something which would have immediately inserted them within the discursive significatory domain of indigenous oral practice. Thus, as we noted earlier, Johnson illustrates the crux of the contradictions at the heart of ethnohistoriography. These are mainly of two orders. In the earlier sections of the *History*, when he is as close as possible to the oral discursive modes, he at the same time adduces Christian and other Western epic principles to explain some of the events. In the later sections, when he is dealing with a new and documentary archive, the oral discursive mode is put in tension with the documentary one, thus showing the difficulties that any ethnohistory has to face in negotiating its own forms of knowledge at the cusp of different cultural sensibilities.

What is more important about the effects of a Western documentary historiography on the indigenous area of knowledge is that it is precisely this effect of narrowing down or completely freezing indigenous orality that takes place in academic historiography whether written by Africans or Westerners. A form of scientific rationalization is imposed upon mythical and quasi-mythical accounts to bring them closer to the empiricist mode of history writing. And there lies the rub: How do we know we are historiographically conveying the 'gnosis' of the indigenous peoples (to return to Mudimbe's phrase) if their peculiar ways of understanding history are subsumed under a form of scientific empiricism? And how then do such histories, having attained cult status, serve ultimately to overdetermine the very ways by which indigenous peoples later imagine their histories?

These are by no means easy questions to answer and they touch at the very heart of Western historiography, which, from its professionalization in the eighteenth century, carefully eschewed any forms of the fantastic and, indeed, looked down upon earlier historiography as somehow debased and/or backward.[12] Which brings us full circle back to postcolonial historiographies in general. From the discussion about the differences between Subaltern Studies historiography and that of colonial discourse analysis, it was evident that in both cases the past was being put to present uses. In many respects Subaltern Studies historiography was much closer to the world-views of the peasants and subalterns themselves. Shahid Amin's essay attests to this. With colonial discourse analysis as practised by Anne McClintock, Homi Bhabha and others, the interpretative modality interposes theory firmly between the indigenous or local sphere and the present. The subaltern, of whom Spivak famously concludes that he or she 'cannot speak', is twice removed from speech in colonial discourse analysis because the psychoanalytic categories that are deployed to adduce the mentalities of the colonized do not partake of the native's own discursive modalities. This is of course not to suggest that there is anything as pristine and pure as an unadulterated native position. Any such pure position is partly a figment of the analyst's imagination. Johnson's own peculiar location between contending sensibilities (Yoruba oral discursive, Christian and Western documentary historiographic) should alert us to the difficulties in the way of adducing any such pure location. However, the business of deploying modalities of reading drawn from contemporary theories of subjectivity or of attempting to locate an oral discursivity within a foreign paradigm, no matter how well-meaning, has to be rigorously questioned so that we do not mistake the historiographic paradigm for the indigenous voice, the theoretical form for the implied content of history. As Dipesh Chakrabarty notes in the epigraph with which we opened this chapter, it is important to make visible the very structure of the forms by which history is narrativized in order that we are made alive to the strategic possibilities of reading the past for present and future uses.

The view that history is not about the past but about the present is by no means a new one. But it is more significant for postcolonial studies where various contending historiographic interpretations of the imperial and colonial past are intimately linked to structural locations in the world today. It would not be enough, however, merely to assert that resistance was everywhere evident in the colonial encounter and to pursue this idea through tropological and discursive readings of the archive. We have to find out whether the forms of historiography being developed in postcolonial studies are really advancing the uses to which the past can be put; whether the past is being rigorously attended to in terms *both* of the empirical archive *and* more imaginative interpretations; and whether the historiographic knowledge thus produced is really sensitive to the voices of the past in all their variegated complexity. It is only then that we will avoid leading the colonized and, ultimately, our audiences into a deeper and bewildered silence.

3
Literature as a Politically Symbolic Act

So far, our journey through postcolonialism has taken us via discussions of interdisciplinarity and of history. I want to bring the two broad areas of the previous chapters even closer by turning to an area which seems at first glance to pertain more to literary studies than to general analyses of postcolonialism. I am concerned here with the relation between postcolonial literature and politics, which can be couched in a variety of ways. I shall be focusing on a number of overlapping dimensions of this relationship, looking firstly at a two-tiered definition of literary postcoloniality provided by Biodun Jeyifo and then moving on to expand this definition by applying it to the work of Salman Rushdie. Rushdie provides a particularly fascinating case study of postcolonial literature and its relation to politics because of the multiple reading practices that are called for by his work. I then focus on the related issue of instrumental definitions of literature and literary value, and on how, in the context of African literature and politics, this calls for a particularly subtle form of literary evaluation. I underline the need for complexity by looking at the trope of culture heroism in Africa. This provides a peculiar intersection of the discourses of literature, politics and civil society. By focusing on this trope, I argue, it is possible to align literary criticism more closely to a materialist analysis of society and culture, especially as the trope of culture heroism can be shown to be a quest for forms of social agency in a period of the transition from traditionalism to modernity in contemporary Africa. The final section of the chapter centres on two works by Ken Saro-Wiwa and Ben Okri to focalize the issue of literary evaluation and related questions of what it is to carry out a literary politics without lapsing into the binary forms of thought that govern public politics itself.

The relation between postcolonial literature and politics proliferates a number of confusions, especially with respect to how exactly
to conceive of literature as a 'politically symbolic act' (to echo
Frederic Jameson). It is evident on analysis that in the hands of
literary critics, though literature is often rigorously defined and the
mode of interpretation applied to it quite detailed and informed, it
is not always the case that the same rigour is applied either to a
conception of politics or, beyond that, to how literature might be
thought to be an engagement with or challenge of, or even contribution to politics. When the authors of *The Empire Writes Back*
(Ashcroft, Griffiths and Tiffin, 1989) and others who share their
perspective insist that postcolonial literature is essentially a writing
back to the former metropolitan centre, they foreclose the possibility of a more complicated pursuit of the question by instituting a singular (and in many respects distorted) view of what postcolonial
writing aspires to, and what kind of politics it imagines itself engaged
in.

There are always elaborate socio-cultural and political dynamics
to the interpretation of the relationship between literature and politics. In postcolonial studies, there are at least three overlapping directions to be taken in identifying these dynamics. First is the proposition
that postcolonial literature is part of a general process of cultural and
political affirmation. In an essay defining a typology of postcolonial
writing, Biodun Jeyifo (1990) provides a cogent analysis that both
echoes and expands the purview made popular by *The Empire Writes
Back*. He takes a two-tiered approach to postcolonial writing, cat-
egorizing it in terms of what he calls the postcoloniality of 'normativity and proleptic designation' and that of 'interstitial or liminal'
postcoloniality. The first category embraces that in which the writer
or critic speaks to, or for, or in the name of the post-independence
nation-state, the regional or continental community, the pan-ethnic,
racial or cultural agglomeration of homelands and diasporas. In
Jeyifo's account, the normativity in this conception of postcoloniality
often entails a return to cultural sources, the projection of a futurist
agenda, and the celebration of authenticity. This dimension of postcoloniality is often saturated with what could be described as an
ethical will-to-identity, an expression of which is that of Chinua
Achebe's regularly cited contention in 'The Novelist as Teacher'
(1975), that he wrote *Things Fall Apart* as an object lesson to his
readers to prove that indigenous Africa had a viable culture before
the whiteman came. That this normativity depends ultimately on a
perception of literature as part of the contest against colonial

hegemony it is impossible to deny, and the implication of 'writing back' to the centre is much in evidence.

Whatever politics is derived from this standpoint of proleptic designation normally intersects with another type of politics, again fed by an ethical imperative, but this time not aligned solely to racial identity. This is the dimension of internal political and social critique which writers and critics feel themselves obliged to undertake on behalf of their people. Neil Lazarus (1990), elaborating a Fanonian perspective on African literature, identifies this impulse as partly an unacknowledged messianism that derives from the heady dynamics of decolonization struggles and the disillusionment with internal political conditions that was their aftermath. African writers feel themselves to be part of a larger social struggle in the quest for absent or vanishing agents of democratic social change. In many respects, this dimension of their practice defines African and postcolonial writers as almost taking over the role traditionally assigned to the press. The same intensity of focus on pursuing social truth that marks the quest of the vigilant press everywhere in the world also informs the work and lives of these postcolonial writers. Politically committed writers join the press to become the fourth estate of the political culture of the postcolony.

Jeyifo's second category, that of 'interstitial or liminal' postcoloniality, embraces what is normally perceived in the West as a metropolitan or hybrid sensibility. Jeyifo notes that 'the interstice or liminality here defines an ambivalent mode of self-fashioning of the writer or critic which is neither First World nor Third World, neither securely and smugly metropolitan, nor assertively and combatively Third-Worldist. The very terms which express the orientation of this school of postcolonial self-representation are revealing: diasporic, exilic, hybrid, in-between, cosmopolitan' (Jeyifo, 1990: 53). He goes on to name Salman Rushdie as the paradigmatic figure of this mode of postcoloniality, along with Derek Walcott, J. M. Coetzee and Dambudzo Marechera. One would of course have to add to this list the names of Gabriel Garcia Marquez, Isabel Allende, and Wole Soyinka in his more cosmopolitan essayistic temper. The two forms of postcoloniality – proleptic designation and interstitial/liminal – are often expressed within the same text, so that sometimes it is preferable to speak of the two poles as a dialectical continuum, rather than as polarized and mutually exclusive entities. This is certainly the case with writers who, though defining a subject matter critical of the colonial heritage, simultaneously attack concepts and ideas within

their local cultures that serve to reproduce colonial frames of reference and practices in the guise of nationalist sentiment. Thus the work
of the best-known postcolonial writers can be read both ways,
depending on the issues to be addressed.

Rushdie and Postcolonial 'Epochality'

Jeyifo's naming of Rushdie as paradigmatic of the interstitial or
liminal postcoloniality takes on added significance when we bear in
mind that his liminality allows him both to claim and to disavow
affiliation to any locality. The direct implication of this in his writing
is that it makes itself amenable to both proleptic and interstitial readings in the terms defined by Jeyifo. More importantly, as we will
see shortly, he mixes various generic codes (realist, postmodernist,
postcolonial, nationalist, postnationalist and transnationalist) which
open his works to different and often contestatory interpretations.
His works often arouse passionate responses because of their in-
betweenness; it is almost as if his books refract multiple sensibilities
that cannot be subsumed one under the other but have to be played
out in radical interpretative contests around them.

The furore over *The Satanic Verses* is worth recalling in this regard.
The novel, about the escapades of two immigrants to London,
Gibreel Farishta and Ibrahim Chamcha, is magical-realist in inspiration and transposes a series of discourses onto each other ranging
from those of Islam and Bollywood right down to the farcical racial
logics of Thatcherite Britain. Also, via the 'theological' fantasies of
Gibreel Farishta, there is a fluid movement between different time
frames from the period of pre-Islamic Jahiliya right through to the
context of a 1980s London. As has been pointed out by many commentators, the novel was particularly offensive to the Muslim community primarily because of Rushdie's attempt to reimagine the
foundational narratives of Islam. It was thought that in doing this
he suggested that the inspiration behind the Quran might have been
flawed by the personally compromised position of the Prophet (see,
for instance, Ahmed, 1992: 169–71; Sardar and Davies, 1990: 115–
20). Another contentious point is that in the novel the Prophet is
called by the nickname reserved for him by the Crusaders in the
Middle Ages, further compounding the view that it was meant as an
Orientalist (*à la* Edward Said) insult against Islam and Muslims. The
novel was published on 26 September 1988. By 5 October of the same

year it had been banned in India. Within a period of six months after
publication it had been banned in South Africa, Pakistan and Iran,
and there had been riots and book burnings in Bradford in England,
Bombay and Islamabad. On 15 February, the Ayatollah Khomeini of
Iran announced a *fatwa* on Rushdie and offered £1.5m as reward for
his life. At the same time as it was causing unease in some parts of
the Muslim community, the novel was also gaining recognition by
literary bodies. In November 1988 it won the Whitbread Prize for
best fiction; 15 March of the following year saw the Nobel Prize
Committee split on whether to consider awarding the Nobel Prize for
Literature to Rushdie.[1]

I should like to make clear at this stage that to me, as to many
people all over the world, the *fatwa* and the subsequent crisis about
Salman Rushdie's safety came as a great shock. It is an act of international terrorism the like of which is unprecedented in the modern
world and should be unconditionally condemned at every opportunity.[2] Nevertheless, even after registering our shock and dismay, it has
to be admitted that *The Satanic Verses* raised critical questions about
literature and its relationship to external reality in the modern world
which have not as yet been fully addressed. Perhaps the most glaring
point has to do with the fact that though operating an essentially postmodern play of discourses, the novel did not succeed in evacuating
such discourses of their embodied entanglements in real-life interpretations of identity for Muslims. In other words, the insertion of
the originary moment of Islam within a postmodernist literary genre
did not evacuate the discourse and representation of Islam of its felt
value for its believers. Thus, the (mis)representation of Islam short-
circuited the postmodernist text's capacity for playful deferral of
meaning and delivered it into a circuit of global political interpretations which, though deriving their energies from an engagement
with what seemed to be a literary aesthetic matrix, in fact had
ramifications that went well beyond the merely aesthetic. As an illustration of this, consider how Ayatollah Khomeini interpreted the publication of the novel:

> Truly, if anyone thinks that colonialism has not and does not persecute
> the clergy which has so much greatness and honour and influence, is
> this not naive? The issue of the book The Satanic Verses is that it is a
> calculated move aimed at rooting out religion and religiousness, and
> above all, Islam and its clergy. Certainly, if the world devourers could,
> they would have burnt the roots and the title of the clergy. But God
> willing, he will continue to be so on condition that we recognize the
> tricks, ploys and deceptions of the world devourers. Of course this does

not mean that we should defend all clergymen, since those dependent, pseudo and ossified clergy have not been and are not too few in number . . .

God wanted the blasphemous book of The Satanic Verses to be published now, so that the world of conceit, arrogance and barbarism would bare its true face in its long-held enmity to Islam; to bring us out of our simplicity and to prevent us from attributing everything to blunder, bad management and lack of experience; to realise fully that this issue is not our mistake, but that it is the world devourers' effort to annihilate Islam, and Muslims; otherwise, the issue of Salman Rushdie would not be so important to them as to place the entire Zionism and arrogance behind it. The clergy and the dear hezbollahis and the respected families of the martyrs must be on guard, not to allow the blood of the dear ones to be wasted through these writings and wrong thoughts . . .[3]

The themes that run through Khomeini's speech show how he interprets the publication of the book as an orchestrated Western attempt to destroy Islam. The association with Zionism seems surprising only if it is forgotten that Khomeini relates this publishing gesture to an entire ensemble of the strategic war against Iran. And it has also to be recalled that in the eight-year war between Iran and Iraq the West was firmly behind Iraq, supporting Saddam Hussein in order to snuff out the perceived threat of the export of revolution that the Iranians signalled. And it was a revolution that would ultimately have targeted Israel. Coming at the end of a disastrous war, when it was evident that his authority as a leader of the international Islamic community had been severely weakened through the vagaries of the war with Iraq, the publication of *The Satanic Verses* enabled Khomeini to renew his position as a warrior on behalf of a globally challenged Islam. That this was not perceived to be the case by Muslims everywhere was not of primary concern; the point was that here the perpetual antagonism between Khomeini's breed of fundamentalism and a perceived threat from the West was interpreted as having to be staged on the site of the publication of a cultural product from the West about the East. In its effects on the material configuration of global politics and of the relation between Islam and Western culture, Rushdie's novel could not have been further from the presumed sanitized spaces of postmodernist experimentalism. The content slipped out of the circuits of traditional interpretations of art and circulated where the content of art is taken as having grave material and political consequences, thus challenging the central premises governing Western liberal free speech in a global cultural economy:

Western liberal free speech has inscribed itself within certain self-generated limits, idealizing free expression even as it suspends the material effectivity of 'language' and the 'world.' At the same time, a host of marxist and foucauldian studies have shown that the conception and evacuation of a privileged space in the Western polity of 'Literature' have taken place since the Enlightenment, as an avowedly negative withdrawal from the world – with the problematization of reference – even as the rhetorical realm of poetic imagination and fiction began to be institutionally opposed to a *corresponding* and *parallel* hyperdevelopment of a factually resonant and materially effective industrial revolution. We are speaking, therefore, within an institutional conjuncture where rhetoric, fiction, subjectivity, and polysemy remain, for the most part, consigned to literature, even as science in this dualistic scheme has arrogated to itself reference, the 'plain style,' and objectivity. While 'Literature' has always held for itself the right to critically intervene in the social and political arena (mediating it from brute techno-economics), it has surrendered (or was rather brought stillborn into existence through the *necessary lack* of) material effectivity.

This is how Srivinas Aravamudan (1989), in reviewing *The Satanic Verses*, interprets the genealogy of liberal free speech, highlighting as he does this the steady insertion of literature into a domain that 'does not matter' while scientific discourse arrogates to itself all the powers of material referentiality. *The Satanic Verses* allows us to see how the dichotomy between the material referentiality of the fictive and non-fictive is often violently sundered in practice. It is instructive to remember, also, that many writers from both the postcolonial world and elsewhere have often lost their freedom owing to their writing being perceived as having specific political implications. Rushdie's case only serves to magnify a continuing conundrum about how art might be thought to relate to political reality.

It might be asserted that the political implications of Rushdie's controversial novel had more to do with contradictory reading agendas that he, as a writer, could never have fully envisaged in writing the novel. The reading publics that Rushdie imagines for his novels can never be fully ascertained, but there is a discursive feature he constantly returns to that allows us to adduce a peculiar form of postcolonial address that he shares with other writers. This feature is one that I want to describe as the 'literary thematization of epochality'. Epochality here is best understood as a transposition of Frank Kermode's concept of the sense of an ending in his book of the same title (1967). Applying insights from the exegesis of biblical eschatology to the literary and cultural products of the West, Kermode argues in this fascinating study that from time to time Western civilization produces a sense of an ending. This sense is somewhat akin to an apocalyptic sense of things, but is secularized and rendered intelligible to a more sceptical non-religious sensibility by the thematization of a sense of exhaustion, ennui or the general sense that things are coming to an end. This is by no means necessarily correlated directly to a real ending; it is the sense of it that matters. If this idea is carried over into the idea of epochality and applied to postcolonial writing, it becomes clear how much postcolonial literature produces precisely the sense, not merely of a beginning, but of a momentous historical configuration. Sometimes this is related to the coming-into-being of imagined communities after independence, such as can be seen in some of the novels of Ngugi or Armah or the plays of Soyinka. At other times, this is a function of a presumed need for social change, with this need being focalized through specially placed characters who are thought to be best situated to carry the burden of social change.

In the Rushdie of *Midnight's Children*, *Grimus* and *The Satanic Verses* and in the Marquez of *One Hundred Years of Solitude* and the Isabel Allende of *The House of Spirits* (not that these exhaust the available examples), the sense of epochality is carefully married to its potential distortion, mockery and parody in a specially constituted form of magical realism. This is thematized in such a way as simultaneously to refract representations of history beyond the texts themselves and to parody them, instituting an equivalence between the discourses of official history and those of fiction and myth. Both Brian McHale (1987) and Linda Hutcheon (1988) make this point in their analyses of the poetics of postmodernism, but neither of them links it to the idea of epochality we are trying to elaborate here. Epochality is thematized in order that the affectivity of beginnings is aligned simultaneously to a questioning of the bases for imagining or representing such beginnings. But, unlike in Kermode's argument, the affirmation and parody of epochality is not designed to engender ennui. The implicit affectivity of the content does not allow for this, even though the formal devices are constantly geared towards raising doubt. It is instructive to note, then, that, unlike his previous novels, *The Moor's Last Sigh* scrupulously avoids any sense of epochality. Moraes's fate in growing at twice the rate of his age is a personal fate and is not aligned to a community's coming-into-being. The vagaries of his family's saga are just that and not the refraction of a larger nation in the background. Indeed, one might assert that, even though *The Moor's Last Sigh* is the same length as *Midnight's*

Children, it is uncharacteristically garrulous. Its magical-realist and postmodernist experimentalism are caught within a self-engendered loop and its form refers securely only to itself. The point about Rushdie's work, then, is that he combines both proleptic and interstitial modes of postcoloniality. His writing is political precisely in the sense that it restlessly projects and confounds a sense of epochality whilst locating this labile sense within a hybrid and globalized form of postcolonial and postmodern address.

The epochal sense makes these interstitial postcolonials political in the sense that they simultaneously assert community and sidestep the bases of such assertions, thus challenging any politics out there that might want to make such assertions unconditional and imperative. It is clear, however, that with *The Satanic Verses*, such a simultaneous assertion and disavowal of the epochal could not be sustained, because for Muslims their religion is not something to negotiate away in history but, on the contrary, is the very prism through which history is to be understood in the first place. One would imagine, apropos this point, that if a novelist set out to denigrate and cast doubt on the pedigree of Jesus Christ and Christianity it would also rankle deeply with practising Christians and would at the very least lead to accusations of grossness and insensitivity.

Some Normative Structures behind African Literature and Politics

There is another type of relationship between literature and politics that needs to be elaborated and thought through. This is the case where literature directly serves instrumental ends in the quest for better social forms of existence. As was pointed out earlier, this idea of literature's political instrumentality in the postcolony extends Jeyifo's category of the postcoloniality of proleptic designation. To a certain degree it is this dimension, but exorbitated into a global feature, that arrests Frederic Jameson's attention in his interpretation of postcolonial literature as predominantly a form of 'national allegory' in his essay 'Third World Literature in the Era of Multinational Capitalism' (1986). Jameson makes his argument in the light of what he sees to be narrow literary curricula in the United States, hoping that these would be expanded to include Third World writing but on terms that would not easily assimilate this literature to an assumed and dominant Western aesthetic. In making this claim, however, he exposes himself to serious criticism about the series of false binarisms he proliferates in his account of the differences between Western and Third World literatures. It is a criticism that is succinctly put by Aijaz Ahmad (1992: 95–122) in his rebuttal of Jameson. However, considering that particularly African writers and critics regularly give interviews defining their work as of a political nature, it is not possible to ignore completely the political dimensions of their representations of African life and society.

Terry Eagleton argues in *The Ideology of the Aesthetic* (1990) that there has been a steady hyper-inflation of aesthetic theories in the West since the eighteenth century, which seems at odds with the fact that aesthetic objects have increasingly come to be commodified. He poses the question: 'Why, more particularly, should this theoretical persistence of the aesthetic typify an historical period when cultural practice might be claimed to have lost much of its traditional social relevance, debased as it is to a branch of general commodity production?' (p. 2). The suggestion here is that as aesthetic objects became gradually detached from circuits of political discourse and entered a commodified domain of popular consumption, the aesthetic domain, which seemed to be nominally apolitical, became the terrain on which quasi-political debates were staged through theories of the aesthetic. With respect to African literature, contrary to the scene that Eagleton paints for the aesthetic field in the West, it is not merely that a seemingly apolitical domain of aesthetics becomes the preferred terrain on which the political is constantly staged, but, rather, that no single discourse in any putative discursive network has been able to differentiate itself from the political. In other words, the discursive network in African life that may be discerned in anthropological, sociological, political and aesthetic discourses can always be read as ultimately political. Thus the conundrum that Eagleton perceives in Western culture in the aesthetic abstractionism that seems to have no bearing on the real nature either of aesthetic production or of real life manifests itself in much of Africa in a completely different equation. African aesthetic theories frequently aim to read literature and politics and political ideology simultaneously. At times this is done in a somewhat simplistic way, with literature being seen as an unmediated mirror of society, ideology and politics, and taken as an excuse for frenzied political analyses of one kind or another.[4] However, to stabilize a discursive network that conflates the literary with the political in Africa for analysis would have to be done in terms of their historicity, their relationship to the past and to a putative *transitional* movement towards the future. Transition and movement are also of the essence because whatever configuration we

happen to focus upon has to be ultimately keyed into materialist tran-
sitions on the continent, the peculiar oscillation between indigenity
and modernity, traditionalism and progress.

One peculiarly tenacious idea that persists in both public *and*
literary discourse in Africa is that of the leader as culture hero. This
idea offers a useful means by which to discuss the intersection
between literary and political discourse in Africa. It is best to follow
the genealogy of this idea through the indigenous domain itself
before relating its mutations in African literature and politics. In a
certain sense, we impose a measure of distortion on what is essentially a very complex reality by describing it as an 'idea'. It is more a
series of ideas and practices that come together in varied social and
cultural settings to foreground notions of heroic agency and action.
These ideas and practices are themselves expressed in different forms
in the indigenous arena, so that it is always important when centring
on any single form for analysis to remember that these constitute an
elaborate network with other forms of expression. Thus, in Yoruba
culture, for example, a whole array of oral expressive forms that
include *oríkì* (praise names and epithets), *alọ* (folktales) and proverbs
can all be taken to capture different dimensions of culture heroism.
At different times these may define a measure of coherence or contestation in the socio-cultural domain. It is important to recall in this
respect what we noted in the last chapter about the Revd Samuel
Johnson's cultural work, where, in writing *The History of the Yorubas*,
he succeeds in bringing together a wide range of oral discourses
within the body of the literary historiography in such a way as to
create a peculiarly indigenous performative emphasis for his book.

As Karin Barber shows in her superb book *I Could Speak until
Tomorrow*, *oríkì* are a means by which to affirm a person's history
and to link them to a larger social organization: 'Composed to single
out and arrest in concentrated language whatever is remarkable
in current experience, their utterance energises and enlivens the
hearer' (1991: 12). The *oríkì* get expressed in different contexts, and
it is arguably the case that, because of their essentially vocative function, they serve not just to enliven the direct target of the praise
names, but the entire communal body as well. Such oral forms serve
to define a form of cultural agency that is recognized by all who
share in that culture. As a form of oral discourse, *oríkì* help ground
culture heroism within the fluid and overlapping historical and social
realities that affect people. Crucially, however, *oríkì* have themselves
undergone significant transposition into the realm of modern life. In
fact, because of the *oríkì*'s constant interweaving of public with

private, and the historical with the present, it is a form that is firmly rooted *in history* and amenable to all kinds of modern appropriations. A parallel discourse of this kind is the South African praise poem, which Leroy Vail and Landeg White (1991) have shown has undergone various historical transformations to become a widely recognized means of addressing and negotiating power.

Oríkì are only one form of indigenous oral discourse that exists simultaneously between tradition and modernity. The same can be said of folktales and folktale motifs. These get repeatedly transposed into new frameworks to reflect changing socio-cultural concerns. Their modes of transformation are interesting in themselves. In an essay entitled 'Little Genres of Everyday Life', Sekoni Ropo traces the variety of transpositions through which folktales have passed in urban Nigeria. These can be roughly divided into three phases. The first is that of the colonial era when folktales and folktale motifs were re-interpreted to present critical perspectives on the colonial administration or the whiteman. The second is in the direct aftermath of decolonization when different political figures came into the limelight and their followers created fantastic stories about them to augment their political capital. Thus it was common in the 1960s to hear apocryphal stories that the WHO had attempted to buy Nnamdi Azikiwe's brain for special preservation (Ropo, 1997: 142). Azikiwe was from the Igbo minority in Eastern Nigeria, and the stories about him served to strengthen their claim to his being the most intelligent politician to emerge out of post-independence Nigeria. In the 1970s Awolowo, of Western Nigeria, also had his share of legends, one of which suggested that he had been spotted on the moon with his wife just prior to the 1979 elections. Both these examples hint at the desire to raise the profile of political leaders and to project them as larger than life, in a part-extension and part-transformation of the ways in which they would have been treated in the indigenous domain.

Sekoni Ropo notices that during the 1980s a different trope of culture heroism becomes manifest in urban Nigeria. This is that of the trickster figure, mainly expressed in stories about ordinary Nigerians who are able to outwit their masters (often political) and make away with large sums of money, posh cars or even the numbers of Swiss bank accounts (pp. 143–5). As Ropo notes, the main feature that distinguishes these urban folktales from the traditional ones (which have a subjective poetic mode, as he puts it) is that they are essentially realist in temper and have real-life characters in a variety of recognizably modern social roles. Significantly, however, at the

same time as the discourse of urban folktale has become focused on
exploring the escapades of various anti-hegemonic trickster figures,
at the higher level of official political discourse there is a move in the
opposite direction of appropriating resources from the indigenous
realm to ground hegemonic discourses and projects: '[A]t the same
time that the masses switched to the anti-hegemonic narrative
form, pro-hegemonic propaganda for such projects as the Green
Revolution, Ethical Revolution, War Against Indiscipline, and Mass
Mobilization for Social Reliance were couched in the subjective
poetic mode' (p. 144).[5]

It could be argued, then, that *oríkì*, folktale motifs and other oral
discursive forms help to define an intermediate stage of modernity.
However, as soon as we begin to use words like intermediate, we are
constrained by a certain 'tyranny of teleology'. As a paradigm of
pre-colonial, colonial and post-colonial politico-historical realities is
deployed, not only is the loss of the vitality of indigenous culture
sometimes lamented, but the role of contemporary discursive forms
is read in terms of the reproduction of a lost indigenous ethos. The
central problems in analysing the mutations of any concept such as
that of the culture hero would have to involve how to describe change
without necessarily being teleological, and how to define the ambit
of the idea so as to discern its lineaments as a form simultaneously
working on history as well as being worked by it. It is important to
perceive the idea of culture heroism in Africa as a form of *process* in
dialectical relationship to a wide variety of forces both material as
well as politico-historical.

The idea of the leader as culture hero gets reproduced by both
politicians and literary writers. For writers, it is frequently seen in the
assertion that the literary vocation is an extension of the role of traditional creative personalities. Thus a popular vocation is inferred but
related as directly as possible to a symbolic nexus in the indigenous
domain. This assertion is of course quite fictitious since the social relations that supported the traditional raconteur are very different from
those that undergird the modern writer. However, this becomes a
form of validation of the African writer's vocation as authentic culture hero. By far the most elaborate and coherent example of this
position is provided in Wole Soyinka's appropriation of the Ogun
myth to define his own ambit of action.

Not only does Soyinka liberally rewrite the terms of Yoruba
mythology to centralize his favoured tutelary deity Ogun; he does this
in the service of a clearly expressed aesthetic and political ideology.
It is, as he affirms in defining the agenda of *Myth, Literature and the
African World*, 'the simultaneous act of eliciting from history, mytho-

logy and literature, for the benefit of both genuine aliens and alienated Africans, a continuing process of self-apprehension' (Preface, p. xi). The adoption of a posture that seeks to address both insiders and outsiders is the one which he elaborates at every opportunity. This is done with a free play of the imagination in a continual productive engagement with the cultural matrix. In a note to his adaptation of *The Bacchae of Euripides*, he acknowledges his debt to his own poem *Idanre*, 'a Passion poem of Ogun, elder brother to Dionysos'. The project of his poem *Ogun Abibiman* was to 'lend' Ogun to the South African liberation struggle, where the Yoruba deity would have led the black host alongside Chaka the Zulu. In another interesting replay of this gesture, he suggests in his after-dinner speech at the Nobel Prize banquet that Ogun is definitely the progenitor of Alfred Nobel and asks that those in the audience unfamiliar with his *Idanre* hurry to the nearest bookshop and secure themselves copies. The occasion seems quite humorous, yet, though the linking of Ogun with Alfred Nobel was no doubt meant to evoke some laughter, it nonetheless falls in line with Soyinka's efforts at projecting his tutelary deity into a wider arena of cultural discourse. And the Ogun appropriations are not limited solely to a projection of cultural significance into a global aesthetic arena. He uses them to define his own political sensibilities. It is not for nothing that he has become for Nigerians a kind of political maverick and buccaneer with whom they fully identify. He expresses in his actions the spirit of an indomitable culture hero who refuses to be suppressed by dominant forms of behaviour.

At the same time as this is taking place in the domain of aesthetics, politicians are also defining their own ambit of culture heroism and attempting to validate their modes of political action by recourse to the indigenous sphere. In an interesting article humorously entitled 'His Eternity, His Eccentricity, or His Exemplarity', A. H. M. Kirk-Greene (1991) shows that all these practices relate to a process of the legitimation of the African leader's status, and that they are of a piece with the taking of titles and epithets for the projection of the leader as a sort of culture hero. Kirk-Greene challenges the Weberian interpretation of charismatic leadership that was applied to many African leaders in the political science literature of the 1960s and 1970s. For him the label of culture hero can be applied to the modern leader who 'consciously and quite deliberately reaches back into the history of his people and, by a positive reaffirmation of their cultural dynamic, simultaneously enhances both his stature and his legitimacy' (p. 174). He names among such leaders Jomo Kenyatta, who expounded a peculiarly Kikuyu vision of Kenya with culturally well-versed leaders like him implicitly at the centre in *Facing Mount Kenya*; Ahmado Bello, who reaches well into a Hausa cultural past to recreate himself in an identifiable cultural mode; Kwame Nkrumah, who had a predilection for praise names and epithets transposed from indigenous discourses of praise singing; and Sékou Touré, in his invocation of the ancient Samore as his ancestor. And lest this be thought to be a feature of 1960s and 1970s African leadership styles, we should remember Mobutu of Zaire and his penchant for animal-skin clothes, which he wore up to his over-throw in 1997. Curiously enough, this object of attire is given a new and startling inflection by Kabila during his long-drawn-out guerrilla war to oust Mobutu. As part of the symbolic paraphernalia that sur-rounded him in his meetings with the international press, Kabila had a flag on which was embossed the logo of Simba, the young lion in Disney's *The Lion King*.[6] This immediately invokes all kinds of narratives, such as those of the globalization of images of heroism, the flow of ideas of rite of passage, and the appropriation of symbols of masculinity, all of which go to show that the images that define culture heroism may not always be wholly derived from indigenous contexts as such. And, still sticking to leopards, lions and the feline fraternity, it is interesting to note how a peculiar form of fractious political materiality was defined for colonial Ibadan around a 'cloth of gold', which had a crowned Olubadan holding a leopard on a leash and which was bought for the big meeting of Yoruba chiefs in 1936 (see Watson, 1998).

Both the discourse of literature and that of politics in Africa are caught up in the processes of defining and establishing parameters for individual agency in contexts where such agency is constantly in a state of flux. They both carry a passion for authenticity. The African state arguably prosecutes its passion for authenticity by imposing a regulative parameter of often questionable legalities, whilst the liter-ary field does this by figuring the difficulties in the way of individual self-assertion in the face of the incoherence of state and society. Thus, I want to argue, both political and literary discourses are at war over the instruments of authentic agency, and, beyond that, of social le-gitimation. This is of course not to suggest that they are equivalent in strength, or even that both projects are equally desirable. The point, though, is that both discourses are ultimately interested in the subject positions of individuals. This battle must not be conceived of in monolithic terms; it is always in a process of transition. The problem is how to conceptualize this transition and to perceive its workings even when it is not apparent.

In many parts of postcolonial Africa, the state engenders what one could fruitfully describe as 'nervous conditions' of political and social existence. This is not due merely to the fact that civil society and the state are inextricably linked, but that the form and direction of civil society are constantly interrupted by the state. Concomitantly, the state itself regularly responds to what it perceives as threatening developments in civil society. This is usually in the direction of greater rather than less centralization and authoritarianism. This is even the case when the centralized state seems to be devolving power to its margins. Nigeria provides an interesting case study, where the proliferation of federal entities comes with a related diminution of the power of these entities to regulate the centre. This can be corroborated almost directly from the evidence of economic incoherence that afflicts many parts of the continent. However, it is not solely in the evidence of political and economic incoherence that the effects of the politicization of the aesthetic sphere may be seen to derive, but from the fact that the incoherence of the African postcolony makes itself existentially 'unforgettable', invading all spheres of social existence to the degree of rendering itself a constant horizon for the interpretation of socio-cultural phenomena. It is almost as if the African postcolony creates its own peculiar phenomenology, its own ability to make itself remembered as farce in the terms outlined by Achille Mbembe (1992a), or as nightmare, in those laid out by Jean-François Bayart (1993). Quite often, its unforgettability is closely tied to the issue of the legitimation of governments. To put matters schematically, one could say that illegitimate power is the most important obstacle to the achievement of individual autonomy in Africa. It is thus not for nothing that this lack of autonomy is thematized in African literature in terms of individuals who are alienated from their societies, and, once recognizing the inexorable direction of their alienation, go mad.[7] On a more general level, Africa's literary history is easily transposable onto the evolution of the nation-state and the growing dissatisfaction with its performance. Literary symbols and metaphors are constantly overloaded with meanings precisely because in the real world everything is an aspect of political power and its constant negotiation.

The passion for authenticity which is itself mediated through certain cultural frameworks must then be seen as being articulated within a fraught area of political and social relations. As we noted earlier in the case of urban folktales in Nigeria, there is a shift from straightforward discourses of heroism attaching to political leaders to more demotic trickster tropes that identify ordinary people as the folk heroes within a corrupt social and political environment. It is evident that these are forms of representation that invite ordinary people to identify affectively with anti-hegemonic stances, even if in jest and only momentarily. In the same vein, both literature and politics indicate different subject positions that are intended to colour people's perceptions, actions, choices and dreams. From the purview of the state, as Mbembe shows, this is in order to create subjects, to subjectify as it were. Conversely, from the point of view of progressive literature, these images of culture heroism are meant to instigate a critique of social structures. There is never anything straightforward about this.

(One point of clarification is in order to help us avoid some potential confusion. Whereas African literary writers and critics are constantly reading the aesthetic domain as if it is directly political, there is no reciprocal gesture from the political domain. Politicians cannot be said to read or deploy the aesthetic field. There does not seem to be anything akin to what Martin Jay (1992) traces in Western circles as the 'aestheticization of politics', in which politics is seen as a thing of beauty in and of itself and celebrated as such, even through acts of terror. Whatever aestheticization may be discerned has to be defined in terms of the paraphernalia of power. These 'contents' are often not just material; they can sometimes be discursive as well, as Achille Mbembe has shown. The point I want to make, however, is that politicians do not rationalize their actions as aesthetic. They are governed by a more direct instrumental rationality. Thus we could say that 'politics' is a necessary figment for the aesthetic domain, whereas aesthetics does not possess the same status in the political sphere. The most obvious conclusion to be drawn from this is that the relation between the two is asymmetrical and that this is so because of the different ways in which they articulate resources of power. This point has to be borne in mind and is one to be revisited whenever an attempt is made to discuss the effects that literature might be envisaged to have on social processes.)

Many indigenous symbols are being shifted from the area of sacred application to make room for new usages in the light of changing socio-cultural imperatives. However, it is also arguable that precisely because it is not entirely possible to disengage the new usages completely from their implicatedness in circuits of authority in the indigenous domain they, rather contradictorily, reproduce the dominant forms of existing modes of engagement with power. It should for instance be noted that many of the symbols of culture heroism are masculine. Both male and female literary writers such as Ngugi, Armah, Soyinka, Achebe and Ama Atta Aidoo produce images of female culture heroism, but these do not by any means have similar parallels within the political and social realm. This can of course be explained directly by the fact that women have had very little direct involvement in African politics anyway, with those who have been in the limelight being demonized or perceived in the light of absent males such as fathers, brothers or husbands. We shall have cause in the next chapter to deal more fully with female authority, changing patterns of female behaviour and the tensions that these produce in both the public and the domestic spheres. For now, I want to turn to the problem of literary evaluation when literature speaks directly to politics and tries to make itself amenable to instrumental interpretations.

Two Literary Examples of the Culture Hero in War and Peace

The final set of issues to be discussed with respect to the intersection of the literary and the political has to do with the basic question of how the thematization of the political in literature helps or forecloses the possibility of imagining a passageway beyond the 'nervous conditions' engendered by the incoherences of the African postcolony. But to answer this basic question we also have to postulate in what ways literature is able to refract social reality while at the same time rendering such social reality unsatisfactory and encouraging us to find ways of transcending it.

To explicate this relation, I would like to propose what might at first seem to be a banal interpretation of literature. To put forward a formulaic definition: literature is that form of aesthetic product that generates a series of perspectival alienations. These perspectival alienations start from its predominantly written and oral expressions and go on to embrace various levels of its form such as characterization, spatio-temporal co-ordinates, imagery, setting, generic codes and ethical inflections. We come pretty close in this definition to echoing the Russian formalists of the early part of this century who argued that literature was grounded in a series of defamiliarization effects. But a difference has to be noted. Whereas the Russian formalist notion of defamiliarization depended strictly upon an understanding of literary history as embodied within the formal structures of literature itself, and quite separable from its embodied social referents, the definition we are suggesting here is grounded on a notion of textual and formal defamiliarizations which are meant to alienate the referent from itself, and ultimately lead to a new view of society that moves beyond the existent, here defined as the dominant of social and political relations. For such a literature of alienation to help discompose and reconstitute political reality, it has vigorously to avoid the dominant forms with which political discourse itself attempts to constitute such a reality. For my purposes here, I would like to suggest that, particularly in Africa, the dominant forms of political discourse have operated mainly in a quasi-metaphysical language of Good v. Evil, of Chaos v. Order, and that in the hands of politicians this has served as a necessary simplification that obscures the real complexities of what takes place in the political domain. In other words, a certain binaristic thinking about rights, citizenship and external relations proliferates in the mouths of politicians in their addresses to their constituencies, so that the political terrain makes itself graspable in essentially binaristic terms when it in fact harbours a dense hinterland of complex relations both to local civil society and to global politics more generally. This binaristic code of politics is seen everywhere in the demonization of political enemies, the apportioning of blame for economic failure on ruthless global trends and the repeated catechisms of duty to the state above all else. This code is designed to divert critical attention from the incoherence and corruption of the state. Most times the questioning of the state leads to the unleashing of violence on the ordinary people.

It is here that a problem not ordinarily recognized makes itself visible. If, following Homi Bhabha's contentions in 'The Commitment to Theory' (1994), we argue that the objective of political critique must be to enable an intervention in political debates without reducing such debates to polarized entities, the issue to be addressed in relation to the intersection of the aesthetic and political domains is the degree to which specific configurations of such intersections actually serve to confirm existing schemata rather than defamiliarizing them and delivering us into a view beyond them. Let me put this another way: if our objective as literary writers and critics is ultimately to intervene in dominant social formations via particularized configurations of literature that ask to be read politically, then there is a concomitant imperative to ensure that such an objective is prosecuted in such a way as not to deliver the popular consciousness directly into the existing shape of dominant political discursive paradigms. What I want to point out is that, to the degree to which literary and aesthetic discourse imagines any possibility of intervention in the social formation, it has to defamiliarize existing categories even as it holds them up to view. This is in order that a double or even redoubled vision takes place. The first is one in which the contours of existing categories are recognized, and the second, simultaneous with the first, is one in which these categories are discomposed and seen as constructions that we can reach beyond. It is important not to see this as occurring in a sequence, even though, through the tyranny of narrative description, we will be forced to discuss the two moments as sequential. It is only in this way that the intersection between the aesthetic and the political can be said to be fruitful for a *liberatory politics*. To outline the terms in which this might be the case and to tie together all the different strands of this chapter, I want to turn briefly to Ken Saro-Wiwa's *Sozaboy* (1985) and, more extensively, to Ben Okri's *The Famished Road* (1992) and *Songs of Enchantment* (1993). I focus here on these books because they centralize anti- or quasi-heroic characters and deploy various alienation effects to help produce a distanced view of politics without being apolitical. These characters bear a family resemblance to the trickster figures of popular folktales, and as such are useful for establishing a critical distance from the political domain. I would like to argue, however, that the ways in which the political domain is imagined in these works have a number of both salutary and negative implications for the kind of politics that can be derived from them. These three texts, in their various ways, help to show the pitfalls in any simple understanding of the instrumental functions of literature and call for nuanced modes of evaluation. These are by no means the only texts that could be looked at. One is even tempted to run through a typology of political literature to show the various ways in which culture heroism is thematized and then linked to the imagining of a liberatory politics. Texts that might be considered in this regard are Ngugi's *A Grain of Wheat*, Achebe's *A Man of the People*, Sembene Ousmane's *God's Bits of Wood*, Wole Soyinka's *Kongi's Harvest* and even Dambudzo Marechera's *House of Hunger* among others.

Ken Saro-Wiwa's *Sozaboy* gives a humorous account of the effects of the Biafra War through a focus on the life of the eponymous hero of the novel. The language of the novel, which in the subtitle is called 'rotten English', is broadly based on pidgin. The language becomes a kind of demotic register which serves as an immediate conduit for subverting received categories. The nature of the narrative is generally picaresque. In a way, the picaresque contrasts directly with the form of the romance quest, a form of which is in evidence in the

Tutuolan form of the folktale, which, as we will discuss later, also lies behind Okri's work. However, though Sozaboy shares something with the heroes of Tutuola's stories in having his adventures related in a picaresque and episodic form, unlike them his are not aligned to either a quest motif or a process of self-discovery. Quite the opposite. His picaresque existence is governed more by the illogical movement of war than by any metaphysical imperatives driving the narrative. His harrowing journeys are not through a forest of demons but through the carnage and irrationalities of war. Furthermore, the picaresque form in the novel is intended to be deformative of teleology. By the end of the story, his home villagers not only believe he has been killed in battle, but, on the advice of a medium, decide that he has not been properly buried and that his ghost is the cause of an outbreak of smallpox in the village. They are advised to catch him and bury him 'proper' so they can live in peace:

> 'Is it so?' I said.
> 'Yes. So we have gone to see juju about the thing. And the juju have told us that unless we kill your ghost, everybody in Dukana must die. So, we looked for money and seven white goats and seven white monkey *blokkus* and seven alligator pepper and seven bundles of plantain and seven young girls that we will give to the juju to make sacrifice.'
> 'Is it so?' I asked.
> 'Yes. And the juju have told us that seven days after he have made the sacrifice, you will return from the place where you have been staying, and then they will bury you proper so that your ghost cannot return to Dukana.'
> 'True?'
> 'Yes. The juju said that your ghost is moving round killing everybody because when you were killed in the war, they did not bury you proper. And anybody that they do not bury proper in the ground with drink and dance after he have already dead, surely his ghost must move round like porson wey no get house until they bury him like proper man.'
>
> (Saro-Wiwa, 1985: 180)

Sozaboy comes reluctantly to believe that he may indeed be a ghost without knowing it. Thus his picaresque adventures have served not to consolidate a firmer communal solidarity, but, quite conversely, to split him from communality. He suffers a dematerialization of his sense of self in a reflection of the effects of the war on his social universe at large.

In this way the novel becomes a deeply disturbing and unforgettable critique of the social and political determinants that produce such an impasse for the individual. For it is obvious that in a state of war any attempts at proper burial are of course impossible. But the curious thing is that Sozaboy's people transfer what is essentially a problem that can only be dealt with through a critical engagement with the political domain onto concern with a piece of local ritual. We might even argue that the political domain in this book, refracting as it does the real politics of the Biafra War in Nigeria, generates a simultaneous coherence (by being situated within the violent binaristic logic of violence, war and escape from these) and incoherence (by concealing the complex dimension of the collapse of the national imaginary of which such a war is only a delayed and violent symptom). However, to the villagers this problematic can only manifest itself in a reified and transposed form in the arena of ritual. The ritual itself is their mode of coping with the grand unknown. But it is a coping mechanism which is evidently inadequate to the task at hand. The strength of *Sozaboy* is that our perception of the novel's political critique is so well managed by the form of the narrative that we are encouraged to look awry at political reality in order to see it properly. And all the time we are meant to see the utter ridiculousness of everything that is placed before us, from the 'rotten English' of the narration, which alerts us to the fact that this is from the first a discourse of subversion, through to the vagaries of the life of the naive picaresque hero, right through to the magnified grotesqueness of war.

Ben Okri's *The Famished Road* and its sequel, *Songs of Enchantment*, seem on the surface to carry the process of defamiliarization to the furthest extreme.[8] The two novels do indeed do this, but they flounder at certain key moments, thus failing to achieve properly the process of looking awry at the political. Defamiliarization takes place in *The Famished Road* and its sequel at various levels. The first is at the level of the characterization of the central character, Azaro. Azaro is an *abiku* child, and though traditionally believed to be trapped as all *abiku* children are in an unending cycle of births and deaths and rebirths he decides to interrupt this process and to remain on earth with his parents. The problem, though, is that even though he takes this momentous decision, he does not completely sunder his relationship with the spirit world. He frequently moves between the two domains of the real world and the esoteric. What is more disturbing, however, is that the switches between the two domains are not within his own volition. He switches between the two realms without warning, and he himself is as much a victim of the errant switches as his readers are of the confusion that this generates for the narrative form. The entire narrative is focalized

through the consciousness of Azaro. Because of this, it has a peculiarly fluid and unsettling quality to it. Even though Azaro is best
understood in relation to the hero of the traditional folktale, the
critical difference is that he has none of the juju or magical assistance
that the hero in the folktale had. Furthermore he lacks any titanic
heroic stature. His incursions into the esoteric world are not couched
in terms of a quest for self-definition in which the hero's titanic
stature is constantly reaffirmed. Azaro is frequently at the mercy of
various spirit figures and quite bewildered by them. Thus Azaro is
quasi-mythic in being an *abiku* child, but is sundered from the titanic
affirmations and quest motifs that govern the folktale narrative structure. This is the first aspect of the defamiliarization that we see in the
two novels.

The rapid and unpredictable shifts between the two realms of the
real world and the esoteric also contribute another aspect of defamiliarization. The narrative is like a tissue of interruptions, with no
promise of return to the precise moments in either realm when the
interruption took place. In addition, setting is itself defamiliarized in
terms of what physicists describe as anamorphic space. This is where
the volume of any given space does not correlate to its spatial parameters. It is the one we normally see in operation in science fiction
where a small room opens up into the universe and back, or a tiny
keyhole is found to be the passage to the entire past of the world.
This anamorphic space also has implications for how time is viewed
because there is a constant process of negotiation between real and
anamorphic time.

Ben Okri also defamiliarizes the anxiety-generating potential that
would normally have been aligned closely with grotesque spirit
figures in the structure of the folktale. In *The Famished Road*, we
encounter various characters who sit uneasily between the esoteric
and the real in their grotesquerie. Such for instance is the case of
various lunatics Azaro meets in the course of his wanderings, one of
whom has eyes that seem not only to be looking awry but are actually multiplied by the presence of flies that congregate around them.
All these sites of defamiliarization allow several conclusions, the most
significant for our purposes here being that Okri has succeeded in
defamiliarizing the moral economy of the folktale. The quasi-mythic
hero is not representative of the Good, and the grotesque spirits do
not represent the Bad; on the contrary, they all occupy a strangely
shifting amoral universe in which moral positions are repeatedly rel-
ativized through the constant shifts in narrative perspective between
the two realms.

And yet the moral economy of the folktale is not entirely done away with. Even as he evacuates it from the sphere of the quasi-mythic folktale hero, Okri transfers it into the domain of the adults, whose existence, it must be noted, is wholly in the real world. Of the characters in *The Famished Road*, it is only Azaro (and another peripheral *abiku* character called Ade) who has access to the spirit one. But though the other characters do not have access to the esoteric economy of the folktale, they subsist within its moral framework. This is done in a highly complex way which I cannot elaborate fully here. Suffice it to say that Azaro's Dad, who is originally a boxer, becomes increasingly identified with the category of Good. This takes place slowly, but then it is clear that Azaro's Dad, also known as the Black Tyger, painfully defines a form of social being for himself that sets him off as a defender of the oppressed. His nickname, recalling as it does Blake's poem, is itself significant. Furthermore, he more than once boxes with spirit figures, all of whom he defeats, though at a cost to his health. At the same time, and moving in the opposite direction, is Madame Koto, owner of the local palm-wine bar and up-and-coming entrepreneur. As the narrative progresses, we are gradually made to lose all sympathy for Madame Koto. She is demonized by her neighbours, accused of being a witch and swallowing other people's children, and finally is X-rayed by Azaro as having unborn *abiku* children in her belly who struggle unsuccessfully to come out.

The trajectory of the development of the two characters is further complicated by being linked to growing political consciousness. The novel itself is set in a vaguely defined period before independence. It is easy to identify the setting as that of inner-city Lagos, but that is not relevant to the current discussion. What is relevant is the fact that two political parties vie for the votes of the people. These are respectively the Party of the Rich and the Party of the Poor. Both parties are highly allegorized and there is no doubt that they are essentialized expressions of the political impulses of exploitation on the one hand and social welfare on the other. However, it is the alliance of the Black Tyger with the Party of the Poor, and Madame Koto with the Party of the Rich, that gives conclusive evidence that the two characters are being scripted according to an overarching moral economy. This moral economy identifies the local bourgeoisie with exploitation, and the wretched of the earth with social improvement. What allows *The Famished Road* to balance itself uneasily on the brink without falling into a simplistic moralism is the fact that the development of the two characters is detailed as one of changing *social relations.* The metaphysical dimension of their character development is never left in doubt, but it is clear that this is subsumed under the category of evolving social relations. Secondly, the novel maintains the uneasy balance by virtue of not allowing all the characters to have equal access to the spirit world. Their access to the metaphysical domain is thus couched in terms of a struggle and is interesting on its own account.

Things take a decidedly different turn with the sequel to *The Famished Road. Songs of Enchantment* is a completely unbalanced text in terms of its moral tone. Unlike the earlier novel, we are from the first never left in doubt that this is a clear-cut war between Good and Evil, represented by the Black Tyger on the one hand and Madame Koto and the Jackal-headed Masquerade on the other. The central conflict is triggered when Madame Koto's car runs over and kills Ade, the other *abiku* child and friend of Azaro. But Madame Koto and the Party of the Rich insist that Ade must not be buried by anyone, on pain of death. Ade lies outside at the mercy of the weather in a replay of Greek tragedy whilst the Black Tyger has to fight it out with Madame Koto for the right to give a proper burial to the child. From the start of the novel we know exactly what is going to happen and nothing surprises us.

What accounts for this 'imbalance', for this sudden reduction of complexity to the form of a politicized metaphysical struggle between Good and Evil? I would like to suggest that the imbalance makes itself felt precisely because, unlike in *The Famished Road*, Okri fails to defamiliarize the governing discourse of the political by which the political domain is viewed. He lapses too easily into binarisms without refocusing on a point beyond them. And this is in spite of saturating this novel with the structure of a folkloric mode. Because the various levels of the folkloric mode (characterization, moral framework etc.) are not in this novel defamiliarized, the political is allowed to govern the implicit moral economy of the folktale form and ends up distorting the aesthetic construction in its own favour. Thus we are given a view of the political which exactly mirrors the simplistic binaristic forms by which it constantly seeks to regulate our engagement with it. What makes it more difficult to grasp the political in this text for what it really is is that its own binaristic economy is being refracted through a folkloric surrogate, thus splitting our attention between the political and the folkloric.

It might of course be successfully argued from the implications of the experimental texts I have chosen for discussion that I am privileging experimental forms of writing as opposed to straightforward realist ones, and that any form of realism, so long as it attempts to engage with the political, is bound to be contaminated and distorted, and therefore cannot be revolutionary. I can only parry such a criticism with some words from Okri himself. In answer to the question whether he was thinking of a possible new way of writing when working on *The Landscapes Within*, a much earlier novel written essentially in a realist vein, he has this to say:

> I wasn't, no. But I've come to realize you can't write about Nigeria truthfully without a sense of violence. To be serene is to lie. Relations in Nigeria are violent relations. It's the way it is, for historical and all sorts of other reasons . . . [I]n an atmosphere of chaos art *has* to disturb something. For art to be very cool, very clear – which, in relation to chaos, is a negative kind of disturbance – or it has to be more chaotic, more violent than the chaos around. Put that on one side. Now think of the fact that for anything new, for something good to come about, for it to reach a level of art, you have to liberate it from old kinds of perception, which is a kind of destruction. An old way of seeing things has to be destroyed for the new one to be born.
>
> (in Wilkinson, 1992: 81)

It would seem, then, that to be truthful to a liberatory politics which starts from the literary representation of the political, one has to liberate art from all sorts of established perceptions. This requires alienation effects at as many levels as possible. This cannot be solely at the level of the representational regimes, whether realist, magical-realist or otherwise, but at all the intersecting levels of language, characterization, generic conventions, moral frameworks and codes of spatiality and temporality. With these we may see the political and yet reach beyond its lulling seductions into another and hopefully more revolutionary understanding.

It is evident from the discussion so far that the two expressions of postcoloniality named by Jeyifo, though sharing different protocols of representation, both face the same problematic of how to link literature to politics without either lapsing into a binaristic code, as we showed to be the case in Okri and Saro-Wiwa, or proliferating so many aporias and slippages as actually to generate the necessity for radical interpretative contestation, as was the case with Rushdie. Though these examples by no means exhaust the literary protocols that would have to be attended to in elaborating the intersection between literature and politics, perhaps one thing that we can take from the examples that we have highlighted in this chapter is that each literary text has to be politically contextualized via a complex series of negotiations. This requires an understanding of literary discourse in its textual ramifications as well as a clear view of the political domain and how a literature might reach beyond the political *through* it. Shifting Jeyifo's terms from descriptive labels into forms of critical practice, it would be possible to redefine the postcoloniality of proleptic designation and of liminality as modes of practice joined together as a single process of reading any politically inflected postcolonial literature. Proleptic designation would then become that reading of the literary which allows it to open up and point to a reconfiguration of things beyond it, while liminality would involve an engagement with the specific alienation effects of the literary that call attention to its special status as a work *working* rather than a product *produced.* The proleptic and the liminal readings would have always to be placed in dialectical relation to each other in such a way that the reading has a motion, an energy that is ultimately satisfied only when reality is looked at in a new way. And this would be the ultimate objective of this kind of reading: thoroughly to engage with the literary, the political and the fraught social space between them in a process of reading literature not as an escape from the nightmare of existence but as a way of changing it.

4

Feminism, Postcolonialism and the Contradictory Orders of Modernity

Writing to Constance Webb in 1944, C. L. R. James said:

> With the increasing opportunities that modern production (and the development of ideas based upon it) gives to women, a new type of woman arises. She is called a career woman. The name is stupid but very revealing. A man is never a career man. That is his privilege. He can have his career, and the finest fruit of his successful career is wife and children. But the woman is called career woman because her 'career' in modern society demands she place herself in a subordinate position or even renounce normal life. The social dice are loaded against her; and the plain fact of the matter is that they are loaded, not only in the economic opportunities, *but in the minds of men.*
>
> (James and Grimshaw, 1992: 144)

His reference point is the American woman but the condition described is relevant to women everywhere. This condition is not to be named simply as that of the contradictory entrapment in a seeming material freedom that is nonetheless subject to prejudicial economic arrangements and the hypocritical patriarchal attitudes of men. For what James describes here to be applicable elsewhere, a different dimension of his description needs to be foregrounded. Namely, this is in the peculiar condition of women taking their rightful place in modernity but having simultaneously to renounce 'normality'. Viewed another way, this could be described as the conundrum of attaining citizenship whilst becoming alienated subjects. This conundrum that afflicts women's lives is arguably greatly aggravated in the Third World, where women's existence is strung between traditionalism and modernity in ways that make it extremely difficult for them to attain personal freedoms without severe sacrifices or compromises.

The instruments of alienation have coincided with those by which an ostensible freedom has been attained. It is a situation which is going to be at the centre of this chapter.

Feminism has been about challenging the representations of women and arguing for better conditions for them. Representation itself has at least two meanings, both of which are relevant to post-colonialism and to feminism. The first and more political one has to do with the matter of political representation, something which even in a democracy arguably never fully satisfies the needs and aspirations of all the people for whom democratic systems are set up. For political representation to be fully representative, it has to be constantly reviewed by those it claims to serve. The second and no less significant definition lies in the area of the discursive, in the ways in which metaphors, tropes and concepts are used to project an image of some person or persons. Discursive representation has serious effects on the lived domain of everyday life and crucially sets up forms of potential agency which are offered as means of defining subject positions in the world. Both political and discursive dimensions of representation are relevant to feminism and postcolonialism, with the two frequently being conflated in general discussions so that the discursive representation of Third World women is often seen as ultimately of political consequence.

Chandra Talpade Mohanty makes the link between the political and discursive dimensions of representation explicitly in her well-known essay 'Under Western Eyes: Feminist Scholarship and Colonial Discourses', where she argues that, though the relationship between Woman and women is not a relation of 'correspondence or simple implication', some feminist writers 'discursively colonize the material and historical heterogeneities of the lives of women in the third world, thereby producing/representing a composite, singular "third-world woman"' (1994: 197). Mohanty's central contention is that this discursively created, oppressed Third World woman is nothing but a homogenized creation of Western feminist discourses whose intent is to set up an object that can be the presumed Other of the Western female culturally, materially and discursively. Even progressive Western feminists do not always escape this tendency, as Spivak shows to be the case in Julia Kristeva's *About Chinese Women* (1977). For, as Spivak points out in 'French Feminism in an International Frame' (1981), Kristeva's study has no real historical basis as the entire foundation for the speculations is library sources. The 'Chinese women' in Kristeva's account are really produced as part of structuralist debates in post-1968 France and point to the politicization of her own feminist position rather than anything directly to do with Chinese women. And so the scene is often set for a series of complex negotiations between an implied hegemonic Western feminist discourse and the heterogeneous conditions of Third World women.

In emphasizing a different dimension of this same problem, Obioma Nnaemeka (1997) argues that the homogenization of the Third World woman also extends into the media representations of traditional marital arrangements, childcare, health and so on in the Third World. Analysing the implications for discussions of polygamy in Mariama Ba's *So Long a Letter*, Nnaemeka highlights the subtle differences in media representations of polygamous relationships in America, such as those of Alex Joseph and his eight wives in Big Water, Utah, and the way in which any such polygamous set-ups in Africa might be viewed by the same media. The critical difference is seen in the manner in which the Josephs' marriages were reported in *Marie Claire*. All the groups of people involved in the relationships – Alex Joseph himself, several of his wives, and the small-town community – are given an opportunity to express their views freely on the marriages. The writers of the article, Ross Laver and Paula Kaihla (1995) describe the eight American women as 'well-adjusted', with a heavy insistence on their freedom and peace of mind. The level of objectivity displayed by the writers and their reluctance to pass judgement on what is clearly a quite unusual arrangement is what is intriguing for Nnaemeka in its contrast to how traditional African cultures are typically reported:

> This report is pertinent to the questions I raise about voice and agency primarily due to the *manner of its telling*. I have written at length on the report in order to tease out the different categories of speaking subjects – the wives spoke, Alex spoke, the neighbours spoke, and the reporters 'reported' without any noticeable insertion of the reportorial voice. The reporters did *not speak for* the Josephs. They treated with respect these 'well-adjusted' women who 'are virtually indistinguishable from typical, modern American women'; they visited the Joseph wives, saw them as reasonable adults who are capable of making personal decisions and choices, *talked with* them, and walked away convinced that the 'living arrangement works.' On the contrary, in the narration of African traditional cultures and the ways in which they are 'oppressive' for women, African women are not accorded the same respect and subjectivity as Alex Joseph's wives; African women are spoken *for, about, and against*.
>
> (Nnaemeka, 1997: 166–7; emphasis in original)

The point to note, as she argues, is the extent of the reification of traditional African practices and their interpretation as impositions on women. The homogenizing tendencies observed by Mohanty and Spivak with respect to certain emphases in Western feminism can then be seen as extensions of a larger conception of the oppressed position of the 'Other' woman common in media and popular representations as well. Though Nnaemeka and others are definitely correct in their diagnosis of the Western media's penchant for focusing on the oppression of women from other parts of the world, it would be going to the other extreme to suggest that some of this is not actually correct, or, indeed, relevant to how discussions of women's position in the Third World are to be debated. The parameters for the discussions should by no means be those set by the Western media, but the corrective to the distortions can also not be a mere debunking, or an inversion of the terms by which the Western media have set up the debates. The problem calls for more subtlety than that.

Another angle that postcolonial feminism has brought to bear on the entire field is in showing the extent to which nationalist discourses have subtly subsumed concerns about women under what turned out ultimately to be patriarchal concerns under the impetus of a nationalist agenda. Once again the discursive and political dimensions of representation are at issue. This phenomenon was evident particularly in the nationalist debates across the Third World, where women's questions were subsumed under larger nationalist ones and local women's experiences were taken as needing defence from the implications of Western feminine models. But in this arena of nationalist concerns, women became more the sites than the subjects of the debates about them, and these 'sites' were eventually construed in ways that rendered women completely alienated and absent from the experiences that were being declaimed on their behalf.

In this chapter I will be touching on these and other issues to prepare for a general discussion of questions of postcolonial women's lives. The focus will be on the degree to which women's oppression makes itself manifest through varying degrees of conjuncture between modernity and traditionalism, especially with regard to conjugal marital relationships and the pressures that are brought to bear on these by extended kinship ties. The critical move will be to historicize the conjuncture as the dialectical meeting point between residual and emergent values, and not as a reified moment of either oppression or freedom. To elaborate the grounds for this focus, I shall first of all attend to the debates concerning bourgeois feminine sexuality in the West and how these could be shown to have often been worked out in relation to empire itself. I shall then turn to the context of India and Africa to draw broadly on issues to do with marriage, domesticity and the relationship between these and civil society and politics in the two regions. The focus on India will be mainly via a discussion of the history of elite debates regarding the position of women and the domestic sphere, whilst the African examples will be used to highlight certain current contradictions affecting women's lives as they seek to negotiate their marital relationships between traditionalism and modernity. As will be seen from the discussion, the focus in both contexts is essentially on middle-class women, primarily because it is they who inherit the profound contradictions of modernity within a mixed traditional heritage. When I use the terms 'India' and 'Africa', it is not to suggest that these are homogeneous categories and that the conditions of women in the two locations were or are always the same. I use these terms to rivet attention on specific contexts which allow for a measure of generalization to enable the opening up of discussion on women's issues. Theory is of no value if it cannot be generalized; however, the purpose of generalization is to bring a particular perspective into view which can then be criticized, qualified or even abandoned once it is seen to have served the purpose for which it was set up. Women's problems can by no means be reduced to that concerning marriage, but I take up this focus mainly because marriage is thought to be a contractual arrangement between individuals (or families), and is hardly ever thought in and of itself to be a concern of policy-makers, or indeed of activists, except in the area of family planning. The serious and useful debates that have been and are being pursued by women's organizations on prostitution, women's labour, the control of women's sexuality and reproductive capacities and the impact of Aids and other factors that affect women have to be supplemented with serious analyses of what lies in the 'invisible' area of marriage that arguably influences the ways in which they construe their identities and articulate some of their deepest aspirations. The somewhat intricate focus of this chapter is adopted in order to place a simultaneous emphasis on macro and micro structures affecting women's happiness and well-being, multiple levels that impose a particular need for subtlety in the discussion of women's issues in postcolonial studies.

The West, Feminine Sexuality and Otherness

Gayatri Spivak argues in 'Three Women's Texts and a Critique of Imperialism' (1985) that certain mainstream nineteenth-century texts such as Charlotte Brontë's *Jane Eyre* reveal the need for Western bourgeois feminism to assert its identity against the 'native' woman. Spivak's argument turns mainly on the place given to Rochester's mad first wife in the novel. Principally, she pursues the ideological correlatives of the novel's relationship to ideas about plantation culture, bestiality and otherness that are arguably part of the ideological background of the novel. The mad Bertha Mason is to Spivak a coding of the native other whose partial beast-like nature has to be somehow contained by the text in order to enable Jane's feminine identity to be fully expressed. It is not for nothing that Bertha burns herself and the Rochester house at the end of the novel. Spivak's arguments are complexly put and she extends her inquiry to address Jean Rhys's *Wide Sargasso Sea* in its 're-writing' of the position of Bertha Mason as well as Mary Shelley's *Frankenstein* and its different perception of otherness, viewed through the frame of the nameless monster.[1]

If Spivak's contentions seem exorbitant and drawn too narrowly from an analysis of literary texts, they gain greater impact when placed alongside other more elaborate discussions of ideas of Western bourgeois feminine sexuality in the imperial period. Gilman (1993) has already noted that by treating sexual and mental pathologies long associated with Jews and Blacks not as external racialized categories but as consequences of civilization itself, Freud offers a whole new discourse for thinking about Western sexuality in relation to race. But it is Ann Laura Stoler's *Race and the Education of Desire* (1995) that provides the more extensive and sustained contextualization of this relation. Her focus is on the discourse of bourgeois sexuality as it was elaborated in Dutch colonialism, but she draws wider implications about European sexuality more generally and suggests that the 'history of Western sexuality must be located in the production of historical Others, in the broader force field of empire where technologies of sex, self and power were defined as "European" and "Western," as they were refracted and remade' (p. 195). The discursive and practical fields in which nineteenth-century bourgeois sexuality emerged were situated 'on an imperial landscape where the cultural accoutrements of bourgeois distinction were partially shaped through contrasts forged in the politics and language of race'. As she notes:

Bourgeois civilities were defined through a language of difference that drew images of racial purity and sexual virtue. That language of difference conjured up the supposed moral bankruptcy of culturally dissonant populations, distinguishing them from the interests of those who ruled ... bourgeois morality was strategically allied with the moral authority of nineteenth-century liberal states.

[The] discourse on bourgeois selves was founded on what Foucault would call a particular 'grid of intelligibility,' a hierarchy of distinctions in perception and practice that conflated, substituted, and collapsed the categories of racial, class and sexual Others strategically and at different times.

(Stoler, 1995: 10, 11)

The main point she seeks to clarify is that Foucault's *History of Western Sexuality* would have been a very different text if he had taken empire into account. Her study is devoted to rectifying this Foucaultian anomaly.

Stoler's is one of a growing number of studies that try to show the links between Western subjectivity and empire. The point that is increasingly highlighted is that different aspects of metropolitan culture derived their main contours and dynamics from being developed alongside an understanding of the realities that imperial expansion had brought to the foreground with respect to other races, other geographies, other flora and fauna and other cultures. The colonies were more than merely sites of exploitation; they were also 'laboratories of modernity' (1995: 15–16).[2]

Another and more invidious factor in the relationship between the West and its others was the much discussed discursive practice of imagining the colonized as feminine and subordinate (see Young, 1995a; Sinha, 1995). At base, these tropes of the colonized were done in a carefully hierarchical manner in such a way that the racial other, figured as female or effeminate, was always in a position of subordination. It is not by accident that this should have been the case, because in the West itself women were placed in a subordinate role in judicial, cultural and historical texts. In *The Sexual Contract* (1988) Carole Pateman shows how debates about the marriage contract in the eighteenth and nineteenth centuries never raised the fundamental question of the power of men over the sexual 'goods' of women. This notion of sexual goods encouraged feminist critics of the marriage contract to raise analogies between the position of women in marriage and that of slaves, servants and workers. An analysis of the subjection of wives, she notes, helps throw light onto other forms of subordination because the marriage contract was essentially a labour contract (pp. 116–53).

Empire, Popular Culture and Female Civility

Popular discourse itself, when figuring bourgeois female civility, was keen to establish a degree of hierarchy between the sexes. The popular imagination in imperial Europe was always fed by a variety of popularly disseminated forms ranging from homilies and sermons to songs, tracts and the theatrical dramatization of ideas and concepts drawn from religion and elsewhere. From at least the sixteenth century, the theatre was arguably second only to the Church as a mass medium through which general cultural ideas were focalized and disseminated. By way of plays about manners and civil behaviour the theatre becomes the prism for focalizing ideas of bourgeois civility that were arguably common in the general culture itself. A fascinating example of such theatre, combining concerns with bourgeois civility with ideas about race and sexuality, is provided in George Colman's *Inkle and Yarico*, a popular pro-abolitionist play first produced in London in 1787. This relatively unknown play is partially a satirization of slaveholders' attitudes to natives; it is a play that draws its pro-abolitionist energies from the depiction of the nobility of the native Yarico in contrast to the dastardly commercial motivations of Inkle, whose life she saves when he is abandoned by his ship on the coast of America. He later tries to sell her off when they get to Barbados in an effort to extricate himself from her and to make it easier for him to marry the daughter of the governor of Barbados, to whom he had earlier pledged his love. One of the key features of the play is its evocation of the commercial interests of the City of London in the period and the links between race, sexuality and projected feminine civilities. The Inkle and Yarico story is now a legend in Barbados and has recently been rewritten as a beautiful novel by Beryl Gilroy (1996) as well as being dramatized in Barbados, Cambridge and London in the last few years. It would be impossible to do full justice to the complex issues of race, class and gender that the play raises. Given a different context, one might even feel tempted to read this play alongside Conrad's *Heart of Darkness*, or even a non-literary text such as P. G. Cain and A. G. Hopkins's *British Imperialism: Innovation and Expansion, 1688–1914* (1993b), to see how their thesis of the place business and commercial classes in Britain had in the expansion and consolidation of empire might be read against the grain by rerouting it through popular couplings of commerce and empire. For our purposes here, however, let me just focus on a few points in the play pertinent to the discussion of the historical inflections of feminine tropes of otherness.

The first few scenes establish the fact that a ship from London has temporarily come aground in a bay on the coast of America. Trudge, Medium, Inkle and others have taken to shore and are now quite terrified of being caught by the natives. Trudge is Inkle's apprentice in Threadneedle Street (spoken of as the nerve centre of the business nexus in London) and has a prominent role in the play as a sort of wise fool, providing robust humour along with wry criticisms of the behaviour of his master and of others he comes into contact with. At the beginning of the play he is with Medium and they are both running around frantically in search of Inkle. They are in mortal dread of being captured by the natives. They pause at a point to get their breath back, and reflect on their absurd situation:

> MEDIUM: This it is to have to do with a schemer! a fellow who risques his life, for a chance of advancing his interest.—Always advantage in view! Trying here to make discoveries that may promote his profit in England. Another Botany Bay scheme, mayhap. Nothing else could induce him to quit our foraging party from the ship; when he knows every inhabitant here is not only as black as a pepper-corn, but as hot into the bargain—and *I*, like a fool, to follow him! and then to let him loiter behind.—Why Nephew!—Why, Inkle.—(*calling*)
> TRUDGE: Why Ink—Well! Only to see the difference of men; he'd have thought it very hard, now, if I had let him call so often after me. Ah! I wish he was calling after me now in the old jog-trot way again. What a fool I was to leave London for foreign parts!—That ever I shou'd leave Threadneedle-street, to thread an American forest, where a man's as soon lost as a needle in a bottle of hay.
> (Colman, 1787: 3)[3]

The stereotype of the native as being 'hot' is a familiar one to students of colonial discourse and should not detain us here. What is of interest is that this early expression of doubt about the rationale for leaving the peaceful shores of England for the dangers of America is later answered by Inkle in terms of what might be taken as an expression of a bourgeois liberal attitude to leisure and travel:

> MEDIUM: Zounds, one wou'd think, by your confounded composure, that you were walking in St. James's Park instead of an American forest, and that all the beasts were nothing but good company. The hollow trees here, centry boxes, and the lions in 'em soldiers; the jackalls, courtiers, the crocodiles, fine women, and the baboons, beaux. What the plague made you loiter so long?
> INKLE: Reflection.
> . . .

> MEDIUM: And pray, if I may be so bold, what mighty scheme has just
> tempted you to employ your head, when you ought to make use of
> your heels?
> INKLE: My heels! Here's a pretty doctrine! Do you think I travel
> merely for motion? A fine expensive plan for a trader truly. What,
> wou'd you have a man of business come abroad, scamper extrava-
> gantly here and there and every where, then return home, and have
> nothing to tell, but that he has been here and there and every where?
> 'Sdeath, Sir, would you have me travel like a lord?
>
> (pp. 9, 10)

Note how, in Medium's words, the unknown terrain is remapped as
the civil(ized) centre of London. This prepares the way for Inkle's
own justification of the need for rigorous mental pursuits in the very
midst of chaos. His rationale for travelling is quite different from the
ostensible one of pursuing commercial interests. His is to acquire
greater polish, sophistication and *knowledge* of the world. Thus
Inkle expresses the interests of the rising middle class which seek to
combine commercialism with a structured cultivation of leisure. And
the chaotic theatre of the 'jungles' of America provides an excellent
if incongruous backdrop against which to express these interests.

If one of the things the play does is to set up a background for
the expression and mockery of business people such as Inkle, it also
provides an understanding of what the male-centred business world
requires of their women. The first inkling of this is provided in the
first encounter between Inkle and Yarico:

> INKLE: How wild and beautiful! Sure there's magic in her shape, and
> she has riveted me to the place; but where shall I look for safety?
> let me fly and avoid my death.
> YARICO: Oh! no, but—(*as if puzzled*) well then die stranger, but don't
> depart. I will try to preserve you; and if you are kill'd, Yarico must
> die too! Yet, 'tis I alone can save you; your death is certain without
> my influence; and indeed, indeed, you shall not want it.
> INKLE: My kind Yarico! but what means must be us'd for my safety?
> YARICO: My cave must conceal you; none enter it since my father was
> slain in battle. I will bring you food by day, then lead you to our
> unfrequented groves by moonlight, to listen to the nightingale. If you
> should sleep, I'll watch you, and wake you when there's danger.
> INKLE: Generous Maid! Then to you I will owe my life; and whilst it
> lasts, nothing shall part us.
>
> (p. 21)

To our twentieth-century post-Freudian sensibility, any association of
caves with women is obviously to be interpreted in sexual terms. What

is more important here, however, is that in saving the lives of Inkle (and Trudge), Yarico's romantic language effortlessly places her as his servant. It is an amorous encounter conveyed in the classic idiom of romantic love, something which in this context has more sombre implications especially because articulated in a text about slavery, thus immediately raising the unhappy possibility of tragedy for her. It is only a small step later from romantic service to slavery when Inkle conspires to sell her off. Even though in their early encounter there seems to be a reciprocal bond of love between them, Inkle feels able to break this bond because he sees her not only as a 'maid' (with all the various connotations of this word) but also always already as a potential slave. It would be disingenuous to press too hard for the analogy we noted earlier in Carole Pateman's comments on the implicit conceptual parallels between wives, servants and slaves, but in *Inkle and Yarico* we see a subtle and troubling elision of all three categories. And this takes place in the play's discursive framing of male–female relationships as an encounter between a potential slaver and his potential slave.

Any doubts we might have had about what people like Inkle really think about women are dispelled later on in the play when he makes explicit his reasons for not telling Yarico he has fallen out of love with her prior to attempting to sell her off. It comes at the point when he is anguishing over how to break the news to her without getting entangled in expressions of endearment and devotion. He wishes he had more time in which to do it. 'I wish', he says, 'this marriage were more distant, that I might break it by degrees.' 'This marriage' is the pre-contracted one between himself and Narcissa, daughter of the governor of Barbados. He continues:

> She'd take my purpose better, were it less suddenly delivered. Women's weak minds bear griefs as colts do burdens: load them with their full weight at once, and they sink under it, but every day add little imperceptibly to little, 'tis wonderful how much they'll carry.
>
> (p. 60)

In discussing *Inkle and Yarico*, we must bear in mind that the play takes pains to mock Inkle's dastardly position and to show up its hollowness; but the point is not so much the excesses of his passivization of women as the fact that they themselves are shown to take on these roles regularly of their own accord, and thus to consolidate the essentially hierarchical gender relations seen everywhere in the universe of the play. The implications of these hierarchies are infinitely more complicated for being staged as an encounter with women as racial others in a progressive pro-abolitionist text. The contradiction in this position could be related to the fact that even such progressive discourses were not entirely free of the racial and sexual hierarchies that structured the dominant discourses they set themselves against. Furthermore, as has been noted by Eze (1997) among others, the Enlightenment itself proliferated such ideas of otherness even whilst elaborating a scientific rationality upon which modern thought was to be grounded. By the middle of the nineteenth century people like Gobineau (1853) and others had fully coupled race and sexuality in arguing for the distinctive foundations of Western civilization, a process which Robert Young discusses in terms of the discourse of 'colonial desire' (see Young, 1995a: 99–117, 175–82).

An additional peculiarity of Inkle and Yarico, which we should note before passing on to the next section, is the degree to which this popular text reifies America in order to create a coherent arena for imagining the otherness of the native whilst proceeding with the business of contemplating a female sexuality amenable to the desires of the bourgeois middle-class male. The most obvious site of this reification is in the scene of half-naked natives in hot pursuit of the travellers that comes early in the text. One must think back to what must have been George Colman's first production in 1787 and the reaction that would have come from his audiences to these figures. If the 'America' that is figured in the play is supposed to invoke for the audience the historical America, then the play deliberately manufactures a number of confusions to allow it to consolidate its racial stereotypes. The 1770s were a particularly turbulent period for blacks in America. The year 1773 saw the publication of Phyllis Wheatley's *Poems on Various Subjects, Religious and Moral*. After an oral examination by the respectable men of Boston to ascertain whether in fact this slave girl could actually have written such poetry, it was to London that she came to find publishers for her poems. And it was to great publicity. She was warmly received by people such as Benjamin Franklin and Brooke Watson, the future lord mayor of London, who it is said gave her a copy of Milton's *Paradise Lost* as a token of his admiration. The publication of Wheatley's poems was nothing short of a media event. The period also saw the beginnings of the American Revolution. In 1775, Lord Dunmore, a Scotsman and the last governor of Virginia, issued an invitation to all slaves of rebel owners to come and fight on behalf of the Crown in exchange for their freedom. Several thousand came together to form the Royal Ethiopian Regiment and to fight alongside royal troops. The period, then, saw blacks in a very active if problematic role in history, something that would not have been completely lost on the citizens of England of the period.

Why, then, does Colman decide to populate 'America' with savage cannibals and to institute a palpable anxiety in the theatrical encounter with it? And, even more to the point, why does he create a native woman with the full romantic sensibilities of a Western bourgeois female in such a context of implicit barbarity? At one level, what Colman does is to conflate a barbaric Africa with a rapidly changing America. He needs the stereotype of the noble savage, but not the noble savage as was emerging in the theatre of the War of Independence in America. He transfers the savages from Africa and places them in America in order to show that these people were not yet *in history*, even if they were historically contesting the hegemony of the slave system in open if limited ways. At a second and more subtle level, he splits the signifier 'native' and reserves the pristine savagery of the imagined native for the warriors while transferring the nobility of the species to Yarico. Colman both reifies and dehistoricizes America whilst at the same time creating a context within which a conception of Western bourgeois femininity can be located that runs completely counter to the implications of the barbaric background. America, then, is the object of a double fantasy, harbouring both the greatest anxieties to do with native others as well as the ambivalence of desire attaching to the trope of the native female as the sexual projection of the Western conquering male. The play could then be said to be producing a subversive abolitionist discourse from the very heartland of reigning racial and gender stereotypes. Thus we see how Stoler's contentions about the inextricable relation between Western bourgeois subjectivity and questions of race and otherness are played out within Colman's theatre, a theatre that was itself contributing to the then raging debates about slavery and otherness at the high point of the abolitionist struggle.

Women as Sites and Subjects

If in the West a patriarchal discourse has regularly helped figure other races in terms of hierarchized gender relations, the curious thing is that this has frequently had resonances in other cultures that also have traditionally placed women in a subordinate position. The fact of patriarchy and of women's subordination is so rampant and cross-cultural that it leads the American anthropologist Sherry Ortner to ask in the 1970s whether this could be attributed to women being universally conflated with nature in a culture/nature divide.[4] For postcolonial studies, it might be argued that it is when a Western patriarchal discourse subtly coincides with local practices in certain historical conjunctures that the true cross-cultural nature of female subordination becomes most acutely evident. But this coincidence does not always manifest itself as a coincidence as such, but as something which on a superficial level seems quite different. In the nationalist context of the decolonization struggles in particular, the conflation manifested itself as a radical opposition, thus beclouding the fact that women were the sites of debates in which they had little voice or representation. For many feminist postcolonial critics, what seemed historically to have been a radical opposition was actually a dialectical relation between similar patriarchal discourses which sought to speak for and to represent women's lives without real recourse to them.

The nature of this phenomenon is best seen in the context of nationalist India and the debates about womanhood that raged among the elite. There were many forms in which the contradictions and discursive complicities manifested themselves. One was around the fraught issue of *sati* or widow burning. The debates raged from the 1820s. As Lata Mani (1989) shows in her superb analysis of the various ways in which the British authorities and the conservative and radical Indians debated the issue, the desire on all sides was to find incontestable reference points within the religious texts of the Hindu tradition by which to evaluate the issue of *sati* and decide upon its historicity and contemporary relevance. There was a hectic debate on the relative merits of custom and Scripture, with Scripture finally taken by the British as being the more authoritative grounds for intervening in the rituals. Crucially, however, the debate was between the British and an indigenous male elite, with the widow herself being completely marginal to the debates. As Lata Mani succinctly puts it: 'Instead women become sites upon which various versions of scripture/tradition/law are elaborated and contested' (1989: 115). This is a point also made by Spivak in her much cited essay 'Can the Subaltern Speak' (1993: 98–104).

Also significant were the debates of Indian nationalists in Bengal from about the middle of the nineteenth century onwards concerning the proper behaviour of Indian women. As Partha Chatterjee (1989) shows, for this issue to be properly linked to a nationalist agenda, it was important for a material/spiritual distinction to be made, with a series of other binary oppositions such as those between modernity/tradition, outside/inside, public/domestic all flowing from this initial distinction. The nationalists resolved the woman issue by a selective appropriation of modernity in which women could gain education but had to be 'good wives' and not aspire to the public sphere. In Chatterjee's view the woman question was recast as one between an Indian spirituality of which women were seen to be the supreme expression and guardians, and a Western modernity thought to be saturated with the worst of materialistic impulses.

A related set of ideas to do with companionate marital relationships and the position of women in them was also part of the discourse which the nationalists were concerned with. In the growing literature on appropriate female manners, there was an insistence that though women should be educated, this education should not be allowed to transform them into *memsahibs* (white women), universally considered to be the epitome of recklessness, disrespect and danger not just for the home but for all appropriate virtues of feminine civility. As Dipesh Chakrabarty shows, again with respect to Bengal from 1850 to 1920, the idea of women's simultaneous modernity and traditionalism displays the curious problematic common in Third World history of evolutionary trajectories moving in the direction of a Western modernity that nonetheless demonstrate a transitional lack on questions of subjectivity. For Chakrabarty, Indian history is paradigmatic of this problem:

> There was, for example, a degree of consensus over the desirability of domestic 'discipline' and 'hygiene' as practices reflective of a state of modernity, but the word *freedom*, yet another important term in the rhetoric of the modern, hardly ever acted as the register of such a social consensus. It was a passionately disputed word, and we would be wrong to assume that the passions reflected a simple and straightforward battle between the sexes. The word was assimilated to the nationalist need to construct cultural boundaries that supposedly separated the 'European' from the 'Indian.' The dispute over this word was thus central to the discursive strategies through which a subject position was created enabling the 'Indian' to speak. What the Bengali literature on women's education played out was a battle between a nationalist construction of a cultural norm of the patriarchal, patrilocal, patrilineal, extended family and the ideal of the patriarchal, bourgeois nuclear family that was implicit in the European/imperialist/universalist discourse on the 'freedoms' of individualism, citizenship, and civil society.
> (Chakrabarty, 1992: 12)

We shall later on take up more fully the question of companionate nuclear marital relationships and the tensions with respect to extended family systems in our African examples. For now, let us just note that the 'lack' in the discourse Chakrabarty describes seemed to grow around the question of whether the educated Indian woman in the imagination of the Indian nationalist was going to be a citizen or a subject. For the term 'freedom' in modernity could never be properly settled without recourse to ideas of citizenship and what its absence meant in the colonial arena.[5] There was no doubt that the elite men contesting Western hegemony were in fact clamouring to be citizens in their own right. It was when it came to women and the domestic sphere that the matter became less clear. The loss of clarity could be said to be directly related to the fact that women were located within the series of polarities that Chatterjee speaks of (materiality/spirituality, outside/inside, modernity/tradition) that were implicitly hierarchical and that were ultimately geared to subserving elite male interests. Recalling James's epigraph about the inherent 'loading of the social dice' with which we opened this chapter, we could restate the problem Chakrabarty identifies here as not just between two contradictory views of the family, but one of the struggle between ideas of citizenship and subjecthood for women articulated within various intersecting Western and Indian discourses in which women remained marginal because subordinate within the patriarchal and hierarchical discourses by which they were represented. This is not to suggest that women did not participate in the making of Indian history or that they were entirely passive in the unfolding historical processes. It is rather to show that in the discursive and ideological environment of their representation they were essentially marginalized and absent. As Spivak notes with respect to the historiography of the Subaltern Studies group,

> The question is not of female participation in insurgency, or the ground rules of the sexual division of labour, for both of which there is 'evidence'. It is, rather, that, both as object of colonialist historiography and as subject of insurgency, the ideological construction of gender keeps the male dominant. If, in the context of colonial production, the subaltern has no history and cannot speak, the subaltern female is even more deeply in the shadow.
>
> (1993: 83)

It is important to emphasize here that what has been generally taken to be a controversial assertion by Spivak of the inability of the subaltern to speak is in this context not about the possibilities of insurgency or resistance; it is rather that in the discursive ideological representation of the subaltern (woman), she is metaphorically unvoiced.[6]

There were times when the split between modernity and freedom generated anguished moments for educated women who stood up alongside their husbands at the forefront of the nationalist struggle. A poignant case is that of Ramabai Ranande, who was married at an early age to the renowned scholar and jurist Mahadev Govin Ranande. Once, rather than make a choice between sitting with either orthodox or reformist women on a visit to the temple, she sidesteps potential conflict by feigning illness. In inexplicable anger at this decision, her husband repays her with a stony silence, which is not mitigated even when she ritually washes his feet. Eventually and in some bewilderment at his anger, she apologizes, upon which he scolds her roundly, insisting that she behave 'according to his will' (Tharu and Lalita, 1991: 288–9). As Ania Loomba notes in discussing Ramabai Ranande's predicament, the 'self-fashioning of the nationalist male thus required his fashioning of his wife into a fresh subservience, even though this new role included her education and freedom from other orthodoxies' (Loomba, 1998: 221). At one level this illustrates the contradictory position of people such as Ramabai caught between a practical affirmation of citizenship in the public arena at the same time as she negotiates a subordinate position within her marital relationship. In a sense Ramabai's problem was with a marital arrangement that was supposed to be inherently companionate and yet instituted an older-style pattern of male dominance in which she had to anticipate her husband's public desires and fulfil them. It is this contradiction between companionateness and hierarchy within marital relationships to which we will now turn, but this time transferring the discussion to Africa.

Nuclear Reactions: Women, Marriage and the Question of Agency

If one wanted quickly to raise the most problematic ideas governing women's and men's different dispositions in marriage, one could do worse than turn to Euripides' *Medea*, a text that by dealing with the atrophying of the basic instincts governing companionate marital relationships and the tragic consequences that arise from this forces a questioning not just of the basis of marital relationships but of the motivations of human actions more generally. The Medea–Jason relationship and the difficulties between them is paradigmatic of some of the issues we will be taking up in this section.

Let us recall the main details of this fascinating story. On the quest for the Golden Fleece, Jason and the Argonauts reach Colchis, where among the impossible tasks set them by Aeëtes, King of Colchis, Jason is asked to sow dragons' teeth from which armed men will rise whose fury will be turned against him and the Argonauts. With the help of the enchantress Medea, the king's daughter, Jason successfully accomplishes the tasks and gets the Golden Fleece. On their way back they have a number of adventures including one in which Medea murders and cuts into pieces her younger brother Absyrtus and scatters the fragments into the sea to check her father's pursuit. In another instance she gets the daughters of Pelias (Jason's usurping uncle) to kill him by immersing him in a cauldron of magic herbs which she tricks them into believing is an elixir of eternal life.[7]

Jason and Medea then come to Corinth where they marry and settle, she as a barbarian foreigner and he as a heroic Greek. When Euripides' play opens, Jason has abandoned Medea and her two sons and married the daughter of Creon, the King of Corinth. One of his reasons is that by marrying her he will ensure that his children become citizens of Corinth. His reasons are informed by a pragmatic coldness and a complete want of feeling and make Medea by turns distraught and incensed. Setting aside the many tragic events that take place in the play (Medea's murder of the princess through the gift of the poisoned gown, her subsequent murder of her two sons to spite Jason and the reasons she gives for doing all this), I would like to focus instead on the reasons she gives Jason for her anger over his betrayal:

> I will begin at the beginning. When you were sent
> To master the fire-breathing bulls, yoke them, and sow
> The deadly furrow, then I saved your life; and that
> Every Greek who sailed with you in Argo knows.
> The serpent that kept watch over the Golden Fleece,
> Coiled round it fold on fold, unsleeping – it was I
> Who killed it, and so lit the torch of your success.
> I willingly deceived my father; left my home;
> With you I came to Iolcus by Mount Pelion,
> Showing much love and little wisdom. There I put
> King Pelias to the most horrible of deaths
> By his own daughters' hands, and ruined his whole house.
> And in return for this you have the wickedness
> To turn me out, to get yourself another wife,
> Even after I had borne you sons! If you had still
> Been childless I could have pardoned you for hankering
> After this new marriage.
>
> (Euripides, 1963: 31)

Two things should be noted about what Medea says here. First is that she helps Jason gain the Golden Fleece in a manner known to 'every Greek'. The adventures she undergoes with him and on his behalf define her as the equal of any Argonaut in terms both of courage and of resourcefulness. She is his companion-in-adventure, much like any of them. It is this crucial factor that underpins what she thinks is a companionate marital relationship between them. The second thing to note is her radical destruction of her own familial ties in order to be with him. She deceives her own father, and, according to the account referred to earlier, even kills and cuts up her own brother. What we read out of this is that to establish the companionate basis of the relationship between her and Jason, she has had to abrogate all other primary blood and familial claims to her devotion. It is this extreme sacrifice for the sake of love that makes her assessment of Jason's betrayal so absolute. Because she has herself negated all ties of kinship to be with him, his attempt at divorce is seen by her in terms of a heartless repudiation of the terms of obligation that should have bound them to each other.

The Medea–Jason relationship may be taken as paradigmatic of the affective foundation of the companionate nuclear family set-up. In expressing this affective foundation in such an extreme form Euripides allows us to see more clearly the many factors that militate against the consolidation of such a relationship. Part of Medea's problem was her anomalous status as both insider and outsider, brave and helpful to the Greek heroic cause but also an uncivilized barbarian. The direct marker of her barbarian nature comes partly in her inordinate anger and partly also in her perception as a sorceress, both of which to Creon require that she be banished from Corinth. It is also partly the fact of her outsider status that Jason uses to justify his going for a Greek woman. His anxiety reflects his perception of the potential damage that the barbarian outsider might mean for his rise in the ranks of a civil Greek polity. If for Medea, her anomalous status as insider/outsider is taken by Jason as a reason for jilting her, it might even be argued that it is precisely this insider/outsider status that women constantly have to negotiate, especially in many parts of the Third World where the establishment of companionate marital relationships has to be achieved in the teeth of traditional ties with extended family systems. This anomalous status is rarely made a contentious point for the position of women, and many women have had peaceful coexistence between a nuclear family arrangement and the ties of the extended family. However, there are various instances where this is not the case, and the business of negotiation is constantly short-circuited by the difficulties inherent in making meaning of the conjuncture of modernity and traditionalism with respect to marriage. This is arguably the case in Africa.

The companionate nuclear marriage in Africa is itself a legacy of Christianity. According to Kristin Mann in her excellent study of the ideology and socio-economic circumstances surrounding marriage among the elite in turn-of-the-century colonial Lagos, the rules governing Christian marriage as expressed in the 1884 Marriage Ordinance not only sought to alter traditional Yoruba inheritance practices, but also gave wives and husbands rights to each other's estates and made Christian wives and their children sole inheritors of a man's property. Furthermore, it disinherited a man's siblings and any children by customary wives or concubines. The Christian form of marriage went through a series of vicissitudes and at various points men chose a dual approach combining a Christian marriage with a traditional union. Furthermore, with increasing economic hardship from the 1890s, Christian marriages were postponed, with men entering into customary unions and waiting till much later to re-establish their marriages on a Christian footing. Unlike the men, however, women as a whole were less ambivalent towards Christian marriage, and when given the choice often opted for that as against the customary one (Mann, 1985; see also Moore, 1988: 119–27). Even though the Christian marriage system is by no means the predominant one among Africans, it is nonetheless the case that an idea of a man and a woman coming together and living away from the extended family system is very popular, especially in the urban areas and among the growing educated classes.

Two key features in the nuclear family arrangement that constantly lead to tension need to be noted. Apart from the fact that spouses are supposed to have equal access to each other's property, perhaps the other key defining factor is the issue of conjugal privacy, where the spouses are supposed to build up their nuclear family together with as little interference as possible from the extended family system or, indeed, from any outside intrusion. Secondly, the Christian nuclear family arrangement is the joining of individuals in love and companionship, rather than the joining of lineages; but it is rare that the nuclear family arrangement is not entangled in other realities that constantly challenge and undermine it. The greatest strain on nuclear conjugal relationships comes from perceptions of the influence of the extended families of both spouses, with the main area of stress coming when one partner, frequently the male, is dominant in decisions about resource allocation. In her book on marriage among civil servants in Ghana,

Christine Oppong (1981) states what can be taken to be a commonly shared observation among urban married couples in Ghana:

> Most of the husbands and wives were noted, either overtly or covertly, to give praise and blame to their spouses for the way in which resources were allocated and decisions taken. They also in several cases, criticized their spouses' kin and associates for their influence, either in diverting resources or loyalty elsewhere or in influencing their partners' attitudes in a way contrary to their interests. The majority of couples referred, at some point, to the marriage and family relationships of other sets of people whom they knew about, including their own parents and relatives and friends. In addition they referred to a number of ethnic stereotypes including Akan and English.
>
> (p. 142)

It is however the case that it is women who end up bearing the main brunt of the contradictions in such conjugal relationships. As I hope to show shortly, this is particularly the case with respect to spousal death, when the full force of extended family claims is brought to bear on the nuclear set-up.

Because of the nature of economic arrangements and, indeed, of the nature of lineage and family arrangements in Africa, the idea of the nuclear family is never allowed to solidify into a clear-cut category in opposition to more traditional forms. In practice there is always an area of overlap between the nuclear arrangement and the claims of extended families. Because of the difficulties in the way of childcare arrangements, especially for middle-class urban women, it is quite often the case that members of the extended family are invited to come and live within the nuclear unit. In other set-ups, the nuclear family unit takes up residence as close to other family members as possible in order to share the burden of childcare and other things. Furthermore, because of the various life-cycle rituals to do with birth, puberty, marriage and funerals in which most Africans, urban and otherwise, are encouraged to participate, there is actually the creation of a two-tiered approach to familial relations, with the nuclear and the extended family ideas acquiring different emphases depending on the contexts in which the nuclear family unit finds itself. Most middle-class marriages in Africa are the combination of two modes: the nuclear conjugal one dominates at home, while the extended family one makes itself felt during traditional family gatherings around life-cycle rituals or at important festivals. But by far the most important set of life-cycle rituals at which the status of the nuclear family faces its greatest challenge is that of rituals to do with spousal death, from the preparation of the body for burial through to the funeral and the disposal of property afterwards. The tension is most acute when the spouse dies intestate, but, as will be shown shortly, the writing of a will is no guarantee that the extended family network will not make drastic intrusions in the decisions taken by the surviving female spouse. The contradictions between modernity and traditionalism affect women most strongly at the death of their spouse, for it is then that the full force of kinship claims on the individual are brought to bear. The question of death heightens the problem immensely because of the issues of property rights which become the key focus of concern immediately after burial.

Stories abound from all across sub-Saharan Africa of the severe treatment that women face at the hands of extended family systems on the death of their spouses. Two particular examples that serve to focalize the contradictions most neatly are the accounts of what is labelled by Kenyans as the S. M. Otieno burial saga in 1987 and that of the confusion surrounding the burial of Joe Appiah in 1990, richly told by Anthony Kwame Appiah as the Epilogue to his *In My Father's House* (1992). The Otieno case is much the more complicated, partly because the misunderstanding between Wambui Waiyaki Otieno and members of her deceased husband's clan had an added political dimension since it was interpreted as a contest between the Luo and the Kikuyu. Wambui Otieno was a Kikuyu and had been deeply involved in the Mau Mau struggle against the British authorities in the period leading up to Kenyan independence. She was arrested several times, and spent a long stretch in prison before meeting her lawyer husband in the early 1960s. Her husband was a highly regarded Luo. By the time of her husband's death in 1987, the balance of power in the country was firmly in favour of the Luos because of Arap Moi's presidency. Moi took over from the Kikuyu Jomo Kenyatta in 1978, and to many observers had steadily instituted a process by which to empower the minority Luo tribe in Kenyan politics.[8] In the introduction to *Mau Mau's Daughter*, Wambui Otieno's autobiography spanning her life from Mau Mau activist, through feminist politician to the painful events surrounding her husband's burial, E. S. Atieno Odhiambo observes that one of the most important themes that has intersected with the formation of Kenyan history has been the 'deep politics of the clan, pitting insiders against outsiders, clansmen against foreigners, original landowners against sojourners' (1998: xii–xiii). In the particular case of Wambui, the events surrounding her husband's burial and her treatment at the hands of her husband's clan resonate closely with the paradigmatic insider/ outsider status we noted of Medea.

The main details of the Otieno Saga are that he died intestate of a heart attack on 16 December 1987. He had said many times both to his wife and to members of his extended family that he wanted to be buried at his home in Nairobi or on one of the farms he owned on the outskirts of the city. The extended clan had different ideas and maintained that as a Luo he should be buried on the ancestral land, about 300 miles away from the city. The matter went to court. The first hearing ruled in favour of Wambui, but after a protracted judicial process this was reversed in the Appeal Court. Many witnesses, including Odera Oruka, Professor of Philosophy at the University of Nairobi, were called to explain traditional Luo customs. In Oruka's answers he sides firmly with the traditional interpretation, at a point even suggesting that a person's will might be set aside if it was thought to violate the taboos of the people. This was supported in the Appeal Court's judgement. The crucial thing in deciding whether a person's choice of burial place is sanctioned by the traditions of the tribe or not is whether a person's house has been properly blessed by parents or relatives with the necessary ceremonies. Without such blessings, the house remains a 'house' and not a 'home' in the traditional sense (Oruka, 1990: 67–83; Otieno and Presley, 1998: 188–91). The point to be noted here is not so much that there is anything wrong with getting such parental or clan blessings, but the fact that even in an urbanized setting, the clan has to sanction the house within which any conjugal relationship may be established. If, as is the case in the Otieno instance, the man has not had recourse to the blessings of his family for personal or any other reasons, his body on death is claimed by the clan irrespective of what nature of conjugal relationship he may have had with his wife. The claims of the wife are completely overruled by those of the clan. Wambui Otieno is a highly urbanized, well-travelled and politically aware woman, as can readily be gleaned from her autobiography. In marrying her husband, she enters a conjugal nuclear relationship in which man and wife are supposed to be equal. What is more important is that during his lifetime her husband was never in doubt about the pre-eminent place that his wife had in his life. There was every indication that she was his closest ally, sometimes even helping to manage his law chambers when he was travelling or ill. But on his death, we see the manifest strain that is placed on the nuclear family arrangement by the very fact of having to be blessed by the extended clan. The blessing of the house, if not sought, is ultimately a curse against the home, something which Wambui and her children discover at great emotional cost.

Anthony Kwame Appiah's account of the wranglings over his father's burial provides a further dimension to women's insider/ outsider status and the contradictions between the nuclear and the extended family systems. Anthony's mother, Peggy Appiah, was an Englishwoman, daughter of Sir Stafford Cripps, one-time Chancellor of the Exchequer in Britain. Her middle-class credentials are unquestionable. Joe Appiah himself was a member of the Ashanti royal house. A renowned lawyer, he had for a long time been a key figure in Ghanaian politics, at a point in the late 1970s being named his country's Ambassador Plenipotentiary, a kind of role between Foreign Secretary and roving ambassador. Unlike Otieno, Joe Appiah does not die intestate. In a codicil to his will, he states explicitly that he wants to be buried in a Church ceremony by his wife of many years and their children. This turns out not to be a straightforward matter. As Anthony Appiah puts it, '[I]n our efforts to conduct the funeral in accordance with my father's desires – expressed in that codicil – we had to challenge, first, the authority of the matriclan – the Abusua – of which my father was erstwhile head; and, in the end, the will of the king of Asante, my uncle' (1992: 294). Anthony Appiah sees the various bewildering events that unfold as part of an almost fairytale reality:

> every attempt to understand what was happening took me further back into family history and the history of Asante; further away from abstractions ('tradition' and 'modernity', 'state' and 'society', 'matriclan' and 'patriclan'); further into what would probably seem to a European or American an almost fairytale world of witchcraft and wicked aunts and wise old women and men.
>
> (pp. 294–5)

In putting matters this way, Appiah renders the events ahistorical, almost willing them to be seen in terms of a quasi-mythical idiom governed by the moral imperatives of the folktale. This can well be understood, considering the apparent heartlessness of the extended family members. But in my view it is precisely the fractious meeting point between a nuclear family idea of conjugal relationships and the claims of an extended family system that needs to be addressed.

The details of the matrikin organization of the Akans (the Ashantis are arguably the best-known of these) is of some interest here. In the matrikin system, the matrilineage is the 'solidary important kin group for incorporating the newborn, for owning property, for supporting the dependent young and old – the unit for performance of important life-cycle rituals especially at death, and the context within which the young or old would always find a home and a source of permanent security' (Oppong, 1981: xx). Because of the essentially matrilineal social structure of the Akans, the most important tie is between mother and child, and between children of the same mother. Thus the rights of uterine siblings override the spousal rights of wives and children, since wives are supposed to retain their identity as kins in their own matriclans and are not integrated into the husband's matrikin. What should interest us here is not so much the question of property rights that derives from this, but the impact of this matrilineal order on the nuclear family arrangements that may be entered into by Akans. For, because the man's property is supposed to pass on to his sister's children, as a rule the greatest interference in any Akan nuclear family set-up comes from other women (i.e. non-wives) in the man's family. This ranges from sisters through to aunts and others. And because these other women in an Akan man's extended family are themselves technically excluded from their own husband's matrikin, they have an added interest in monitoring what happens in their brother's home, irrespective of whether this is a traditional or more modern nuclear arrangement. Thus we see that a great deal of pressure is brought to bear on the very idea of conjugal privacy, one of the central tenets of the nuclear marital relationship.

These details are significant for reinterpreting the seemingly heartless actions of Appiah's Aunt Victoria, his father's younger sister. Importantly, however, Aunt Victoria was also married to the Asantehene, king of the Ashantis, and had played a very influential part in Ashanti affairs. It is Aunt Victoria who leads the vanguard against Peggy and her children's claims to being the rightful people to decide on the funeral arrangements. On the Appiah side were senior officials of the Methodist Church of which his father had been a member, and on Aunt Victoria's side was the considerable authority and clout of the Ashanti stool. The initial trigger of conflict was around the precise dates on which the wake, the funeral itself and the subsequent burial were to take place. The dates the Appiah family settled upon seemed to have coincided with those of a major public ceremony in which the Asantehene had to be involved. They were called to the Asantehene's palace and were asked, by way of very sophisticated euphemisms, to alter the dates. This they were not prepared to do, as they had already got the sense that Aunt Victoria was preparing to take over the entire business of the burial from them. Quite in contrast to the Otieno case in Kenya, the Appiah family got strong support from the media, general public and even members of the Ashanti royal family itself. However, the grounds on which support was given to the Appiah family varied from a clear desire to fulfil Joe Appiah's wishes to a more curious desire to oppose Aunt Victoria, who it was thought was 'influencing' the Asantehene and trying to deploy the power of tradition for her own benefit (Appiah, 1992: 304). A process of demonization gradually unfolds around Aunt Victoria, strengthened by rumours that the food sent from the palace to the Appiah family might be poisoned. Her shift into the mode of the wicked woman of fairytales is complete.

And yet this process of demonization has to give us pause for thought. Where are our sympathies really supposed to lie in relation to the events Appiah has so carefully described? To Nkiru Nzegwu (1996) the whole of *In My Father's House* is an attempt to assert a patrilineal discourse in place of the matrilineal heritage that governs Ashanti life. The demonization of Aunt Victoria and of Appiah's extended family system is taken by her to be the culminating point in various references in the book to specific Western ideas of the family. Without necessarily agreeing with Nzegwu's polemical proposition, it is nonetheless useful to note that because Aunt Victoria is demonized *as a woman*, she herself represents the other pole of the contradiction between the nuclear family relationship and the claims of the extended matrilineal family system. The anguish she must have caused Peggy Appiah as an insider/outsider, whose status is further complicated by her being English, is not to be denied, but it also has to be noted that Aunt Victoria's demonization is part of another discourse that affects strong women more generally. Whereas in the Otieno case the campaign against the Otieno family was led by S. M. Otieno's younger brother in what appears to have been a largely masculine cohort, the opposition to the Appiah family was led by their father's sister. Secondly, when the pro-Wambui faction in the Kenyan press sought to launch a debate against the traditions, they did this by isolating heartless patriarchal men in the Luo clan for attack; contrastively, in the Appiah case, it was the excesses of women such as Aunt Victoria that became the centre of attention. Wambui was of course constantly criticized by her detractors for being a detribalized and disrespectful woman, but it seems to me that in both cases it was partly the assertiveness *of the women* in question that was put on trial at the bar of public perception. Anthony Appiah is himself in a somewhat awkward position. His allegiance rightly lies with his immediate family, and his rationale for standing up to the extended family at a time that must have been very trying for him and his immediate family is completely defensible. And yet, precisely because of the emotionally charged context in which he is constrained to interpret Aunt Victoria's actions, he lapses into the dominant patriarchal discourse that is used to explain away the behaviour of strong women as anomalous. From the other end of the conjunctural attitudes impinging upon nuclear family relations in Akan culture – other women in the extended matrilineal family system – Aunt Victoria expresses what must be the confusing position of uterine siblings who are themselves caught between traditionalism and modernity when confronting the marriages of their brothers. As we noted in the previous chapter in relation to Madame Koto in Okri's *The Famished Road*, the demonization of strong women is a major feature of patriarchal discourses when it is thought that masculine domains are under threat from women. Her case uncannily mirrors that of Aunt Victoria and the processes of demonization that attend their behaviour. The clash is always between residual and emergent values; and in this case it is women from both sides that are caught betwixt and between.

Going back to our central concern about the uneasy place of wives caught between the nuclear family arrangement and the extended kinship network, it has to be noted that in both the Otieno and Appiah cases, the true extent of the transitional crisis makes itself fully felt only after the husband has died. It is almost as if on the death of the husband, the women are thought to be powerless and have to be made to submit to the dictates of tradition, irrespective of the fact that the central parameters of conjugality within which they may have defined their lives for many years go contrary to any secondary role given to wives by tradition. This tension, definable in a simple way as that between modernity and traditionalism, persists even when women are gaining greater education, freedom and the ability to define the main terms of their marital relationships by their actions both inside and outside the home. This state of affairs, to go back again to James and Chakrabarty, enforces a renunciation of normal life and institutes a lack in the formation of the modern African woman. This lack, conveyed through the subtle negotiations necessary for affirming feminine individualism in the face of blatant patriarchy and the claims of traditional systems, often produces great anguish and bewilderment for women and creates what might be described as a contradictory modernity for them. And, unlike what is seen in Wambui Otieno's fiercely uncompromising nature that allows her to persist in setting the record straight about herself as an individual, or in the Appiah case where there is at least one highly educated individual in the family with the commitment and the means to attempt to render the conflicts intelligible, many ordinary African women end up silenced and bitter in the face of these contradictions.

There is no simple answer to the questions raised in this discussion. For one thing, there is no denying the fact that the extended family system is a very important aspect of any African's identity. Its benefits are too many for it to be dismissed lightly. But there is also no doubt that there are many problems with the system for women. Many of the rituals that affect women and marriage in different parts of Africa, from child betrothal practices to rituals of wife 'abduction' and rituals that women are exposed to after the deaths of their spouses, actually conceal serious issues of coercion, consent and freedom. It seems to me that it would be highly productive to bring women's issues on the continent in closer alliance with discussions of human rights and constitutionalism. This is a point also made by Ronald Thandabantu Nhlapo in his discussion of women's rights and the South African Constitution in his contribution to UNESCO's *World Culture Report* (1998). But this would not be to set a simple dichotomy between customary law affecting women and the more modern idiom of human rights. On the contrary, as Nhlapo argues, this requires a practice-by-practice assessment of cultural behaviours. In alliance with sensitive law reform, traditional behaviour can be coaxed into a dialogue with constitutionalism and human rights without 'alienating its adherents or forcing a confrontation between so-called Western values and African values' (p. 133). Nhlapo writes from the position of a member of the South African Law Commission and his gradualist approach is perfectly understandable. But this would have to be speeded up by the joint efforts of everyone, both male and female, in repeated examinations of the implications of traditionalism and modernity for the everyday lives of people. In other words, the law (whether customary, constitutional, human rights or otherwise) should be of concern to everyone. It may be a good start for Law Reform Commissions across Africa and elsewhere in the Third World to take the first but crucial step of starting debates about the contradictions between the different legal discourses affecting women. There is no knowing where this would lead, but the point is that no law can be good law if it does not have the participation of the people for whom it is made. And for this to be meaningful, they would have to be fully informed, at all levels and in accessible language, of the concepts that affect them in their everyday lives. This must be of pressing concern for women, because of the various intersecting discourses of both traditionalism and modernity that seek to render them subordinate. But, as I said a short while ago, the problem is not solely a women's problem. We are all, both men and women, thoroughly implicated when tears run unwiped down anyone's face. If postcolonial feminism is going to be of any use to women caught between traditionalism and modernity, it has to be able to provide an idiom whereby the condition of such women can be discussed both by them and by those interested in their condition. But stopping at this would be a betrayal. Ultimately, the project must be to join such women not just in the critique of patriarchy and of traditionalism, but in the careful construction of better structures by which women can express and fulfil their deepest aspirations, whether these are within marriage or outside it.

5

Postcolonialism and Postmodernism

The terms 'postcolonialism' and 'postmodernism' are both extremely elusive to classify and the attempt to bring them together might be thought only to compound the difficulties further. For some critics, any attempt to fuse the two in a common theoretical inquiry is bound to occlude serious problems of the degree to which the unfinished business of late capitalism differently affects postmodern and postcolonial conditions. More crucially, it is also argued that the postmodern is part of an ensemble of the hierarchizing impulse of Western discourses, and that even though it hints at pluralism and seems to favour an attack on hegemonic discourses, it is ultimately a-political and does not feed into larger projects of emancipation. To collocate the two, then, is somehow to disempower the postcolonial, which is conceived to be more concerned with pressing economic, political and cultural inequalities (Sangari, 1987; Tiffin, 1988). Indeed, for some commentators, such as the Nigerian Denis Ekpo, postmodernism is nothing but another stage in the West's crisis of consciousness:

> The crisis of the subject and its radical and violent deflation – the focal point of postmodern critique – are logical consequences of the absurd self-inflation that the European subjectivity had undergone in its modernist ambition to be the salt of the earth, the measure and master of all things.
> For cultures (such as ours) that neither absolutized, i.e. deified, human reason in the past nor saw the necessity for it in the present, the postmodern project of de-deification, de-absolutization of reason, of man, of history, etc., on the one hand, and of a return to, or a rehabilitation of, obscurity, the unknown, the non-transparent, the

paralogical on the other hand, cannot at all be felt like the cultural and
epistemological earthquake that it appears to be for the European
man. In fact, it cannot even be seen as a problem at all . . . [W]hen such
a being settles for the indeterminate, the paradoxical, the strange and
absurd, it is probably because he bears no more resemblance to
the man as we know him, especially here in Africa; he is a post-man
whose society, having overfed him and spoilt him, has delivered him
over to irremediable boredom. Nothing therefore, stops the African
from viewing the celebrated postmodern condition a little sarcastically
as nothing but the hypocritical self-flattering cry of the bored and spoilt
children of hypercapitalism.

(Ekpo, 1995)

For Ekpo postmodernism has to be seen as the hubristic consequence
of a desire to dominate the world, one that, linked to the universalizing rationality of science and anthropology, has to face its own
unravelling when confronted by the loss of empire. For critics such
as Hutcheon (1989) and Connor (1997: 263–8), however, there is a
productive way of seeing the two as mutually reinforcing. The two
may be brought together in common thematic, rhetorical and strategic concerns, especially as these are brought to bear on questions of
marginality. And so an affinity of concerns and strategies has been
deemed applicable on behalf of both terms, at least in the area of literary studies.

   In this chapter, I take up the relation between postmodernism and
postcolonialism. As in previous chapters where two seemingly
opposed concepts or discourses have been at issue, my emphasis will
be on exploring the conjuncture between the two and their mutual
illumination of conditions in the contemporary world. After a first
section in which I identify some of the main concerns of postmodernism, I move, via a brief recall of some central concepts of postcolonialism, to merge the two and to explore postcolonialism *as*
postmodernism, and vice versa. To aid in the dialectical mediation of
the two, I look first at questions of identity under the pressure of
images of luxury under late capitalist image culture (but whose roots,
I argue, can be traced back into the period of colonialism). The
second site on which I try to show the relevance of the two is in the
area of media representations of race and otherness that are focalized through programmes such as *The X-Files*. By linking police
veridical methods to questions of otherness, normally coded as the
esoteric, *The X-Files* produces a peculiar affect that has to do with
law and order in the cityscape that is concomitantly related to discourses of race and class.

The Concerns of Postmodernism

Postmodernism is related to a literary and philosophical tradition of representation which could be said to have its own peculiar historical and social trajectory in Western thought. Some postmodernist critics maintain that no reality can be thought of outside the way in which it is represented, and that any attempt to do so is to ignore the implicatedness of any perspective within the very object that is being described and vice versa (see, for instance, Natoli, 1997: 5–8, 21–5). Because the desire of what passes under the rubric of postcolonial theory is frequently concerned with representational discourses, postcolonialism also regularly takes representations as the primary target of analysis, with material conditions being accessed only insofar as they can be related in varying ways to representational regimes. A simple way of viewing this similarity would be to see both theoretical terms as being the descendants of what has been called the 'linguistic turn' in the social sciences and humanities, but this approach is not always helpful as it does not take account of the different emphases the two areas place on the relation between representation and a possible praxis, something to which we shall attend more fully in the third part of this chapter.

There are other areas of perceived overlap between them. The shared prefix 'post' in postcolonialism and postmodernism aligns them both to similar problematics of temporal sequence and transcendence in relation to their second terms, colonialism and modernism. The relation of temporal or other supersession raises problems of continuity and rupture for both terms, something which has been pointed out in different directions by critics alert to the easy triumphalism inherent in such 'posts'. Alex Callinicos (1989) shows how much the definitions of postmodernism actually reproduce definitions that had been applied to high modernism, while Anne McClintock (1992) provides a stimulating critique of postcolonialism and shows how much, in its implicit temporal trajectory, it ends up reproducing elements of Enlightenment notions of progress which it seems inclined to challenge. On the other hand, the 'ism' in both indicates their shared mutuality as second-order meditations, which, even though not coalescing into clear-cut ideologies, nonetheless seek to distinguish themselves from central positions in their various fields of inquiry. Both are thought to be second-order meditations upon real (and imagined) conditions in the contemporary world, and are to be taken seriously as contributing to an understanding of the world in which we live.

A fruitful way to proceed in defining the potential conjunctures and distinctions between the two terms is to attend to their different theoretical inspirations and ultimate social referents. As a means of mapping out the theoretical terrain of postmodernism, it is perhaps best to typify it according to a number of regular concerns. These concerns get different treatment in the hands of different critics, and there are bound to be disagreements on what things are most representative of the postmodernist paradigm.

A key area of dispute is how postmodernism is to be related to modernism. Ihab Hassan, one of the earliest commentators on postmodernism, addresses the question by schematically discussing the differences between modernism and postmodernism. He sets out the differences in the form of a table (1985: 123–4), part of which is reproduced below:

Modernism	*Postmodernism*
romanticism/Symbolism	paraphysics/Dadaism
form (conjunctive, closed)	antiform (disjunctive/open)
purpose	play
design	chance
hierarchy	anarchy
mastery/logos	exhaustion/silence
art object/finished work	process/performance/happening
distance	participation
creation/totalization/synthesis	decreation/deconstruction/ antithesis
presence	absence
centering	dispersal
genre/boundary	text/intertext
root/depth	rhizome/surface
interpretation/reading	against interpretation/misreading
narrative/grande histoire	anti-narrative/petite histoire
master code	idiolect
paranoia	schizophrenia
origin/cause	difference-différance/trace
determinacy	indeterminacy
God the Father	The Holy Ghost
transcendence	immanence

These are mainly stylistic oppositions and it runs the danger, as Harvey (1989) has pointed out, of reducing complex relations to simple polarizations. What Harvey shows in his discussion of this table in the context of the wider questions of definition more generally is that Hassan draws on a variety of fields as diverse as linguistics, anthropology, philosophy, rhetoric, political science and theology in setting up the distinctions (1989: 42–65). Thus, Hassan's table attempts to encompass all aspects of contemporary society and culture and to show how elements within them distinguish them from modernism and mark them out as postmodernist. These schematic polarizations, though useful as a starting point are by no means beyond dispute. In the area of architecture, for instance, there have been disputes about the ways in which contemporary buildings are either modernist or postmodernist. One such disagreement has been between Charles Jencks and Frederic Jameson on the status of John Portman's Bonaventure Hotel, with the first seeing the hotel as late modernist and the second interpreting it as postmodernist (see Jencks, 1980: 15, 70; Jameson, 1991: 38–45).

As can be seen from the debates on terminology, the discussion of what constitutes postmodernism often highlights borrowings from linguistic metaphors and their application to social and cultural discourses. Indeed, the genealogy of postmodernism has to be traced to the poststructuralism(s) that proliferated in the 1960s. For some, postmodernism is the operationalization of concepts developed initially within poststructuralism. At a rather basic level, it is the split in language between the sign and its referent, the understanding that language does not actually name an objective reality that has acted as the main import from poststructuralism into postmodernism. This split between sign and referent is then taken also to be homologous with a series of other splits, such as those between history and its narrative representation, and between the author's intention and the meaning(s) of the text.

At one level, then, postmodernism can be typified as a vigorously anti-systemic mode of understanding, with pluralism, borders and multiple perspectives being highlighted as a means of disrupting the centralizing impulse of any system. This in itself has a fascinating history in Western philosophy and has been discussed by Robert C. Holub (1995) in terms of the ways in which, from the period of German Romanticism, the maxim, the apothegm, the aphorism, the anecdote and the essay were used as a discursive means of expressing the irreducibility of human subjectivity to totalized frameworks. Holub analyses this with reference to three historical moments in Western philosophy: the elevation of the fragment into a legitimate literary and philosophical genre in the early writings of Friedrich Schlegel and Novalis; the scrupulous plurality in the thought of

Friedrich Nietzsche and his attempts to take apart the fundamental categories of Western thought through various attacks on conceptions of the subject, value, representation, causality, truth-value and system; and, finally, the critique of totality expressed in poststructuralist thought. Holub comes to two important conclusions in his account. The first is that the three phases have different understandings of totality. For the Romantics he discusses, the fragment, though seeming to stand in contrast to any totalized whole, was thought to be capable of capturing the essence of totality. Thus the fragment was ultimately itself totalized and wound up being a 'religiously recuperated totality' (p. 89). In Nietzsche's work, on the other hand, it is evident that his robust attacks on totality are themselves undergirded by an implicit impulse towards totalization. This is best seen in the oppositions in the antagonistic value scales he frequently sets up in the course of his philosophizing, which he labels variously the Dionysian and the Apollonian or Socratic, the Greek and the Judaeo-Christian, or describes by the oppositions good v. bad and good v. evil. Holub notes that on all such scales two common features are evident: the first term is always valorized over the second, and the second and non-favored designation or category is viewed as an 'outgrowth of sickness, deceit, deception, or an illicit attempt to gain and secure power' (p. 94). In poststructuralist thought, exemplified for Holub by the work of Lyotard, the same entanglement with a totalizing impulse is evident, particularly in Lyotard's implicit claim to oversee all historical development while tracing the factors that have led to the postmodernist loss of belief in metanarratives (p. 98). The important thing for us here is not so much whether Holub's own account fully explicates the central anti-systemic impulses behind postmodernism or not, but that historically, the anti-systemic focus on fragments and other forms of apodictic discourses has been related to specific historical and aesthetic configurations.

Jean-François Lyotard in his book *The Postmodern Condition* (1984), provides another dimension to the anti-systemic disposition in postmodernism. Among other things, Lyotard argues that both scientific knowledge and ordinary anthropological knowledge are governed by narrative. However, there is a historical break from about the eighteenth century, when science suppresses forms of knowledge that depend upon narrative. The crucial distinction comes when the mode of assigning truth-value in scientific knowledge is set apart from the ways in which such assignings are achieved through narrative in everyday knowledge. For Lyotard, the central feature of the postmodern condition is an incredulity towards metanarratives produced by science, Marxism and Enlightenment theories of progress, and one of the ways in which the postmodern is set to counter the institutions and discourses that seek to validate such metanarratives is by way of 'the atomization of the social into flexible networks of language games' (pp. 17ff). Lyotard's position might be fruitfully aligned to that of the Frankfurt School's contention that scientific universalism comes at the price of the peripheralization if not distortion of specificities. For postmodernism, it is precisely this problematic excess that is widened and rendered into the dominant epistemological truth of existence under late capitalism, with a number of strategies produced to support this key informing premise. These include a focus on indeterminacy, ambiguity and deferral; on the deliberate fragmentation and misarticulation of the text, whether this is conceived of as social or literary; on the proliferation of aporias where meaning is deliberately made unretrievable; and on a carefully parodic style that appropriates everything from tradition, history and other genres and respects nothing. There is a focus on surfaces, on play, on the dissolution of boundaries and on narrative and other jump-starts that do not necessarily lead anywhere. The key theoretical terms in postmodernism are dissemination, dispersal, indeterminacy, hyper-reality, normless pastiche, bricolage, *différance*, aporia, play and suchlike.

The third major concern of postmodernism to be highlighted in our account has to do with the way in which the contemporary condition of globalized economics and culture is interpreted. Again following on from the implications of the linguistic turn already mentioned, postmodernist thinkers have attacked economistic models of interpretation of social reality in favour of more attention to representation. Marxism was the prime candidate for critique, and the nature of the postmodernist rereading of Marx is best seen in the work of Jean Baudrillard. Classical Marxism has a three-tier interpretation of the growth of the market and its central feature, exchange-value. For Marx, the phase of industrial production is that in which things are produced primarily for exchange; use-value becomes secondary to exchange-value, unlike the case that might be thought to have pertained under feudalism, where only a small proportion of what was produced in handicrafts, agricultural products etc. was available for exchange. The third phase discussed by Marx is when abstract values such as love, virtue and knowledge, previously thought to be immune from market forces, themselves enter into the realm of exchange-value. For Baudrillard, in works like *The Mirror of Production* (1973) and *The Orders of Simulacra* (1983), it is no longer possible or desirable to separate the second from the third stage since in the 'post-industrial world' (Bell, 1973) all abstract human qualities, images and representations have become part of the economic world. Thus Baudrillard argues that a 'political economy of the sign' has come to predominate in contemporary life, to the degree that all reality, including the economic, is ultimately understandable in relation to signs. Television, the media and popular culture then become significant areas of analysis for postmodernists because it is in these areas that the economy of the sign is best seen in its varying operations.

This post-industrial scenario is thought to proliferate a number of important social and cultural features. As David Harvey puts it in *The Condition of Postmodernity*:

> Postmodernism also ought to be looked at as mimetic of social, economic, and political practices in society. But since it is mimetic of different facets of those practices it appears in very different guises. The superimposition of different worlds in many a postmodern novel, worlds between which an uncommunicative 'otherness' prevails in a space of coexistence, bears an uncanny relationship to the increasing ghettoization, disempowerment, and isolation of poverty and minority populations in the inner cities of both Britain and the United States.
> (1989: 113–14)

Harvey contextualizes this within a larger discussion of shifts in economic patterns. Like Baudrillard, he believes that postmodernity is due to the vast assimilation of more and more areas of life to the logic of the marketplace in place of the clear division of economic interest between labour and capital along with clear patterns of social antagonism and identification. But unlike Baudrillard, he focuses intently on the material and social referents that might be thought to undergird the economy of the sign in the first place. There is now a 'space–time' compression brought on by accelerations in travel and communications. Under these conditions, production is now organized on a global scale, with the manufacturing process being spread out across many countries and plants, with each being responsible for a minor part of the finished product. This contrasts sharply with the model he describes as exemplified in the car-maker Ford, where cars of the same make were made in the same plant and distributed to thousands of consumers all over the world. Such a form of production was centralized, dedicated to the mass production of minimally varied items, and was driven by economies of scale demanding and providing stable and continuous patterns of employment. In the post-

Fordist era, economies of scale are replaced by economies of scope, where shifts in demands of taste and fashion are met by increased differentiation in the product (Harvey, 1989: 125ff). Within such contexts, and given the 'uncommunicative otherness' that reflects the ghettoization of minority populations, one then sees how multiculturalism becomes the 'praxis' by which a sense of identity is negotiated within a seemingly incomprehensible postmodern social realm.[1]

Some of the overlap between the anti-systemic concerns of postmodernism and those of postcolonialism can be gleaned from a definition of postcolonialism advanced by Homi Bhabha:

> Postcolonial criticism bears witness to the unequal and uneven forces of cultural representation involved in the contest for political and social authority within the modern world order. Postcolonial perspectives emerge from the colonial testimony of Third World countries and the discourses of 'minorities' within the geopolitical divisions of east and west, north and south. They intervene in those ideological discourses of modernity that attempt to give a hegemonic 'normality' to the uneven development and the differential, often disadvantaged, histories of nations, races, communities, peoples. They formulate their critical revisions around issues of cultural difference, social authority, and political discrimination in order to reveal the antagonistic and ambivalent moments within the 'rationalizations' of modernity. To bend Jürgen Habermas to our purposes, we could also argue that the postcolonial project, at the most general theoretical level, seeks to explore those social pathologies – 'loss of meaning, conditions of anomie' – that no longer simply cluster around class antagonism, [but] break up into widely scattered historical contingencies.
> (Bhabha, 1992: 437)

Lyotard's understanding of the incredulity towards metanarratives that he argues defines postmodernism is evident in Bhabha's formulation here, with the difference that Bhabha's formulation seeks to highlight the fight against perceived inequalities as central to postcolonialism.

Differences between postmodernism and postcolonialism seem pronounced when the their different social referents are disentangled from their representational domains and brought out into the open. Postmodernism references a particular socio-cultural configuration in the West and theorizes globalization from an essentially Western standpoint, generalizing about global economics and culture as they are seen from the vantage point of the Western metropolis. As has been noted earlier, postmodernity is the era of surfaces, of the flattening out of affect, of multiple and shifting subjectivities, and of the total subordination of the real under the irreality of the images generated by visual culture under capitalism. And yet, on the other hand, one of the central problems which brings the two closer is on the question of the double vision that a peripheral existence in the world engenders. This doubleness can be theorized in many ways. Du Bois provides something of a significant lead in the area of African American subjectivity when he writes in 'The Souls of Black Folk' (1997) that the African American is a product of double consciousness:

> It is a peculiar sensation, this double-consciousness, this sense of always looking at one's self through the eyes of others, of measuring one's soul by the tape of a world that looks on in amused contempt and pity. One feels his twoness, – an American, a Negro; two souls, two thoughts, two unreconciled strivings; two warring ideals in one dark body, whose dogged strength alone keeps it from being torn asunder.
>
> (1997: 615)

Coming from different theoretical and personal inspirations, writers such as Frantz Fanon in *Black Skin, White Masks* (1967) and Ngugi Wa Thiongo in *Decolonizing the Mind* (1986) and others have also theorized the same idea in postcolonialism, both in the domain of subjectivity and in that of language more generally. In all these texts, a seeming situation of ontological crisis is ultimately traceable to material conditions. But their material conditions are mediated through images and perceptions and entangled in a series of discourses that attempt to alienate the racialized consciousness from itself and obscure the conditions that sustain the ontological split in the first place.

Reading across the 'Posts': Towards a Methodological Agenda

Without attempting to read the two fields in their fullest comparative possibilities (something which would be self-defeating if not utterly hubristic), I want at this stage to focus on two areas as a means of pointing out possible directions that such a comparative approach might take. The two areas I want to focus on are (1) that of the problematic nature of identity-formation in the light of aestheticized images of luxury, and (2) the 'political unconscious' of popular filmic and televisual images of otherness and the implications these have for the *reception* of otherness in the metropolitan West. I do this drawing examples from postcolonial and postmodern texts as well as with reference to the popular television series *The X-Files*, among others.

The social life of images

Something of the potential for a fruitful cross-reading of concepts between postmodernism and postcolonialism can be extrapolated from Arjun Appadurai's introductory essay to *The Social Life of Things* (1986). In this stimulating essay, Appadurai boldly joins Baudrillard to Simmel, Mauss and others to define how exchange-value is created for commodities through what he carefully elaborates as their 'social life'. This, he shows, is not a secondary offshoot of exchange relations but is part and parcel of economic exchange and the creation of value in all societies. His comments are much too complicated and rich to be properly summarized here, but for my purposes I want to focus on the comments he makes about the work of Sombart (1967). Sombart argues that the principal cause of the expansion of trade, industry and finance capital in the West was the demand for luxury goods, principally on the part of the newly rich, the courts and the aristocracy. He locates the source of this increased demand, in turn, in the new understanding of 'free' love, sensual refinement and the political economy of courtship during this period. To Sombart fashion becomes a driving force for the upper classes, who are satiated only by ever-increasing quantities and ever-differentiated qualities of articles of consumption (Appadurai, 1986: 36–7). Appadurai makes a direct link between Sombart and certain postmodernist theorists before adding his own interpretative gloss to Sombart's ideas:

> In his emphasis on demand, in his key observations about the politics of fashion, in his placement of economic drives in the context of transformations of sexuality, and in his dialectical view of the relationship between luxury and necessity, Sombart anticipates recent semiotic approaches to economic behaviour, such as those of Baudrillard, Bourdieu, Kristeva, and others.
> ... For our purposes, the importance of Sombart's model of the relationship between luxury goods and early capitalism lies less in the temporal and spatial specifics of his argument (which is a matter for historians of early modern Europe), than in the generalizability of the *logic* of his argument regarding the cultural basis of demand for at least some kinds of commodities, those that he calls luxury goods.

I propose that we regard luxury goods not so much in contrast to necessities (a contrast filled with problems), but as goods whose principal use is *rhetorical* and *social*, goods that are simply *incarnated signs.*

(Appadurai, 37, 38)

Following Appadurai, we can see how a focus on commodities as incarnated signs allows us to discern more clearly the economic basis for the double consciousness that I spoke of at the end of the last section. Two literary examples will help bring this point home. In 1915, a play was produced by the Ghanaian nationalist Kobina Sekyi called *The Blinkards*. This play seemed on the surface to be merely a dramatic satirization of the up-and-coming newly rich who (mis)approporiate what they think are forms of Western bourgeois civility and luxury items as a means of giving themselves a distinctive standing among the local population. There is much that is pathetic and hilarious in the dramatization of the concerns of this class of people. Among other things, Mrs Brofusem, who has returned to Ghana with her husband after a brief spell in England, insists on speaking English to her husband and her servants. What is more intriguing, however, is that she also insists that her husband smoke his cigars and drop the ashes on the carpet in the living room. The English, she insists, do this to give the carpets a special look. But she is not the only one afflicted by this misapprehension of bourgeois domestic social practices; as the action unfolds a local farmer, Mr Tsiba, brings his daughter to live with Mrs Brofusem, so that she can be brought up in the proper ways of civilization as only the redoubtable Mrs Brofusem is thought able to instil. But Mr Tsiba is inspired by an odd sense of doubleness, part of which is due to the fact that he keeps a small book with him of English sayings and proverbs which he tries to translate directly into his understanding of life. The results are unsettling:

MR TSIBA: Er – Mrs Brofusem, some book I have reading say 'All modest young ladies blush at certain times.' I look in the dickhendry, and I see 'blush' means 'to redden in the face,' also I look 'modest,' and I see 'chaste.' I know 'chaste': the minister explain this to me. But I think 'blush' is some English powder for face. I have never seen it here. Order some for my daughter I have many cocoa . . .

MRS BROFUSEM: (*Laughing*) Ah! Blush: Your daughter can't be able to blush.

MR TSIBA: (*Offended*) You mean my daughter too raw? I say I give her to you free, gratis. Make her blush. I will pay.

MRS BROFUSEM: I mean her skin don't allow it to be clear when she will blush.

MR TSIBA: But she has fine black skin, – velvet black. My great-grand-mother she say, in old times, the blackest ladies are most beauti-fullest. I think my daughter's skin is alright.

MRS BROFUSEM: You don't understand—

MR TSIBA: Ma'm I went to standard seven. I understand—

MRS BROFUSEM: I don't mean to say you don't understand English. How can you talk what you don't understand? You understand English but you don't know that white people's skin is transparent; so you can see the blood running into their faces when they are having some emotional state.

MR TSIBA: Ah! What fine big words you use. 'Transparent – Transparent'. Wait (*Takes out a pocket Dictionary, and looks in*) Ah! here it is: 'Transparent – that may be seen through, clear.' (*To himself*) Well, my daughter's skin is clear, my skin is clear, my wife's skin is clear. We get no sickness. (*Reflects a moment*) Oh, 'see through: I see! I see! Very funny. 'Transparent' is like glass: no colour; so it is the blood make him red. You call that 'blush.' All right! Teach Barbara all the things.

(Sekyi, 1974: 32–3)

It is interesting to note how the hapless Mr Tsiba has to trace the liminal meanings of English words through the dictionary. In piecing such meanings together, of course, it is evident that he is never able to come to a thorough understanding of their full significance. This is of course a function of his semi-literacy; but more important is the fact that the dictionary atomizes the meanings of words and treats them largely in isolation from their full cultural context. The inklings of a postmodernist problematic are in evidence here. But this has to be seen alongside the larger colonial and postcolonial problematic of double consciousness. Mr Tsiba is bringing his daughter to be trained so that her 'market value' in the marriage world can be augmented; in choosing this option he simultaneously enters the realm of imagined Western fashion and thus allows the further consolidation of a Western idea of selfhood which, as Sombart argues, comes from the sexual economy that ultimately undergirded the industrial expansion of the eighteenth century in the first place. But Mr Tsiba has to square these new ideas of feminine desirability which he wants for his daughter with indige-nous ideas of beauty. As he recalls it, his great-grandmother always said that the darker the skin, the more beautiful. Because the play is essentially a comedy, it resolves the contradictions happily, allowing us to laugh at these people on stage while remembering the more tragic ways in which this doubleness was played out in the social life of the newly educated classes in the period.[2]

Another good example of the incarnated significatory valence of commodities, this time taken from African American literature, is provided in Toni Morrison's *The Bluest Eye* (1993). This jump to African American literature is strategic.[3] *The Bluest Eye* is at a primary level about the crisis of identity faced by the teenage Pecola Breedlove, who, because of the dysfunctional nature of her family and her own lack of beauty and grace, craves for blue eyes in the forlorn hope of gaining herself acceptability. But the 'blue eyes' have entered a commodified domain; they are no longer just part of the white man's anatomy. Aided by marketing, images of blue eyes are found on dolls, cups, films and even sweets, and become a disembodied object of aesthetic intensity. Though this is by no means the place to pursue a full study of this phenomenon, it would be interesting for example to trace how this objective fact – blue eyes – is detached from its objective domain and then transferred into the domain of commodification, accruing an exchange-value through its social life, and becoming a desirable commodity to 'own' as a means of identity affirmation. One might, in such a study, cast a passing glance at the eyes of Dr T. J. Eckelburg in F. Scott Fitzgerald's *The Great Gatsby*, which, implanted on an oculist's fast-fading billboard, nonetheless create the social conception of the eyes of God in the novel. One might also study the Black Consciousness Movement of the 1960s and 1970s and the popular culture that it spawned, the ways in which the 'I am black and proud' of the likes of James Brown was a reaction to this commodification of blue eyes and white ideas of beauty. How do such objects shift epistemologically from a human domain through a quasi-theological one and into an area of aesthetic commodification? What are the moments of intensity in this process, and what social formations disguise *and* support their transformations?

The important thing for us at this point, however, is the effect that the desire for blue eyes has on Pecola. Partly at the mercy of an image culture, and partly because of the domestic crises of lovelessness she is constantly exposed to, she gets a split consciousness. For it is patently clear to her that she cannot get blue eyes, and yet she insistently desires them. When she does finally get the blue eyes, after being raped by her father and through the agency of the religious charlatan Soaphead Church, she is completely split within her psyche and becomes mad. She can only attain the aestheticized object of a commodified image culture by tragically doubling herself, being her own ontological interlocutor with an immediacy only allowed the insane. At the same time, this self-doubling can be interpreted as a doubling due to the material conditions of dispossession of which she is a victim. And she is not alone in this. Her father, Cholly, labours under an intense sense of alienation because he had been brought up not knowing his father. He sets out to find his father in his late teens and, after following a laborious trail, meets him in a gambling house. But his father does not recognize him, and rudely rebuffs him when Cholly attempts to introduce himself. The shocked Cholly runs outside and breaks down in tears, involuntarily wetting himself in a gesture of infantilization. His doubleness is instituted from this point and is further compounded by a sense of economic failure. The only way he can find to resolve this contradiction within himself is through alcohol and violence. Raping his daughter is the final signal of the atrophying of his humanity. *The Bluest Eye* is at all levels ultimately an existential crisis whose roots lie deep within the brutal racial hierarchies that govern society, constrain economic opportunities and becloud these under the alluring aestheticized domain which breeds and frustrates the desire for self-fulfilment.

Are these examples postcolonial or postmodern? They appear amenable to both perspectives. In both of the cases we have looked at, abstract or concrete categories are interpreted as efficacious signs of identification and become invested with desire. They are first and foremost incarnated signs, and mark, as Appadurai points out, a 'register of consumption'. But they are signs that are not entirely free of power; there is a certain discursivity in both cases that places the desired objects within cycles that define a nebulous but regulative capitalist or Western or white area of power. Mrs Brofusem and Mr Tsiba in Sekyi's play define themselves in relation to a Western bourgeois civility, one that cannot be fully attained precisely because the incarnated signs of luxury they activate and aspire to conceal behind them a complicated hinterland of Western cultural significance. For Pecola, the problem is obviously more pressingly ontological. Having blue eyes is not in itself enough; for the blue eyes to be efficacious in giving her a sense of worth, she would also have to be part of the middle-class ethos defined by the family captured in the words of the primer with which Morrison opens her text. Without reducing the two theoretical perspectives to simple polarities, we might say that the key dimension that postcolonialism forces us to consider is that of agency, whilst the postmodernist angle would make us settle on the economy of the image, and the potential for the fragmentation of subject positions. For postcolonial theory, the question of agency is crucial because merely identifying the purview or ambit of the regulative parameters set up by images is not enough. The next step has to be how such images ought to be subverted or how, if at all, their effects are to be challenged with a view to setting up a better order of effects. As the Igbos of Nigeria succinctly put it, 'When we ask where the rain is hitting us, it is to prevent us from getting wet in the future', or, in another useful formulation, 'The anthill survives so that the new grass will have memory of the fire that devastated the savannah in the previous season.'

Films, TV and otherness

Following this thread on agency, it is important to note a difference between postmodernism's interest in image culture and the multiplication of realities, and postcolonialism's focus on the politics of representation. For some postmodernists, the proliferation of images is a reflection of a potentially empowering subjectivity, one that allows people greater leeway in continually reimagining themselves. This is how Douglas Kellner puts it in *Media Culture*:

> My analyses suggests that in a postmodern image culture, the images, scenes, stories, and cultural texts of media culture offer a wealth of subject positions which in turn help structure individual identity. These images project role and gender models, appropriate and inappropriate forms of behavior, style and fashion, and subtle enticements to emulate and identify with certain identities while avoiding others. Rather than identity disappearing in a postmodern society, it is merely subject to new determinations and new forces while offering as well new possibilities, styles, models, and forms. Yet the overwhelming variety of possibilities for identity in an affluent image culture no doubt creates highly unstable identities while constantly providing new openings to restructure one's identity.
>
> (Kellner, 1995: 257)

Even though this notion of freedom cannot by any means be taken as a generalizable opinion, it is interesting that it is asserted at all as a form of the possibility for the individual's appropriation of the postmodern moment. In postcolonial theory, the emphasis is placed elsewhere. Whereas representations, especially residual colonialist ones, proliferate everywhere, it is by no means the case that the mere recognition of their proliferation gives access to freedom; such proliferations must be understood in their hegemonic or counter-hegemonic implications before they can be aligned potentially to questions of freedom.

Something of the difference in the implications of the two positions for the issue of freedom may be glimpsed from the implications that televisual and filmic images of otherness have for postcolonial diasporas, and beyond them for multicultural agendas in general. Stam and Shohat (1994) point out that the beginnings of Western cinema coincided with the intensification of empire in the late nineteenth century. This had a correlation with the content of films, especially as the medium was used for documentary and propaganda purposes in the heyday of empire. Popular images of the cinema helped to secure an image of otherness whose efficacy it is difficult to deny. From Tarzan to Disney's Aladdin, the popular televisual and filmic media have succeeded in creating images of otherness that, even though a part of the proliferation of images that postmodernists speak of, nonetheless attempt to stabilize subliminal images of otherness whose contestation can never be completely successful until their import in a hierarchical world is fully grasped.

This contention is given even greater relevance if seen in the light of the changing demographics of cities in the West and the historical implications these have had for imagining individual subjectivity. The Western city, as an idea and peculiar place for the meeting and mingling of strangers, was an important organizing paradigm behind modernism. Many well-known characters of the modernist novel struggled for an identity within the hustle and bustle of the city, and this struggle for identity provided the rationale for their interiorization and the focus on the mediation of the external bustle through the psychology of the individual. While modernism relentlessly defined the individual against an engulfing urban background, it also succeeded in producing an important opposition between interiority and exteriority, the individual and the masses. But, crucially, it also subsumed under this typology a dialectic of otherness, in which the individual sensibility was shown to have to shore up a sense of (in)coherence in the face of the burgeoning and spreading city. These typologies by no means die with the waning of modernism, and postmodern culture has repeatedly returned to a number of these typologies in the face of the changing demographic configuration of the city. There is, for instance, a more subtle logic to be seen at play in the *film noir* genre of the 1950s, where filmic techniques sought to inscribe the typology of otherness on the landscape of the city itself. In the various metropolitan cities in which *film noir* was set, such as Los Angeles, New York, Detroit etc., it was clear that a post-war mass of non-white populations was moving into the major cities and, thereby, producing anxiety about urban space. The *noir* films of the 1950s confronted this phenomenon, but not directly. They grappled with otherness by inscribing the polarities of race and of good and evil within the dynamics of filmic technique itself. This was realized in the foregrounding of the peculiar affectivity tied to the perambulations of the civic hero in the dark, mean and lonely streets of the city. Julian Murphet puts the point succinctly in his nuanced analysis of the 'racial unconscious' of *film noir*:

> These run-down, dark, mean and empty streets resound with the fear and hatred of a race/class faction that has lost its hold over them. The anger and bewilderment of the protagonists as they run along these avenues, casting nervous glances into every niche and side-alley, is as much an expression of bereaved loss as it is of haunted terror.
>
> (1998b: 29)

If *noir* is taken to be a 'modernist' filmic genre, supremely subtle in conceptualizing the shaping forces of otherness in the city, it is no less true to say that this concern retains its force in current popular TV series such as *The X Files. The X Files* is a curious hybrid. On the one hand it is clearly a police-detective drama, with a subliminal sexual synergy between the two cops Scully and Mulder. (It is perhaps not idle to note that Scully always keeps her lips partially apart, even when she is not speaking, in a barely concealed sexualized gesture much reminiscent of advertisements in women's magazines.) More important, though, is that the series is specifically about the esoteric crimes that consistently baffle the established protocols of investigation and which the police protagonists of the series are always brought in to tackle. 'The truth', as the opening words in the title score say, 'is out there.'

The series is predominantly set in the city, and in many respects extends one of the concerns of the *film noir* genre, namely the ontological inscription of otherness onto the geography of the city itself. In one particular episode called 'Teliko: The Case of the Missing Pigment' this concern with an ontological otherness manifests itself at both the explicit level of the story as well as at the level of the cityscape.[4] The episode opens with a flight from an African country which we later learn is Burkina Faso in West Africa. One of the passengers gets up to visit the toilet, and, while washing his hands, looks up and sees something off-camera that obviously frightens him. The scene is cut back to the passengers in the plane and we see a flight attendant asking people to prepare for landing. Asking about the whereabouts of the missing passenger, she goes into the toilet and, on seeing the body of the man, now dead, screams. He is chalk white and no longer black. The action begins.

We are next taken to the police department where we follow Scully and Mulder on their early attempts to make sense of a spate of strange deaths of Black men from inner-city areas. The cadavers, all of African American men, are distinguished by the uncanny chalk whiteness that seems completely inexplicable. Things resolve themselves into a clearer pattern when a new character is quickly introduced who happens to have travelled on the flight from Burkina Faso (and of whom we caught a brief glimpse coming from another toilet in the plane). He is Samuel Aboah, and seeks immigrant status that would allow him to remain and work in the United States. As the programme unfolds we are gradually given more information about Samuel Aboah. He is visited by a Black social worker who promises to help him get his papers; captures another victim in whom he induces a kind of trance-like state by shooting him with poisoned darts from a small reed-like object; is momentarily interrupted by the police inserting the reed-like object into the nose of his victim; and is later captured and sent to hospital but makes a dramatic escape. There is a final showdown in which the Black social worker and Mulder are almost made victims of Samuel Aboah before he is shot in the stomach by Scully.

This truncated account by no means conveys the tension and mystery/thriller-like impact of the episode as the two detectives attempt to unravel the mystery of the missing pigment. But the 'truth' is pieced together methodically. It turns out that Samuel Aboah is a member of a tribe in Burkina Faso who have been rumoured to kill other tribesmen regularly, and, magically, to leave them chalky white. For the Burkinabe victims of this strange plague, this can only be the sign of a feared magic. But Mulder unearths a more rational explanation. Aboah's tribespeople are, according to him, in an earlier stage of evolution, when their bodies lack the capacity for producing the life-sustaining melanin that is the cause of the black pigment. But without it they cannot live. Their solution to this is to kill others and somehow to drain them of their pigmentation to supplement their own deficient supplies. This is what leaves their Black victims chalk white.

A number of things need to be highlighted if this remarkable episode is to be fully understood in relation to the typology of othering that we noted earlier. The first thing is the subtle integration of the esoteric, in this case identified in Samuel Aboah's mysterious vampire powers of draining melanin, with the discourse of illegal immigration. At a point during the film, Scully asks Mulder why this melanin-deficient African tribesman should want to come to America in the first place. His answer is revealing. He has come, Mulder says, for the same reasons that all people come to America, to enjoy freedom, a place to live, and to work. However, this universal desire for American life is in this episode criminalized, firstly by the fact that Samuel Aboah is nothing other than a melanin-extracting vampire and secondly by the fact that he seems so desperate to get residence that he is prepared to use any means, fair or foul. Thus, the esoteric is criminalized and linked to the illegal immigrant.

Samuel Aboah is an 'illegal' in another respect also. He is an illegal immigrant into a more advanced stage of human evolution. It is perhaps not entirely accidental that his surname is the Akan name for animal. In his case he is underdeveloped even in respect to other African tribespeople. When he comes to the United States, his entrapment in an earlier stage of evolution reveals itself also in the curious tools by which he captures and works on his victims. Opposed to the guns of the detectives, his mouth-blown weapon is a throwback to superseded stages of civilization. Curiously enough, however, this evolutionarily retarded species is linked in the programme to a more modern African in the person of the Burkina Faso ambassador to the United States. It is from him that Mulder learns about this strange tribe in a story the ambassador tells from his childhood about the death of a cousin of his. The ambassador, it turns out, has had the body of the man killed in the plane secretly sent back to Burkina Faso for a post-mortem examination in the hope that some light might be shed on his own cousin's uncanny death. But the tale the ambassador tells is clearly meant to be opposed to Mulder's more elaborate and scientific explanation. Aboah is to Western civilization what the Burkina Faso ambassador is to Mulder: evolutionarily and scientifically retarded species respectively.

If this play with otherness manifests itself in such a blatant way, it is folded back into the informing logic of *The X-Files* by being staged in the recognizable geographical background of the inner city that is repeatedly revisited in the series. The inner city is a chronotope. As Bakhtin defines it, the chronotope is a time-space organization that calls up a specific affective response and allows us to relate to image-specific spatio-temporal and historical co-ordinates. Many of the *X Files* episodes end in chases through dark streets and alleys. Even though these dark streets are by no means racially coded, it is also the case that inner cities, especially in the United States, have a specific demographic character. The chronotope of the alleyways and dark streets, then, serves to signal a concern with the otherness of the cityscape even as a variegated racial (and class) demography is written onto it.

A critical question remains to be answered. In what ways can a TV series such as *The X Files* be submitted to a postmodernist reading? It is a curious hybrid form, embodying a belief in the supernatural as a principle of relativizing scientific rationality. This is captured most critically in the fact that the other people in the police department regularly scoff at Scully and Mulder's often bizarre explanations for events. However, and this is a regular movement in the series, the esoteric is always submitted to veridical police procedures and, ultimately, shown to be explicable in scientific terms. But the scientific terms of explanation no longer remain the same. The contact with the supernatural leads to various kinds of short-circuiting of the rational procedures to be applied. In the pigment episode we have described, for instance, this short-circuiting is shown in the fact that no rational explanation is offered for how the draining of the melanin out of Samuel Aboah's victims is supposed to have been done. Also, no explanation is given for how, even granted that he is able to drain his victims of melanin, he is able to inject or take it into himself to give him his life-sustaining blackness.

Police departments in all big cities face increasingly strident criticisms about their competence in combating crime. Crime, the 'other' of the civic and of law and order, is frequently seen to be uncontainable. But it is uncontainable for specific social causes. The genius of *The X Files* is to transfer these causes onto the esoteric, whilst simultaneously placing emphasis on the supremacy of a newly sensitized mode of police work. All the esoteric characters in *The X-Files* are strangers, visitants from elsewhere, not fully integratable into the spheres of civil order. Most of them reside on the social peripheries of the city (naturally, one might add) but this periphery often coincides with destitution and the more run-down areas of the city, where the lower classes and racial minorities are traditionally known to reside. The esoteric is coded along a specific chronotope of the city, which, as was the case in the genre of *film noir*, hides a particular racial unconscious. The discourse of scientific veridical police procedures is always shown to be found wanting; however, this apparent questioning of the efficacy of police procedures is not meant completely to replace it with a postrealist or esoteric procedure. On the contrary. The postrealist or esoteric is shown to subtend the rationalistic discourse of science. Ultimately, just as the esoteric other is contained by the handcuffs of scientific police procedures, so is the social other, whether racial minority or lower class fraction, contained by the apparatuses of power.

How, we might ask, does all this fit into a postcolonial understanding of the world? What sustains *The X Files'* imagining of otherness is not merely the strangeness of the esoteric, but its coding as opposed to the law and to civic order. Mapped onto the chronotopes of the dark alleyways of the inner city, this other of the civic order is then easily imagined as that other which resists the law or, more usually, fails to be fully integrated into the civil order. In the Teliko example from *The X Files*, this other is of course the illegal immigrant who lives among the ethnic minorities of his own colour and preys upon them. Thus, the image of otherness in *The X Files* is conjoined to a major concern of political systems in the West: how are illegal immigrants to be surveilled, checked and policed considering that they are so 'different', so given to 'uncivilized' behaviour and so utterly and irredeemably other? It is not only police departments that are interested in surveilling otherness. The police represent one of the instituional apparatuses that most strongly articulate this interest. But the interest in surveilling otherness is dispersed everywhere, sometimes making itself manifest in the question, 'Where do you really come from?' constantly asked of newly arrived immigrants, to second- and third-generation children of immigrants, and, most irritatingly, to those of mixed descent in the various postcolonial diasporas of the West. For, the question 'Where are you really from?' is never an innocent one; it is a question of origin that, posed to particular subjects, and in particular contexts, also involves a question of return (see Visweswaran, 1994: 114–40). Thus the city chronotopes of *The X Files* and other series like them have to be seen in a general popular anxiety about the very constitution of Western identity in general. This cannot be taken solely as a postmodernist question of the dissolution of the centrality of the West; it is a postcolonial one as well because the demographic changes in the West today cannot be thought of outside the various histories of empire (and slavery, in the case of the United States) which stretch back into previous centuries. And the mass media are critical in the dissemination of specific understandings of the West's history and its relationship to the rest of the world. A postcolonial perspective allows us to see how these media relate to continuing problems of racial anxiety in the world today and how we might think of a way of transcending such anxiety.

Postmodernism as Postcolonialism

I would like to conclude polemically by suggesting that postmodernism can never fully explain the state of the contemporary world without first becoming postcolonial, and vice versa. The cross-reading of the two domains that we have attempted provides some pointers to possible directions. The first thing to note is the need to factor images, tropes and texts simultaneously into specific socio-cultural domains while at the same time attempting to alienate them from themselves by reading them against other images, tropes and texts that do not seem to share historical similarities. The purpose of this would in my view be not only to 'look awry' as Slavoj Žižek (1991) puts it, but to force the phenomenon under analysis into a mode of alienation or estrangement from itself by means of which it would be made to deliver a truth-value that ramifies far beyond its own domain of circulation. This does not preclude the filling in of context. On the contrary, the specification of historical context is one of the first principles to be observed. But this has to be aligned to a more pressing requirement. Following the insights about the proliferation of perspectives that postmodernism offers, it is useful to try and fill out as many dimensions of context as possible, even when these might seem to contradict each other at various points. In our transfer of Appadurai to a reading of Sekyi and Morrison, for instance, we applied his ideas to two texts from very different contexts, one being that of late nineteenth-century cultural nationalism in West Africa and the other that of early 1970s African America. The point of it was to estrange the two texts from their normal grids of interpretation and to show how a similarity of effects could be said to have impinged upon the formation of subjectivity in both contexts. In this comparative approach, it would be critical to attend to certain inherent dangers in comparative analysis. Marilyn Strathern (1991) makes interesting observations about precisely these problems in respect of anthropology.

The next plank of reading postcolonialism and postmodernism together is of course to try and grasp the social life of ideas, whether these inhere in images of fashion, as was the case in the Sekyi and Morrison texts, or in popular cultural images of otherness, as was observed in the example from *The X Files*. The point here is to unearth incipient or fully formed social values both in their formation (in terms of process) and historicity (in terms of completeness from the perspective of the moment of analysis). In doing this we would arguably be going a step further than Appadurai by moving the discussion of commodification from the domain of things to embrace that of images as well, while sidestepping the more extreme forms of postmodernist and postcolonial interpretations that hyperinflate images and take them as unmediated stand-ins for society and culture. Thus the images of otherness in *The X Files* were related in our account to general problems of the surveilling of immigrants and racial others in the West. The key thing would be not to hyperinflate images dubiously, but to read such images alongside other socially relevant configurations. Finally, however, any cross-reading has to have a commitment to integrate the analysis into a larger affirmative project. This is by no means easy when both theoretical domains (but more especially postmodernism) run shy of making definitive ethical and evaluative statements about the phenomena they engage with. The fear of being thought prescriptive and hegemonic is one that most people no longer think worth risking in a world of pluralism. I happen to think otherwise. Recognizing that there is much destitution, poverty and sheer despair in the world, it seems to me increasingly imperative that the risk of appearing prescriptive is one worth taking if one is not to surrender completely to a debilitating anomie brought on by the apprehension of persistent social tragedies. Those who lose their limbs to landmines, are displaced through refugee crises or merely subsist in the intermittent but regularly frustrated hope that the world can become a better place cannot wait for complete moral certitude before they take action to improve their existence. It is partly in the implicit (and often real) alliance with those who, to appropriate a phrase from Julian Murphet, 'keep running all the time simply to keep pace with events' that we ought to take courage to make ethical judgements even in the full knowledge that we may be proved wrong. To this larger picture, and in the service of this larger affirmation we ought to commit our critical enterprises. Both postmodernism *and* postcolonialism have a part to play in this.

6
Parables from the Canon: *Postcolonializing* Shakespeare

Every major rethinking of literature and theory has a way of returning to particular texts, whatever the theoretical resistance to the very
idea of a canon; and often to discover that what was canonical was not
so much, or not just, the text in question but the received readings of
it, its normalization as a cultural icon or familiar construct.
Patricia Parker, *Shakespeare and the Question of Theory*

In the course of writing this book I have developed a good deal of
respect for the vitality of irrationality, and of the power of stories to
lead people to act in ways that are difficult to comprehend.
James Shapiro, *Shakespeare and the Jews*

Let me make explicit a methodological procedure which most readers
will have discerned in the course of these pages. In every chapter, I
have frequently had recourse to literary examples in either setting up
the grounds of my argument, or in outlining the contours of a particular problem to be investigated. At no time, however, has literature been
turned to for its own sake. It has always been to illustrate something
beyond itself either in the broad intersection of imperialism with
ideologies of gender, as was the case in chapter 4, or to define the
space between literature and the domain of politics, as was the case in
chapter 3, or to help in adducing a notion of subject formation that
arguably operated in the high point of colonialism and persists after it,
such as was the case in the last chapter with the discussion of Kobina
Sekyi's *The Blinkards* and Toni Morrison's *The Bluest Eye*. These
straightforward literary examples have also been augmented by a
searching focus on the implications of the use of tropes and metaphors
in postcolonial theory and in contemporary culture generally. This we
saw in chapter 1 and in the later part of the last chapter, respectively.

I make explicit this literary dimension to the present book not just to remind my readers of my role as a literary critic, but, more importantly, to point out the fact that no interdisciplinary model is innocent of bias. In other words, every interdisciplinary configuration harbours a particular inflection which itself accounts for the nature of the interdisciplinary 'knowledge' that is produced. But there is another reason why I bring up this methodological issue, and that is to suggest that because literature is always caught within different contexts of significance ranging from the purely aesthetic through to the sociological and the political, it is in fact necessary to place the literary in an explicit dialogical and dialectical relationship with all of these fields. This has always been attempted in this book with varying degrees of success.

The need to read the literary in a dialogical or dialectical relationship to other spheres becomes most pronounced when we are discussing issues of the literary canon and its role in the formation of cultural values in the contemporary world. It is to this issue that this final chapter will be devoted, with the ultimate objective of attempting to *postcolonialize* Shakespeare, arguably the most important single figure of the Western canon. My concern here is not so much to rehearse the heated debates to do with canon formation and how it is to be expanded (or not expanded; there are two sides to every canon), something which is competently dealt with in books such as Paul Lauter's *Canons and Contexts* (1991), but rather to show how the debate can be joined by an informed ideological critique of particular texts that seeks not to stop at such critique but to rescue some insights from the texts themselves for thinking about the world and our place in it. This is carried out with a view to extending the notion of pedagogy of liberation that has been associated with Paulo Freire and others. It is a chapter that will combine ideological critique with a clear view to addressing matters of teaching Shakespeare postcolonially.

Ania Loomba and Martin Orkin's recent *Post-colonial Shakespeares* (1998) sets some of the terms in which this postcolonializing might take place. It is the first time in Shakespeare studies that an entire volume has been devoted to postcolonial readings of Shakespeare. In their useful introduction, Loomba and Orkin suggest that the energies for what has become postcolonial readings of Shakespeare were already in place in the revisionist studies of the new historicists, Marxist and feminist critics of the 1980s and 1990s. These studies provided fresh insights into the relation between Shakespeare and attitudes to race, class and gender in the early modern period, and also enabled a consideration of the extent to which some of these attitudes persist in the West today. What these kinds of Shakespearean studies suffered from, however, is that they did not attempt to set past and present in a dialogue that might help Shakespeare to be reread via current debates about racism and vice versa. Furthermore, the debates within postcolonialism itself on issues of racism, hybridity, colonial discourse analysis and other issues were not central to the illuminating analyses that these earlier critics produced or to their view of how a social practice might be conceptualized. As Loomba and Orkin point out, 'revisionist studies of Shakespeare need to be concerned with these [postcolonial] *questions both when they reinvestigate the past and when they analyse the present*' (1998: 7; emphasis added). Thus the essays in the collection range from straightforward revisionist interpretations of Shakespeare from the perspective of colonial discourse analysis to more localized readings that transpose his works onto present-day concerns such as those on the question of land reform in South Africa (Nicholas Visser) and the relationship of Jerusalem to early modern English nationalism from the perspective of twentieth-century Israel (Avraham Oz). It is to this project, that is, reading Shakespeare to illuminate early modern England as well as present-day postcolonial issues, that this chapter will be devoted.

I shall proceed first of all by outlining Shakespeare's global popularity, something which to most people would seem so obvious as not to need further demonstration. But I outline his global popularity in a particular direction, namely in the ways in which he has been appropriated to bolster up ideological positions on both the right and the left and provided means of self-identification in both the West and the postcolonial world. The next step will be to establish different parameters of ideological readings of Shakespeare, mainly through the different ways in which he has been aligned to popular culture in the eighteenth and nineteenth centuries, periods of his full canonization, and in the twentieth century, the period of his providing an international multifaceted cultural idiom *after* empire. I shall then focus the discussion on *The Merchant of Venice* as a means of highlighting issues of the economic and cultural nexus, and of race, class and identity in early modern England to do with Jews, Jewishness and otherness. I shall then proceed to postcolonialize *The Merchant of Venice* by focalizing contemporary concerns with multiculturalism and other postcolonial issues through the framework of the previous section before concluding with comments on an engaged pedagogics of liberation.

'Not of an Age but for All Time'

Ben Jonson's observation of the value of Shakespeare for all time is by now a truism. Through educational curricula all over the world, Shakespeare has demonstrably become international cultural property without equal.[1] Individuals everywhere turn to Shakespeare for images by which to interpret personal and social realities. And this goes far beyond Nigel Lawson's notorious sentiment that Shakespeare was without a doubt a Tory.[2] This sentiment, though seemingly laughable, is actually part of a long-held tradition of 'using Shakespeare as a national icon of conservative continuity' (Cohen 1993: 21). Terence Hawkes describes how *The Tempest* was interpreted during the First World War to express a Germanophobic reading in which the English, Prospero-like, are obliged to put a stop to the Caliban-like Germans in a struggle ultimately thought to be about the ascendancy of a national language for international discourse (Hawkes, 1985). And in the 1980s Secretary of State George Schultz was credited with saying with respect to American policy towards Nicaragua that the US would not become 'the Hamlet of nations' (Cartelli, 1993).

It is not only in the hands of the powerful that Shakespeare has nestled. After the chaotic events in Nigeria following the annulment of the country's presidential elections, literate and semi-literate people kept referring to the then head of state, General Ibrahim Babangida, and his wife as Macbeth and Lady Macbeth. This extended a common traditional discursive practice whereby people judged to have transgressed all bounds of decency are demonized and thought to be possessed by evil spirits. The Macbeth analogy also signalled a reinterpretation of Babangida's Machiavellian chicanery, which when he was in favour with the people had earned him the nickname of 'Maradona'.[3] In apartheid South Africa, *Othello* was a play that was practically outlawed. It was hardly ever produced. This was because the interracial marriage and its unravelling under the impact of Iago's machinations spoke to a hidden political concern in the apartheid realm which could not be addressed in the open without the exacerbation of tensions.[4] And in Soviet Russia, *Hamlet* was the favoured play of the dissident underground in which Elsinore was interpreted as a series of prison cells, with Hamlet cast as the rebellious individual committed to putting an end to the regime of unfreedom.[5] As Jean E. Howard and Marion F. O'Connor point out in concluding their introduction to *Shakespeare Reproduced* (1987), 'Shakespeare is constantly reproduced in the general discourses of culture and is used to authorize practices as diverse as buying perfume, watching Masterpiece Theater, or dispatching troops to far-flung corners of the globe.'

An assumption shared by the various interpretations we have highlighted is that Shakespeare is amenable to instrumental readings. In other words, it is possible to read this globalized cultural icon as a means for social understanding or for specific interventions in the real world. But straightforward instrumental readings sit rather uneasily in Shakespearean criticism. In Shakespearean scholarship concessions to a vaguely instrumental interpretation are made either when reading his texts as embodying universal principles detachable from their ideological and material contexts of production, or in the hands of cultural materialists and new historicists as mediations of ideological contradictions during the early modern period. The first variety is by far the more popular in both Shakespearean teaching and research, and is associated with many of the major Shakespeare critics from Samuel Johnson to Harold Bloom. These figures have provided some of the most astute and enduring interpretations of Shakespeare; however, their readings are constantly critiqued by the more politically oriented writers working from Marxist, new historicist, feminist and postcolonial perspectives (see, for example, Dollimore and Sinfield (1994), Drakakis (1985), Belsey (1985), Ryan (1995) and Loomba and Orkin (1998) among others). Though these two forms of criticism are distinct in many respects and have radically different implications for how Shakespeare is conceived of as relating to real-life concerns, at the risk of distortion I want to suggest that they illustrate weak and strong instrumental interpretations respectively. At heart both types of reading suggest that it is possible to appropriate Shakespeare for an interpretation of real life. The weaker form, which in effect harbours an exegetical impulse applicable across the whole range of canonical texts, reads literature essentially as a self-enclosed activity which nonetheless harbours insights that can be transposed into an understanding of universal human and social conditions across contexts and times. The second, stronger version aligns the exegetical reading more closely to the ideological contexts of literary production, attempting not merely to specify a historical context (something which they share with all serious interpreters of canonical texts) but also to bring into view the processes of ideological formation that are arguably inherent in the very formation of metaphor, genre and language. In the stronger readings, the Shakespearean texts are interposed into an arena of social struggle, a struggle that is meant not just to illuminate the formation

of sensibilities in the period in which the plays were originally produced but to show up the genealogy of ideas that arguably persist in
varying forms to the present day.

The question of popular appropriations, and the relation between
these and more academic-oriented analyses of Shakespeare, have not
been entirely lost on scholars. The twentieth-century appropriations
we noted earlier do not at all exhaust the varieties of uses to which
the Bard has historically been put. The task of aligning popular
appropriations of Shakespeare to those of Shakespearean specialists
has been taken in new directions in recent studies influenced by new
historicism, cultural materialism and cultural studies. To typify just
two contrastive models of such gap-bridging studies, however, I
would like to comment briefly on Jonathan Bate's *Shakespearean
Constitutions* (1989) and Slavoj Žižek's *Looking Awry: An Introduction to Lacan through Popular Culture* (1991). These will help
specify the broad parameters of my own critical appropriation of
the Bard.

Bate's book, covering the period 1730–1830 when the process of
Shakespeare's canonization could be said to have been consolidated
in earnest, looks at a variety of popular sources to gauge the 'after-
life' of the Bard. For him, cartoons are an especially important area
for analysis because

> in an age without photography and television, when newspapers were
> not illustrated, caricature was the principal medium through which the
> public derived their images of politicians and State affairs. A study of
> the presence of Shakespeare in caricature in that period is the nearest
> equivalent to a study of his presence in television in our period;
> that is to say, it is a study in popular iconography. Furthermore,
> Shakespeare's life in Georgian graphic satire evinces not only the cen-
> trality of the plays to English culture, but also the process whereby
> they are forever being re-created, appropriated in the name of con-
> flicting political and aesthetic ideologies.
>
> (Bate 1989: 2)

The book is organized as a series of historical, chronological and thematic sequences, with the examination of popular satirical representations followed by an exploration of theatre, their relationship to
political debates and to the commentary of Shakespearean and cultural critics such as Hazlitt.

In Slavoj Žižek's more interdisciplinary account, Shakespeare is
not central to the task of introducing Lacan through popular culture
as such. He takes his place among many other ideas and images from

the cinema, jokes and science fiction taken from popular culture.
Žižek undertakes a thorough 'looking awry' at all the texts he
deploys, reading the high and the low alongside each other in order
'not only to explain the vague outlines of the Lacanian theoretical
edifice but sometimes also the finer details missed by the predominantly academic reception of Lacan' (1991: vii). He undertakes this
cross-reading by means of what may be described as an oscillatory
practice. He oscillates very rapidly (one almost thinks, frenetically)
between Lacanian theory, high culture and texts from popular culture
in such a way as to illuminate their shared potential for disclosing
Lacanian psychoanalytic categories. In one particularly brilliant
reading he sets *Hamlet* alongside horror films such as George
Romero's *The Night of the Living Dead*, John Carpenter's *Halloween*
and Sean S. Cunningham's *Friday the Thirteenth* to suggest that they
all exemplify issues of interrupted burial rites and how the consciousness of improper burial rites acts as a constant interruption of
the reality of social arrangements within these texts (1991: 23–7). As
will be recalled, Shakespeare's play has a fair number of characters
who die untimely deaths (King Hamlet, Ophelia, Polonius, Hamlet
himself), whose proper rites of burial become a key factor in the relationships among the remaining protagonists. In Žižek's reading, all
the texts he isolates for comment are pressed to illustrate the often
difficult psychoanalytical categories of Lacan. But the other implication to be drawn from his reading is that anything that can illuminate
the problems of social existence, whether it be philosophical, psychoanalytical, literary or popular cultural, has to be read with equal
seriousness and *at the same time*. The simultaneous cross-reading of
the popular with the high literary should not becloud the fact that
all such readings are ultimately ideological. The 'equal' seriousness
applied to the two fields is designed to support a particular perspective on the world, in Žižek's case the Lacanian interpretation of subjectivity and identity. Thus the equalization of the high cultural and
the popular is not to be assumed to be value-free, something which
must be borne in mind later when we transpose *The Merchant of
Venice* to a reading of liberal ideology in certain present-day journalistic and popular cultural texts.

Bate's study is more clearly historical and raises different problems about relating Shakespeare's texts to various political and social
contexts. But taken together, both writers allow us to raise the question of the relationship between sequence, simultaneity and disjuncture in attempts to narrow the gap between popular cultural usages
and more academic ones. In Bate's account the historical sequence is

necessary as a means of spelling out the relationship between the various discourses he is interested in. Furthermore, the time span he covers requires an explicitly sequential account to be able to make sense. His account allows us to see the relationship between the popular, the political and the literary-critical. However, by being done sequentially, it is not always that he establishes a dialectical engagement among the three domains of analysis. Though all the chapters are fascinating in themselves and well documented, the chapters on Hazlitt at the end of the book only sporadically reach back to recall the popular appropriations of the cartoonists and satirists. Thus, though indicating significant ways in which the gap between the high cultural and the popular might be bridged, Bate's methodology only indicates this as a tantalizing possibility with an implicit gap between the three domains still being retained. Žižek produces a problem at the other end of the scale with his oscillatory practice. He seeks to render the high cultural and the prosaic as analogues of each other, but analogues whose resemblance can only be discerned when they are wrenched from their normal circuits of circulation and made to serve the specified Lacanian theoretical end. The entire procedure depends on our ignoring other dimensions of the text that would contradict the Lacanian reading. Once a wider canvas of significance is brought into view (or if we happen not to agree with the Lacanian interpretation), the oscillatory practice seems a clever but irritating trick to seduce us into agreement with the model being deployed.

The nature of these two problems of sequence and simultaneity can also be related to a third one to do with the inherent disjunctiveness of comparative frameworks more generally, whether these are comparisons of high cultural texts with popular ones from the same period or across different epochs. The prefatory anecdotes of the new historicists, criticized by many traditional Shakespearean critics as unhistorical if not intellectually irresponsible, could be taken to suggest a disjunctive framework of interpretation that highlights the conjuncture between text and context while at the same time distancing and alienating the two from each other. The incoherence that is created in the work of new historicists is in itself a reflection of the necessary disjunctiveness that is involved in locating Shakespeare within transgressive comparative frameworks. In any comparative approach, it would be critical to attend to certain inherent dangers in comparative analysis. Marilyn Strathern makes interesting observations about precisely these problems in respect of comparative anthropology. Observing in *Partial Connections* that 'complexity is intrinsic both to the ethnographic and comparative enterprise', she points out how in the attempt to demonstrate the social and cultural entailments of phenomena, simplification is necessary for complexity to be made visible (1991: xiii). She adds further:

> The perception of increasable complication – that there are always potentially 'more' things to take into account – contributes to a muted skepticism about the utility of comparison at all. However, anthropologists do not produce this sense of complexity unaided. *Their discipline has developed in a cultural milieu committed to ideas of pluralism and enumeration and with an internal faculty for the perpetual multiplication of things to know.*
>
> (pp. xiii, xiv; emphasis added)

Her remark about the cultural milieu in the West of pluralism *and* enumeration is particularly relevant for any cross-reading, comparative or otherwise. These impulses have to be relocated within grids that allow for challenges to be posed to any overweening systemic or hegemonic rationalization – not, it has to be noted, as a means of merely negating the systemic or the hegemonic, but to bring these into dialectical confrontation with their denied logics. In a postcolonial critical practice of wresting parables from the literary canon, this issue of disjunctiveness would have to be kept constantly in view, precisely because of the danger of inadvertently collapsing reality onto the literary and reading them as somehow equivalent. As we noted in our discussion of postcoloniality and interdisciplinarity in chapter 1, this danger is particularly common in postcolonial studies because of the influence of poststructuralist modes of analysis.

Secular Parables from Shakespeare

In the light of the instrumental readings that are regularly applied to Shakespeare, one might argue that through the ages he has been seen to provide 'secular parables' by which the purely literary material from his work is transposed into understanding real-life contexts. And, as we noted earlier, this is not solely a concern of popular culture but a practice that both politicians and ordinary people turn to, sometimes with seemingly coherent views in sight and sometimes merely under the impress of specific conditions to which a momentary recourse to Shakespeare seems the handiest response. To parry charges of irresponsibility in any sustained attempt to read Shakespeare as providing such secular parables, however, the

Shakespearean text has to be read first of all in terms of its 'historically produced semantic potential', as Metscher (1979: 36–8) puts it, but in such a way as to make it amenable to appropriation into contexts quite different from those envisaged by the text itself. I want to read Shakespeare not just as providing secular parables, but providing parables of materialist historical processes and contradictions. In doing this I want to appropriate Shakespeare strategically for an examination of questions of otherness across race and class in the contemporary West, themes of obvious relevance to postcolonial studies, and not new in Shakespeare studies either. In this I am continuing the discussion started in the previous chapter, but in a different direction.

Though in various radical readings of Shakespeare *The Tempest* and *Othello* have been the favoured texts for discussions of colonialism and otherness, it is to *The Merchant of Venice* I would like to turn to specify a postcolonial reading.[6] Unlike the two other more obviously postcolonial texts already mentioned, *The Merchant* has had very little attention from postcolonial critics. This is in part due to the fact that an implicit mimeticism enters into postcolonial analyses. *The Tempest* is read as representing processes of colonialism, whilst *Othello* is easily grasped as depicting the plight of that minority black fraction in the West that is both accepted in public discourse and reviled in private. This mimetic identification of Shakespeare's texts with specific processes and figures is not altogether avoidable, but it seems to me somewhat to foreclose the possibility of extending a radical postcolonial reading to other Shakespearean texts that could be thought to raise similar postcolonial issues to those raised in *The Tempest* and *Othello*. Plays as varied as *As You Like It, Antony and Cleopatra, Coriolanus* and the first Henriad all seem to me to offer fruitful opportunities for a postcolonializing interpretation. My reading of *The Merchant of Venice* in this vein is only a rudimentary indication of what could yet be done by people interested in postcolonial studies.

To proceed into the next phase of the argument, however, it is important to specify more clearly what we might have to consider in rereading *The Merchant of Venice* as a parable of materialist processes and contradictions. I use the term 'parable' not in the straightforward sense of the potential interpretative closures of religious texts, but in the more open-ended sense gained from the philosophical and secular parables of writers such as Adorno and Horkheimer (such as in their rereading of the myth of Odysseus and the Sirens in *Dialectic of Enlightenment*), Jorge Luis Borges (such as in 'Tlön, Uqbar, Tertius' and 'The Garden of Forking Paths') and Italo Calvino (such as in *Invisible Cities*). Though these three are separated by time, culture, and genre, in their writing of secular parables they all share the desire to trigger a process of examination rather than instituting a clear one-to-one relationship between the parables and a presumed reality. Their parables are thus first and last *processual*, the crucial thing being the process of exploration itself rather than any set conclusions. Crucially also, they all make their secular parables amenable to multiple and often contradictory inter-pretations. In speaking of materialist processes and contradictions, my interpretation also coincides with Marxian analyses of *The Merchant* which have sought to elaborate its refraction of contradic-tions within capitalism in early modern England. The one important difference in the current reading, however, is that I will be arguing for a more insistent focus on the conflict between economy as economics and economy as culture, or, in other words, for a distinc-tion to be drawn between the play's emphasis on an incipient politi-cal economy and its articulation of the conflict between this and a cultural economy.

As has been noted by several commentators, *The Merchant*, like Shakespeare's other comedies, can be discussed in terms of certain peculiarly Shakespearean formulas. The romantic comedies such as *As You Like It, A Midsummer Night's Dream* and *Twelfth Night* and even *Much Ado About Nothing* all have as their central concern the development of a companionate love relationship between young lovers. I prefer the term 'companionate love relationship' to the pre-dominantly used one of 'romantic love' because I believe that the romantic comedies are not just about romance. They are also about friendship and equality between romantic lovers even when these seem to lead to and are subsumed under the sign of marriages presided over by father figures at the end of the plays. The young lovers invariably have to overcome certain obstacles in order to con-summate their companionate relationships properly. The impedi-ments are at least of three kinds: (1) misapprehensions about the nature of true love as in the case of Orlando in *As You Like It* or Orsino in *Twelfth Night*; (2) negative sentiments of anti-comedic spirits (Malvolio and his like); (3) impediments deriving from severe social contradictions. The third tier of problems can fruitfully be labelled the problems of the social text of the comedies, the dimen-sion of social contradictions which has to be confronted for there to be a proper reintegration of the lovers with the society at large. This feature has regularly been interpreted as the socially affirmative nature of the romantic comedies. It is unarguably correct. Shakes-peare has various ways both of setting up the problems of the social text and also of resolving them. Sometimes the problems of the social text are articulated in such a way as not to be entirely separable from the articulation of the anti-comedic sentiment embodied either in individual characters or as part of the implied ethos of the universe of the play. In *Twelfth Night*, for instance, the problem of the social text has a double focus, making itself seen partly in the sour character of Malvolio as well as in the predominating spirit of misrule. What Sir Toby Belch and Sir Andrew Aguecheek represent is the carnivalesque comedic spirit detached from any sense of social responsibility. Thus, the comedic is brought close to its own potential negation: the carnivalesque spirit of misrule is dangerous for self-governance, for the stability of domestic arrangements and, ultimately, for the proper articulation of a socially responsible humour. *Twelfth Night* displays an attenuated form of the social text compared with, say, *As You Like It* or *A Midsummer Night's Dream* where there are specific problems of injustice and of parental injunctions respectively that are shown to pose recognizable risks for the lovers as well as for the social polity more generally.

The Merchant of Venice compounds all the elements of Shakes-pearean comedy by instituting a problematic within the social text which forecloses the possibility of grasping it simply as a formulaic comedic genre. *The Merchant* refuses completely to harmonize the contradictions that are exposed, and is exemplary of a dramatized 'coexistence of contradictions', to echo William Empson in *Seven Types of Ambiguity*. But the coexistence of contradictions, which Empson notes as pervasive in the play but interprets as due to the contradictory articulations of the characters, is not reducible solely to the contradictory articulations of the characters. It has a more subtle effect in terms of the social text of the play. For one thing, there are various interconnecting aspects of the social text which impinge upon any interpretation of the anti-comedic spirit we might like to settle on. At one level, Shylock is similar to characters like Jacques in *As You Like It* and Malvolio in *Twelfth Night*. Like them, he is the anti-comedic spirit that has to be exorcized or recontained to enable true companionate love to be fully consolidated. But there is a major difference between him and them. Unlike them, his Jewishness is an irreducible factor in the play, and the play interweaves an anti-Semitic discourse whose ramifications are only properly understood with recourse to the formation of Englishness in the early modern period. As James Shapiro points out in his well-documented book

Shakespeare and the Jews, from which the second epigraph to this chapter is taken, myths about Jews had a certain resilience and were refracted in *The Merchant of Venice* and in other plays of the period which had Jews as characters. The myths varied, but the ones that were most relevant to *The Merchant* were those that postulated that Jews participated in ritual murder (circumcision often being thought to be the first step to this), were usurious and mean-spirited and generally had a relentless antipathy towards Christians (Shapiro, 1996: chapter 3). The Jew was the prism through which social anxieties and phobias were refracted, often without any reference to real Jews themselves; the Jew 'continued to figure as a point of reference in early modern England for a wide variety of social and theological concerns that ultimately had little to do with Jews themselves' (p. 111).

For both Shylock and the other characters in the play his 'Jewishness' is relevant for circumscribing their social relations. Shylock is variously described by the others as the 'alien', 'the stranger cur', 'a kind of devil' and a 'faithless Jew'. He himself, on being invited by Bassanio to dine with them, replies with obvious irritation:

> Yes, to smell pork, to eat of the habitation which your prophet the Nazarite conjured the devil into: I will buy with you, sell with you, talk with you, walk with you, and so the following; but I will not eat with you, drink with you, nor pray with you.
>
> (I.iii.29–33)[7]

We shall return to this passage later, but for now let us just note that his Jewishness short-circuits the process by which he can be reduced to a literary formula or trope within the dramaturgical schemes of Shakespearean romantic comedy. This is arguably not the case with Othello, where all the insults that are directed at him occur behind his back, never to his face. At any rate *Othello* allows the eponymous hero an undisguised tragic stature and centrality to the culture of Venice which, joined to the various levels of the theme of appearance v. reality in the play, forces us to look well beyond the surface of his skin colour and into his fractured humanity. In the case of Shylock, his racial difference is a critical cultural factor which consistently manifests itself both in the self-articulations of the Jew himself and in the way he is perceived by the Christians. Shylock is a character who has to be read as a *social* stereotype and a *dramaturgical* formula simultaneously; it is impossible to subsume the one under the other.

At another level, the social text of *The Merchant* expresses an interesting contradiction between economic rationality and cultural ethos. In a fascinating reading of the play inspired largely by the New Criticism, A. D. Moody (1964) observes how within the insistent materialistic preoccupations of the characters there is regularly a conflation of a religious language with a more economically driven discourse. These preoccupations are suggested very early in the exchange between Solanio and Salerio.

SOLANIO: Believe me, sir, had I such a venture forth,
    The better part of my affections would
    Be with my hopes abroad. I should be still
    Plucking the grass to know where sits the wind,
    Piring in maps for ports, and piers and roads:
    And every object that might make me fear
    Misfortune to my ventures, out of doubt
    Would make me sad.
SALERIO: My wind, cooling my broth,
    Would blow me to an ague when I thought
    What harm a wind too great might do at sea.
    I should not see the sandy hour-glass run
    But I should think of shallows and of flats,
    And see my wealthy Andrew dock'd in sand,
    Vailing her high top lower than her ribs
    To kiss her burial . . . Should I go to church
    And see the holy edifice of stone,
    And not bethink me straight of dangerous rocks,
    Which touching but my gentle vessel's side
    Would scatter all her spices on the stream,
    Enrobe the roaring waters with my silks,
    And, in a word, but even now worth this,
    And now worth nothing?

                                    (I.i.15–36)

In Moody's view, what is shown in Salerio's speech is not 'a simple preoccupation with the world, but the expression of that preoccupation in an idiom adapted from the pulpit'. Crucially, however, 'Salerio reverses the preacher's logic and draws a wholly secular moral, ignoring any life beyond death' (Moody, 1964: 11–12). The conclusion that Moody draws from this, and from another instance pertaining to Portia where she declares near the end of IV.i that she was 'never yet more mercenary' (mercenary and mercy both having the same Latin root *merces*, meaning reward or fee), is that the characters speak of their earthly preoccupations via a quasi-religious idiom. One quite obvious implication to be drawn from this is that the characters are so driven by their materialistic concerns that all other discourses get coloured or pressed into the materialistic framework. This is of course not to impose a blanket condemnation of the efficacy of their world-views. The play takes pains to show that the Christians' enlightened self-awareness, though contradictory at various points, still sustains a positive attitude to the world. The much larger point I want to draw out, even while agreeing with Moody, is that this conflation of a materialistic idiom with a more religious discourse is actually one dimension of the dialectical contradiction between a discourse of economy and a discourse of culture that is captured so subtly in the play, and whose contours are relevant to interpretations of economics and culture even till the present day.

Shylock's own insider/outsider status allows us an immediate entry into the nexus of culture and economy. Shylock is spat upon by Antonio, completely denigrated by the Christians, hated by his daughter and misunderstood by all. But to grasp the nature of his own hatred of the Christians, we have to attend to an important feature of the social text which articulates the cultural/economic contradictions hinted at earlier. Marxian interpretations have painstakingly elaborated the ways in which a capitalist economic rationality and the struggle between different economic models are captured in the play. The play, in the words of Walter Cohen (1982), 'offers an embarrassment of socio-economic riches'. Cohen shows how the play, in a dual reflection of real economic conditions, assumes a recognizable but contradictory relationship to economic realities in England and Italy, a bifurcation which is 'a consequence of the fundamental contradictions in Shakespeare's social material' (p. 774). For, historically, the implicit distinction that is drawn in the play between usurers and merchants has different implications deriving from the differences between Italian and English economic history. Whereas in Italy merchant-usurers were in fact significant in promoting new forms of banking and therefore consolidating an emergent form of capitalism, in England a wedge was drawn between merchants and usurers, with the usurers being portrayed as having a potentially damaging effect on the economy and on moral standards. Furthermore, the emergent capitalist class of merchants aligned themselves with an agrarian landed gentry, something figured in *The Merchant* in the alliance between Portia, Bassanio and Antonio at the end of the play.[8]

Historically, every period saw denunciations of usury in England and elsewhere. In the England of the last third of the sixteenth century these denunciations occurred at the same time as money-lending was being seen as an inescapable economic necessity. The concept of usury underwent a radical transformation between the usury statutes of 1571 and 1624. The landmark Usury Statute of 1571 permitted individuals to obtain 10 per cent interest on loans. The House of Commons in 1624 struck out the declaration in the statute suggesting that usury was against the law of God, and in the period between the two statutes usury itself as a concept shifted gradually from meaning any loan at interest to one that meant the giving of a loan at an exorbitant rate. By 1626 attitudes had shifted so much that English moneylenders could buy a copy of *Money Mongers: Or the Usurer's Almanacke*, which set out 'the necessary tables of interest, the usurer's gain, and [the] borrower's loss'. Yet at the same time, as Shapiro argues, 'even after the 1571 statute permitting usury, individuals who lent money at unacceptably excessive rates were prosecuted'. Thus, the economy of England in the early modern period had to accommodate the obvious necessity of new modes of business financing whilst still struggling to confront some of the moral contradictions involved in moneylending in the first place. The implied schism between interest and usury enabled a projection of the negative part of the equation elsewhere whilst the more positive aspects were retained for definitions of economic rationality. And it was the Jews who were associated with the negative pole in myths, literature and popular belief (Jones, 1989: 145–74; Shapiro, 1996: 98–100).

The social text of the play illustrates this contradiction. At one level, the Christian ethos of the play disavows the mode of business financing represented by Shylock. And yet at another, precisely because the imagined Venice of the play is a mercantile economy, the mode of business financing represented by Shylock is absolutely essential for its sustenance. Yet more important for our interpretation here is that this contradiction between an implied Christian ethical order and a necessary economic practice which is the material basis of that order captures the meeting point between 'cultural' economy and 'economic' economy. The Christians have to be understood not just as exemplifying a specific kind of belief system, but as demonstrating a way of consolidating social exchanges that would ultimately undergird the economic exchanges themselves. This allows a reinterpretation of the partying spirit we see in the play. Belmont, a veritable dream world saturated with music and moonshine, is a place where there is no work. Portia's wealth, unlike the hardwon wealth of the Venetians, is not sustained by labour. Stephen

Greenblatt defines the difference between Portia's and Shylock's attitudes to wealth as pertaining to the relation between a manipulation of liquid assets and the presence of land. It is germane to our discussion:

> In Shakespeare's play this economic nexus is suggested above all by Shylock's usury, but it is also symbolized by his nonparticipation in Venetian society, his cold, empty house, and such subtle indicators of value as his hostility to masquing – 'the vile squealing wry-necked fife' (2.5.30). All of this is in sharp contrast to Portia, who has plenty of liquid assets; she can offer at a moment's notice enough gold to pay Antonio's 3000-ducat debt 'twenty times over' (3.2.306). But her special values in the play are bound up with her house at Belmont and all it represents: its starlit garden, enchanting music, hospitality, social prestige. That is, the economic nexus linking Portia with her environment is precisely not instrumental; her world is not a field in which she operates for profit, but a living web of noble values and moral orderliness.
>
> (1990: 43)

Greenblatt is correct in this interpretation except for one point. The economic nexus linking Portia to her environment is not directly instrumental, but she does deploy her wealth instrumentally to augment her social ties. These social ties cannot be consolidated outside the cultural patterns established for the dominant Christian culture of the play. But they are cultural patterns which in their turn feed into the economic nexus. When Antonio spits upon the Jew, he does this for both cultural and economic reasons. The cultural and the economic are interlocking and overlapping nexuses through which the characters shape their relationships with other characters and with themselves.

Another way of interpreting this contradictory dimension of the play is in terms of a split between an abstract instrumental sociocultural network deriving partly from a notion of intrinsic value and the attempt to switch off individuals selectively according to their relevance in fulfilling goals processed in that network. The operational word here is 'network'. The Christian characters are ultimately interested in consolidating a social network. This social network, always also economic, is consolidated by entering into certain circuits of social circulation in which money and wealth are not allowed to define value even while they are being made central to the sociocultural circulation. In our own modern times, even with the rapid expansion of capitalism and its incursions into the service industry and all areas of everyday life, the economic is, ordinarily, rarely seen as a direct expression of the cultural. However, if one wanted to get a contract in Hollywood, one would hire an agent. The agent is nothing other than a cultural player, a networker whose networking expertise is placed at the service of the economic motive.[9] In *The Merchant*, we see a curious entanglement of the cultural and the economic when the cultural refuses to acknowledge its dependence on the logic of the economy while being sustained by it. What *The Merchant* expresses is the historical meeting point of emergent and residual values played out across the conjunctural relationship between economics and culture.

Curiously enough, Shylock embodies precisely the same conjunctural economic/cultural logic but from a marginalized and self-marginalizing perspective. His reasons for hating Antonio are significant in this regard:

> I hate him for he is a Christian:
> But more, for that in low simplicity
> He lends out money gratis, and brings down
> The rate of usance here with us in Venice.
> If I can catch him once upon the hip,
> I will feed fat the ancient grudge I bear him.
> He hates our sacred nation, and he rails
> (Even there where merchants most do congregate)
> On me, my bargains, and my well-won thrift,
> Which he calls interest: cursed be my tribe
> If I forgive him!
>
> (I.iii.37–47)

The reasons embrace religious (I hate him for he is a Christian) and economic ones (He lends money gratis and brings down / The rate of usance here with us in Venice), but then enter a vague liminal arena of racial/religious ones in talking about an 'ancient grudge'. By starting with cultural reasons and implicitly prioritizing them over economic ones, Shylock is arguably unable to grasp the social constructedness of the conjuncture of the economic and the cultural. He beclouds his motivations by adducing a 'natural' racial genealogy reaching back to the genesis of the two religious traditions to account for his hatred. This recalls to mind the Salerio–Solanio exchange we noted earlier, with the difference that Shylock's intersection of the economic with the cultural serves both to confuse and to magnify the motivations for his hatred of Antonio. His character is partly atrophied by the denial of his humanity by the Christians and partly by his own self-insertion into the contradictory mode of articulation of the economic with the cultural.

It is evident from the intensity of his hatred that its roots are far from simple. Shylock seems to have absorbed the intensity of the stereotyping process and made of it his own peculiar instinctual reflexes by which to visit vengeance upon Venetian society. His consciousness of himself is constructed within the intersubjective relations he is obliged to have in a society that stereotypes him, but from which he absorbs the stereotyping predilections in his turn. More than that, Shylock has what might be described as a neurotic exactness born out of his peculiar relationship to money; one which leads him to a series of literalizations in his views on the Christians, the law and even on the nature of his economic and cultural motivations. Even his much cited 'Hath not a Jew eyes' speech can be read in this light. He seeks an egalitarian extension of communality on the basis of a literal interpretation of what it is to be human, interpreting the fact that because he has the same anatomical features as the Christians, they should accept him as equal. But society never refuses an egalitarian extension of humanity to its others solely on the basis of the presence or absence of human similarities; it is often done by the invocation of invisible intrinsic values which cannot be challenged solely by referring to a common humanness. Shylock's neurotic exactness is born out of his dissociation from the social circuits of interaction to which, because of his contradictory economic and cultural position, he sets himself in opposition. When he refuses Bassanio's invitation to dine and refers to his Jewish antipathy to pork, he is also expressing the difficulty of entering their circuits of social circulation from a narrow and culturally relative perspective. In this relativism he rehearses the dominant social structural order and creates his identity within the intersubjective space provided for him by the culture. It is this conjunctural and intersubjective personal location and his position as simultaneous insider/outsider that provides the most fruitful opening for reading him and the play as a parable of materialist contradictions and processes applicable to our own postcolonial concerns.

Shakespeare's plays habitually pose problems by repetition and variation and it is always important to think of the dynamics of the whole. In a fuller discussion of *The Merchant*, the Christians would have to be more carefully distinguished and the polemical argument around Shylock's Jewishness would have to be complicated with reference to Jessica's position in the play. We would also have to see Belmont not simply as a magical place and the opposite of Venice.

We would have to contest the view that the dominant morality in the play is essentially 'Christian'. At an even higher level of complexity, we would have to address the issue of how the canonical text makes itself available for particular interests and for rereading and the fact that the historical gulf between Shakespeare's time and any contemporary real-life context we might like to apply his texts to sometimes results in the obscuring of the ideological complexities of the plays. It would also be interesting in a more elaborate account of *The Merchant* to discuss, for instance, the historical significance of religion and the place of religion within the resistances to and suspicions of capitalism in its early forms; the extent to which the play distinguishes Shylock as an individual from Shylock as a Jew; the problem of performance and the way in which Shylock as a dramatic figure shifts in meaning whether he is played by a non-Jew (which was for a long time the case) or by a Jew, and how this is highlighted in various ways. We would also have to trace the history of the difficulty of secular claims regarding Jewishness as a racial category rather than as a religious identity, and the impact of the Holocaust as a historical parameter in any understanding of the play now. Furthermore, if the analysis of the play is forced into contemporary religious/racial politics such as those between the PLO and Israel or in Northern Ireland, a completely new dimension would be opened up. In the section that follows, I turn from an analysis of the relation between culture and economics in the play to a discussion of that relation in the context of contemporary liberal discussions of the welfare state in Britain. In doing this, I only indicate one potential direction in which a postcolonializing reading of *The Merchant* might be taken. The application of insights about the play to the issues that follow is meant to act as a stimulating pointer to ways of recontextualizing *The Merchant* and Shakespeare more generally within seemingly disparate concerns to help in rendering his texts more directly useful for understanding the heritage of the *post*colonial world.

Cultural/Economic Rationalizations of Liberal Ideology

There are obvious routes which the attempt to take *The Merchant* as a parable for our own times could take. These could include reading Shylock's location as emblematic of the insertion of other races within the Western economy and their difficult and problematic rise to different measures of economic influence. Another dimension might embrace the persistence of myths attaching to various 'others' such as Blacks, Hispanics, south-east Asians, Turks and Algerians in the United States, the UK, Germany, France and other metropolitan countries. These would themselves be worthwhile pursuits and would yield valuable insights. But there is another, more complex and ultimately more fruitful route which involves taking the entire world of the play as a means by which to understand the ideological processes that undergird any system of values, in this particular case the peculiar value system given expression at the conjunctural site between economics and culture in their concealed but mutual interdependency in the contemporary West. I want to read this conjuncture in terms of right-wing ideologies of otherness across race and class, and how they manifest a subtle pseudo-universalism to undergird the business of social othering. This is not to suggest that Shakespeare's play by any means supported a right-wing ideology. The play is not easily reducible to any such programmatic statement. What remains true, however, is that in Shylock's defeat by the Christians, their world-view is meant to predominate. Even after all their own chicanery and contradictory standpoints are taken into account, the play sides with their values as opposed to those of a neurotic exactness expressed by Shylock. However, because Shylock's being a Jew is arguably an irreducible part of his representation both in his own eyes and in those of the other characters, any modern reading of the play has also to contend with the sense of his having to be recontained, through his enforced conversion, into a dominant Christian civil order for the dominant society to prevail in its business. These and other issues will be taken up in our parabolic transposition.

To refract issues of diaspora and identity fruitfully in the contemporary world through *The Merchant of Venice* a number of serious qualifications have to be made. The first and perhaps most important is that the figure of Shylock has to be translated into a general cipher of otherness within a dominant Western culture, whatever the given or assumed racial identity of that other. Secondly, the discussion has to be made applicable to less economically privileged fractions, fractions that inhabit an insider/outsider position but do not have the benefits of economic power by which to negotiate their stake in the dominant culture which is their host or adopted land. Furthermore, it is important to note with Stuart Hall that in today's West, race is often 'the modality in which class is "lived", the medium through which class relations are experienced, the form in which it is appropriated and "fought" through' (1980: 341). The conflation is by no means unproblematic, but as we shall soon see, right-wing ideology often pursues its pseudo-universalist logic by means of racial motifs. As we noted in chapter 5, the very demography of many Western cities ensures that the poor are often racial minorities.

When right-wing politicians such as Jean-Marie Le Pen and others maintain that France is for the French and that Black people cannot truly be said to be French, they ignore the degree to which Frenchness is itself a labile category whose content is filled in by events like the 1998 World Cup and relations with its former colonies. Thus it is that the multicultural nature of the winning French World Cup team poses a serious problem to purist notions of French identity. The team that won the final match against Brazil was a mosaic of multiple cultures with key players like Zinadine Zidane (Algerian parents), Youri Djorkkaeff (of Armenian extraction), Patrick Viera (born in Senegal), Marcel Dessailly (of Ghanaian extraction) and Lilian Thuram (parents from Guadeloupe) all able to claim a dual culture, one French and one other. And I use the word 'extraction' to denote parentage here advisedly because all these figures have been extracted from somewhere else before becoming French. France's win over Brazil allowed the French to express a French national pride which swept across the nation and made complete nonsense of the right-wing calls for racial purity. The title of a special cover article of the *Guardian* dealing with French reactions to the win spoke it all: 'Black and White and French All Over'.[10]

Right-wing thinking does not always pursue its agenda of racial and class othering along the blatant racial logic of people like Jean-Marie Le Pen. It is much more sophisticated than that. The energies of right-wing ideology are often directed to the pursuit of a pseudo-universalism about the dangers to the welfare state from imagined threats and negations. For such threats to be rationally presented, however, it is always necessary either to render race and class interchangeable or to conflate the first with the second. The structure of this pseudo-universalism in contemporary debates about welfarism is hinted at by Slavoj Žižek in an essay entitled 'Multiculturalism, or, The Cultural Logic of Multinational Capitalism' (1997). Žižek notes how contemporary multicultural societies consolidate their critique of the welfare state by magnifying the condition of its most marginal elements and interpreting these as that precise threat to the welfare system itself. The universal is tested with reference to its apparent negation; thus, for instance, single mothers are thought to be the prime instance of the negation of the civilized values of the welfare system. But for this to be able to be articulated at all, it has to include the content of a popular social longing, in this particular instance the idea of 'family values'. In other words, the right wing often poses as a *defender* of a pseudo-universal humanism whilst steadfastly attacking the welfare system.

Something of this move can be gleaned from an essay by Matthew Parris entitled 'It's Good to be Needed' in *The Times* of 9 January, 1998. The argument, though at one level quite simple, is complexly put and centres on the old motif of the welfare system being like a giant surrogate parent. The invidious suggestion here, however, is that the welfare state indirectly deprives real parents of the need *to be needed*. The complexity of the position comes from how the essay develops its central insight. It opens not on the streets of London, but in a bus trip in Peru and takes us along a steady journey guided by the formulas of the first-person participant-narrator:

> To those who travel by bus and train in the Third World, something in the poignancy of the image I try to recapture below will be familiar. I was on a small bus going from Pisac to Cuzco in Peru. The road takes a high pass over the mountains, and at sundown – it was sundown – the air freezes quite suddenly.
>
> Some passengers slept, others stared out of the window, huddling blankets around them. The man and woman in front of me, of mixed Indian and Spanish blood, tended their little girl.

So opens this classic (and one must say well-written) piece of realist scene setting. But it is the girl on whom our attention is next focused. She is 'perhaps nine, and a Down's syndrome'. It is clear that her parents, though obviously poor, tend her lovingly. After a while the mother falls asleep, and the task of looking after the distracted child among a sea of strangers is left to the man. The little girl eventually falls asleep, at which point the man glances round apologetically. ' "My daughter", he said. Then folding his arms again around the sleeping child, he smiled at her with an expression of infinite tenderness. His smile had a sort of rapture.'

Our first impression on reading this is: how touching. There is a clear nobility conveyed about the couple and their attitude to their daughter. But that is to miss the point about this portrait, for it is actually being used as a means by which to contrast other attitudes towards parenting in both the Third World and the West. The contrast is made painfully evident in another town, Puno, where the writer sees a 'pathetic, rat-like retarded boy' who was placed on display on the pavement with a sign beside him. On this sign was written 'To the public: The Overseer of Minors places at your disposition a boy, certifying of the same, that he was abandoned by his family at the age of four, lived in different households and places, and was taken away by the authorities and brought to this town. He has nothing. Whoever might wish to adopt him . . .' But apparently nobody does. But the contrast is not entirely innocent of an interpretative slant. Note for instance that the first child, whom we are supposed to admire, is described as a Down's syndrome, while the second one is described as 'rat-like' and 'retarded'. The point which Matthew Parris is at pains to make is that the second child's parents have abandoned him precisely because they lack the true milk of parental kindness. That this might actually be a good argument in support of the welfare system does not strike Parris.

A number of subtle assumptions about what constitutes 'the family' play across Matthew Parris's essay which it is important to specify. The first, and most carefully concealed, is the 'universal' idea of the nuclear family unit. He says in relation to the first family that they were 'completely alone in the world' like 'a small boat on a wide and treacherous sea' and that 'there will have been absolutely nothing to fall back on materially and nobody, nobody [note the repetition for effect] to share the load with'. This implies that there are no extended family networks and that the family units he sees in his travels in the Third World are identical with the nuclear family unit of Western culture. This, of course, is patently false. As we noted in chapter 4, this is by no means beyond contestation in the Third World. But the central assumption governing this entire contrastive portrait is that there are universal values of parenting evident everywhere and which welfarism threatens. The question of poverty is utterly immaterial in his account. Indeed, he asserts in a strangely patronizing way, that to have added to the couple's monthly income 'would have contributed nothing to the joyfulness of the father's smile, nor diminished it either'. One is curious to know whether Matthew Parris had bothered to ask the father about his financial preferences before making such a ridiculous statement. But the point about this distortion is that it is meant to subserve the larger programme of pursuing a pseudo-universalist argument whilst attacking welfarism.

Later on in the essay, the real logic of the entire piece is made manifest. The point to note, according to him, is that though social and welfare policy is usually seen in terms of its needful clients, 'a need we seldom discuss is the need to be depended upon', something which is 'speculative and intangible, impossible to quantify'. And so we are brought to the crux of the matter: 'When a safety net is placed by the State under the life you hold in your hands, the instinct to protect is frustrated. You cannot feel depended upon when, in the ultimate, you are not.' So there we have it. The welfare system leads to an atrophying of basic instincts, here figured as the parental instinct to protect. At no time have those who join weekly dole queues been explicitly condemned, but once it is remembered that the readership of *The Times* is made up mainly of middle-class people, it is clear that the real victims of this atrophying process are the lower classes. And it is those who do not share in the universal principle of parenting who can be seen across cultures reaching as far as Peru. Not only are those who rely on the welfare state a drain, they are actually only partly human, even though they may not know this.

The pursuit of pseudo-universalism in right-wing thinking and its implicit invocation of race is by no means as sporadic as might be thought from reading an occasional piece such as that of Parris. The *Spectator* of 18 April 1998 ran a lead article entitled 'The Third World in Britain', in which Anthony Daniels argues that the welfare system in the UK was repeating the same mistakes it made with respect to socialist Third World countries such as Tanzania in the 1960s and 1970s. The main thrust of the argument is the homology between giving aid to Third World nations, which he argues was diverted into greasing unaccountable party bureaucratic apparatuses, and the social welfare system in the metropolis which only goes to underwrite the public funding of 'psychopathy and irresponsibility'. But Daniels makes another point, similar to that raised by Parris, namely that welfarism atrophies the human spirit. In his case he sees it firstly in the victim mentality that it produces in those who depend upon the welfare state, and secondly in what he sees as the channelling of liberal middle-class guilt. Citing Lord Bauer, he writes,

> one of the roots of the disastrous doctrine of Thirdworldism was liberal middle-class guilt. This guilt attaches not to one's individual conduct, of course, but to the way the world as a whole is organised, from which one has undoubtedly benefited. This guilt liberated one to behave as one chose: for what was a little peccadillo such as betraying one's wife compared to the inequitable and unjust distribution of income in the world?
>
> Such 'guilt' is really disguised self-importance. It makes the middle classes responsible for everything in the world: not a sparrow falls, but it is the duty of the middle classes to rescue it. In fact the middle classes need a large population of lame ducks – and there's no one lamer than an illiterate psychopath – to assure them of their own providential role in society and history.

The shocking perversity of the logic should not becloud the fact that Daniels is trying to speak for his version of the 'human spirit', here expressed as the social conscience of the middle class. It is a social conscience he sees as perverted precisely by the very existence of the welfare system, which, oddly enough, is nothing but a surrogate for middle-class charitableness. It is in these ways that the real process of the othering of the underclass and of race takes place, and not just at the level of strident calls for immigration control. For, as can be observed in both cases, right-wing thinking always reaches for other less privileged worlds (in both these cases the Third World) as a means of grounding its ideas of universalism. This suggests a necessary and inextricably dependent relationship between middle-class liberal ideology and its imagined others. The Christians' identity in *The Merchant of Venice* is partly dependent on their having the figure of Shylock to demonize; as we have already noted, in sixteenth- and seventeenth-century England, the growing need for new modes of business finance went hand in hand with a desire to project the negative aspects of moneylending onto the quasi-mythical figure of the Jew. Analogously, as can be gleaned from the two journalistic pieces we have looked at, liberal ideology seems to require various others almost out of necessity in order to consolidate a pseudo-universalist argument.

But the pseudo-universalist argument has to be disentangled also at the level of the conjuncture between economics and culture. In both the above cases, the focus on parental values and on a social conscience are implicitly calls for putting culture above the reach of economics. Cultural values, declaimed here as ethical ones, are supposed to act as a bulwark against the economic rationality thought to be articulated in the welfare state. The fact that this sanitized cultural location of cultural-cum-ethical values is actually undergirded by the ideological presuppositions about individual autonomy, individual responsibility, ideas about the family and other such touchstones of capitalist thinking is not allowed to be made manifest at the surface of the right-wing accounts. We are of course in a completely different historical configuration from that of the sixteenth century to which *The Merchant of Venice* was directly addressed, but the fact still remains that the contradictory co-dependency of economics and culture has a complexity which is subtly formulated in Shakespeare's play. And the tenacity of the cultural/economic conjuncture and the obfuscations around it are not to be taken lightly.

The discussion cannot be closed completely without looking briefly at the degree to which the underclass itself frequently conspires in the process of its own othering within late capitalism. We see this process replayed time and again in talk shows such as the *Jerry Springer Show*, where the underclass of American society is regularly encouraged to fight out differences over transvestism, parental abuse, extra-marital sex and prostitution for the televisual consumption of global audiences. Significantly, most of the pugilistic displays derive from disagreements about sex and sexuality. For the critics of the welfare state, these TV shows provide the images by which society's underbelly can be hypostasized and rendered into a stereotype of civil chaos, the Other of civility and civilization, the threat towards the concept of 'family values'. Going back again to *The Merchant of Venice*, however, we have to note that the negation of civility that the *Jerry Springer Show* regularly puts on display is only an explicit representation of a major contradiction riddling the larger society itself. This is the fact that as an institution, marriage, taken as the prime conduit for the articulation of family values, is itself increasingly being put under the pressure of social contradictions. The problems include childcare arrangements, the difficulties in the way of working mothers, the gender roles accorded men in the workplace, the strain put on familial relations by increasing economic migratory tendencies and even the very images of consumption proliferated enticingly by televisual entertainment and advertising. The pressures and contradictions have reached a point at which marriage is no longer able to provide the secure ties to hold the family together as it was thought to do in previous times. Thus, when the single mother or the transvestite is isolated for castigation, society as a whole attempts to divert attention from the threat to family values that comes from the increasing splintering and commodification of the idea of sexuality and the family itself.

There is a strong temptation at this point in the argument to draw a parallel between what we described as Shylock's neurotic exactness as a peculiar reaction to his problematic position inside Venetian society, and the seeming pathologies of the gladiatorial underclasses on the *Jerry Springer Show*. It would seem attractive to interpret the pugilistic reactions of these underclass gladiators as the reflection of their own problematic subjectivization within the incoherent orders of the economic/cultural nexus we spoke of. But that would be a mistake. A big mistake. What we see in the Springer show is a reification of sexual and social aberration projected as if it is a naturalized feature of the underclass. Nothing could be further from the truth. The middle classes themselves are riddled by the same aberrations that we see in the underclass; the difference between them is that the middle classes do not normally deliver their aberrations to the commodified procedures of global television. To put it another way: the aberrations of the middle classes are often kept secret, they are private, whereas those of the underbelly are rendered public so that they can be projected as that other of civility and of law and order. It is interesting how televisual culture is providing the means for this subtle reification to take place under the gaze of millions.

Methodologically, there is a point when a firm wedge has to be placed between literature and real life, for though literature may disclose certain perspectives on reality, it is dangerous to see it as providing direct metaphorical or even allegorical correlatives. By this I want to factor into my model of taking secular parables of materialist processes from Shakespeare for postcolonializing purposes that it is always necessary to pay careful attention to the range of disjunctures that lie in the comparative transposition of art to life. We do not seek new forms of allegories from literature; what we seek is to grasp the complexity of both life and literature dialectically as well as materially, that is, in detail.

Conclusion

If in this account I have at various points suggested a conflation of race with class, it is for strategic reasons, for it is my belief that the pursuit of social justice has to be carried out on several fronts simultaneously. Furthermore, it is important to note that if any underprivileged social category (seen in terms of race, class or gender) is under pressure, there is a concomitant effect on the other underprivileged fractions. This is particularly acute when all three underprivileged and contested categories are manifestly important for shaping a radical postcolonial pedagogical agenda. For such an agenda to be properly elaborated, a firm connection between analytic and material categories has to be constantly kept in view. Additionally, we should be bold enough to dislocate literature from its normal circuits of sanitized commentary to enable the cross-reading of ideas from literature to society and vice versa. An excellent place to start is from the canon itself, for the issue is not whether to study writers in the canon or not, but how we interpret them and what we use them for.

In this effort, it is useful to remember the words of bell hooks in her suggestively entitled book *Teaching to Trangress: Education as the Practice of Freedom*:

> The unwillingness to approach teaching from a standpoint that includes awareness of race, sex, and class is often rooted in the fear that classrooms will be uncontrollable, that emotions and passions will not be contained. To some extent, we all know that whenever we address in the classroom subjects that students are passionate about there is always a possibility of confrontation, forceful expression of ideas, or even conflict.
>
> (hooks, 1994: 39)

It is evident from her extensive discussion of engaged pedagogy that the classroom is often the crucible of latent social tensions which are often subsumed under the very pedagogical imperatives that govern the socialization of individuals. This subtle subsumption takes place in at least three mutually re-inforcing contexts. The interactions between teachers and students may take place within a structure in which an implicit hierarchical relationship between teacher, as unquestioned arbiter of value, and student, as disciple or apprentice, constantly forecloses the possibility of a performative democratic exchange. Competence is rewarded in place of risk-taking and the classroom context implicitly reproduces attitudes of conformity that make of students successful citizens but shallow individuals. Or, in predominantly single-race contexts, race (and class, and gender) are either not treated at all or in such a way as not unduly to destabilize the tacit values of the dominant group. In these contexts such troublesome categories are truly 'othered' and never allowed to disturb the inherently unquestioned values that ultimately undergird systems of hegemony and domination. But it is perhaps the third scenario that is the most invidious. Here, in the multicultural classroom context, even when attention is paid to the realities of race, class and identity, this is carefully managed so as to delink them from lived experience in order to detonate their potential explosiveness. This delinking is sometimes done, as bell hooks indicates, in order not to allow potentially unmanageable tensions to come to the surface to destabilize the dynamics of the classroom.

If we focus on these putative scenarios in what might seem to be an exceedingly schematic manner, it is only to suggest the need constantly to defamiliarize our teaching methods in the bid to consolidate a productive sense of what we do. And most importantly, we need to be ready to take risks; those out there in the throes of postcolonial contradictions, who will ultimately be affected by the conceptual and analytical categories we employ, take risks daily. To experiment with a radical pedagogy is a minor risk compared with what the inheritors of the colonial legacy everywhere in the world are obliged to live with.

Notes

Introduction: Postcolonializing

1 For further discussions of decolonization and postcolonialism, see Lazarus (1990), Williams and Chrisman (1994), Sekyi-Otu (1996) and Parry (1994).
2 See Hulme (1992) for a general discussion of this point; also Bishop (1990); Viswanathan (1990); Eze (1996).
3 See, for example, Quentin Skinner's fine introduction to *The Return of Grand Theory in the Social Sciences* (1985).
4 See for instance, the definitions and examples of minority discourse given in JanMohamed and Lloyd (1990).
5 See Ortner (1984); Fish (1989); Clifford and Marcus (1986); Palmer (1990).
6 This is taken from gr@pbs.port.ac.uk, 18 January 1996. It is likely to have been cross-posted several times on many Internet discussion groups, making it almost impossible to ascertain its original source.
7 I take this idea about the 'shape' of the labour market from Rouse (1991), 13.
8 See Sekyi-Otu (1996) for a fascinating discussion of the creative uses of the dialectic in Fanon's work, from which something of what I am arguing here can be glimpsed.

Chapter 1   Instrumental and Synoptic Dimensions of Interdisciplinarity

1 All this information is taken from a review of the 1997 MLA conference in the *Times Higher Educational Supplement*, 9 January 1998.
2 I deliberately add the description 'epic' to all three works to indicate their amenability to literary interpretations of a particular kind. These do not by any means exhaust any potential list that one might like to draw up, though, as is easily seen, I focus mainly on texts that have a significance for postcolonial studies.

3 There has been a serious re-evaluation of the Frankfurt School and their contributions to current theories ranging from postmodernism through to cultural studies and postcolonialism. In terms of postcolonialism, the most sustained attempt to think through the implications of Adorno has been that of Varadharajan (1995: 43, 55–66). See also Lazarus (1987) and Radhakrishnan (1990) for illuminating discussions of Adorno in the context of varied postcolonial concerns.

4 For this it is best to consult Jay (1973); Jameson (1990); Arato and Gebhardt (1997); Jarvis (1998).

5 This feature of his writings may be fruitfully discussed in terms of his idea of the non-identity between the subject and the object or of concepts and objects. The most sustained exposition of this idea is to be found in his *Negative Dialectics* (1973). But see also Martin Jay's exposition of Adorno's views on totality in general (1984); and, for a more elaborate account tracing Adorno's deployment of dialectical analyses across the full range of his work, see Jameson (1990), already cited.

6 This list is taken from Mbembe's response to his critics (1992b: 129).

7 On the limitations of such equivalence between literary texts and other domains, see Tejumola Olaniyan's critique of Mbembe in his essay in *Public Culture* 5.1 entitled 'Narrativizing Postcoloniality: Responsibilities'. Olaniyan opens his essay by first showing how texts like Soyinka's *Opera Wonyosi* seem to almost prefigure Mbembe's scatological discussion of the postcolony. But he then goes on to show the radical differences between the two writers and the weaknesses in Mbembe's dissolution of binarisms and the pursuit of equivalences between different domains in their place.

8 Bhabha's writing has drawn sharp criticism from people pursuing different methodologies. See, for example, Dirlik (1994); Lazarus (1993); JanMohamed (1985); Miyoshi (1993); Chrisman (1990); Parry (1994).

9 It has to be noted that several disciplines that have had to deal with postcolonial societies have staged some such debates between theory and practice. One of the most lively has been that taking place among African philosophers. See, for instance, Hountondji (1996) for an account of African philosophy as part of a larger system of theoretical reflections, and Serequeberhan (1994) for a discussion of the need to constitute African philosophy as a form of praxis rather than just theory.

Chapter 2 Postcolonial Historiography and the Problem of Local Knowledge

1 The essays and monographs on the subject are quite extensive. But for different emphases in the last decade alone, see Hobsbawm (1987),

on the links between metropolitan class tensions and the evolution of empire; Hyam (1990), on empire as the place where the inhibitions (particularly sexual) of bourgeois European cultures were increasingly set aside; Cain and Hopkins (1993a, 1993b) on the impact of the City of London and 'gentlemanly capitalism' on the evolution and decline of empire; Stoler (1995) on the degree to which Western sexual ideologies were dependent on debates about sexuality within empire itself; and Bayly (1996) on the links between networks of information gathering and the consolidation of empire, especially in India. As can readily be seen, these books cover a wide variety of focuses, ranging from the economic and technological to the cultural and even sexual modalities of empire.

2 The sources I draw on for my ideas on the methodology of historians are many and varied, but the main ones are Carr (1962); White (1973); LaCapra (1985); Tosh (1991); Jenkins (1991, 1995). It has to be noted that the history writing I am interested in here is the professionalized genre that traces its inspiration ultimately to von Ranke in the nineteenth century. Before the professionalization of the genre it was not always that history writing could have been said to be following the methodology I describe here.

3 See LaCapra (1985), esp. chs 1 and 3. And, for a critical evaluation of how the debate is presented in history classrooms, see Jenkins (1991), esp. chs 1–3.

4 For an assessment of some of the implications of Lord Acton's project, see Dawson (1996), 604–6.

5 See Frank (1967); Amin (1974); Rodney (1969).

6 Jim Murray, Director of The C. L. R. James Institute in Manhattan, New York, personal communication, July 1997.

7 It is important to note at this point the degree to which this type of criticism, i.e. the one that asserts that 'though you are trying to produce something different, yours is no different from that which you are differentiating yourself from', has, under the impulse of poststructuralism, become a dominant and almost axiomatic mode of cultural criticism. It is important also to see how much this method, not quite dialectical, always possesses a whiff of dialecticism but never in the service of producing a synthesis of existing ideas, but, rather, highlights the mutual contaminations of seemingly opposed ideas in the interest of undermining them. This is by no means to cast a negative light on what I think is O'Hanlon's superb analysis. However, this is a trope of criticism that itself needs to be historicized and deconstructed, and not just in postcolonial studies.

8 See Young (1990, 1995); Moore-Gilbert (1997).

9 Criticisms of Said that have paid attention to this point include Young and Bart Moore-Gilbert, already mentioned. For a more wide-ranging critique of Said, see also Ahmad (1992), ch. 5, along with MacKenzie (1995).

10   See ch. 2 of Quayson (1997). For an even more extensive and detailed discussion, see Doortmont (1994).
11   I am indebted to Karin Barber of the Centre for West African Studies in Birmingham for this brilliant metaphor about the constitution of oral materials in traditional cultures.
12   For more vigorous discussions of these points, see White (1978) and Rosaldo (1988).

Chapter 3   Literature as a Politically Symbolic Act

1   All these details are taken from Appignanesi and Maitland (1990).
2   In the first week of October 1998, while I was revising this chapter, it was announced that the Iranian government had agreed to withdraw support for the blood money on Rushdie's life. They however declined to annul the *fatwa* as this was a theological matter that was irreversible. This major concession came after massive international diplomacy. The British government, members of Article 19 and the Iranians should all be commended for this, but it still remains to be seen whether Rushdie's freedom will be constrained by the existence of the *fatwa*.
3   From a message by Ayatollah Khomeini addressed to the instructors and students of religious seminaries, *BBC Summary of World Broadcasts*, 24 February 1989, in Appignanesi and Maitland (1990).
4   The *locus classicus* of this tendency in African literary criticism is Chinweizu, Jemie and Madubuike (1980).
5   For further discussion of various deployments of ritual symbols and practices in modern-day Nigerian social life and politics, see Apter (1992), where he discusses the 1983 Nigerian elections, and Drewal (1992), where she highlights the uses of masquerade festival rituals in relocating the social standing of a 'big man' in the politics of a locality in western Nigeria. Both of these serve to expand further our notion of intermediacy.
6   See a report on Kabila in *The Times*, 12 March 1997.
7   A classic example of this would be Awoonor (1972); also Armah (1974) and Marechera (1978).
8   For more elaborate discussions of the ideas in this section see Quayson (1997), ch. 6, and Cooper (1998), ch. 4.

Chapter 4   Feminism, Postcolonialism and the Contradictory Orders of Modernity

1   Moore-Gilbert (1997) provides what I think to be the most extensive recent account of Spivak's work. See his chapter on Spivak (pp. 74–113),

where he discusses 'Three Women's Texts and a Critique of Imperialism' along with various other works by her. See also Young (1990) for the earliest extended account of her work to which most later commentators are indebted; also Childs and Williams (1997); Gandhi (1998) and Loomba (1998).

2 For various analyses of the links between different aspects of metropolitan culture and empire from urban and prison architecture through to art and mathematics, see Mitchell (1991); Mintz (1985); Wright (1991); Rabinow (1989) and Bishop (1990), among others.

3 I have modified the spelling of some words slightly to bring them in line with modern usage.

4 Ortner (1974). For an excellent discussion of Ortner's views along with those of others, see Moore (1988).

5 For a further elaboration of this point, see Mamdani (1996), where he argues that the distinction between the 'citizen' and 'subject' was critical to the formation of different classes of colonial subjects in different urban and rural settings in Africa.

6 For a sharp criticism of Spivak's idea of the speechlessness of the subaltern, see for example Parry (1987).

7 This account is taken from Harvey's handy *Oxford Companion to Classical Literature* (1994: 41–2). For a fuller discussion of the cycle of stories concerning Medea and their various mutations, especially in the medieval period, see Morse (1996).

8 For a very fascinating recent account of the complexity of ethnopolitics in Kenya, see Ndegwa (1997).

Chapter 5   Postcolonialism and Postmodernism

1 For accounts of how multiculturalism has become the preferred praxis of postmodernism, but for critical accounts, see Žižek (1997); Mercer (1992); McLaren (1994).

2 The notion of the double consciousness of the period is given full treatment across the West African region in the various essays in Farias and Barber (1990).

3 Even though there are significant differences between any putative postcolonial condition and that of African America, it is arguably the case that the history of slavery and the peripheralization of blacks in that culture make them amenable to a postcolonial analysis. For a recent discussion of this point in relation to new multicultural pedagogies, see the special issue of *Wasafiri* 27 (1998) devoted to African American literature, especially the interview with bell hooks, and the essay by Julian Murphet (1998a) on Anna Deveare Smith and the question of the staging of racial identification.

4 First broadcast on 18 October 1996; shown on BBC 1 in the UK in September 1997.

Chapter 6 Parables from the Canon:
Postcolonializing *Shakespeare*

1 For critical accounts of the dissemination of Shakespeare through educational curricula, see Hawkes (1986); Holderness (1985) and Sinfield's answer to a mock examination question on Shakespeare and education (1994).

2 The opinion was stated when he was Margaret Thatcher's Chancellor of the Exchequer in an interview with Terry Coleman (*Guardian*, 5 September 1983). For a further discussion of Lord Lawson's opinion, see Heinemann (1994).

3 I was at the University of Ibadan at the time, but my impressions on the use of Shakespeare were gleaned from the numerous political discussions I had with all manner of people, from lecturers and administrative staff right through to bus drivers. For interesting comments on the place of Shakespeare and other literary models in the formation of literate and semi-literate sensibilities in Africa, see Mazrui (1968). African stage interpretations of *Macbeth* abound; one, by Nigerian playwright Rufus Orisayomi, called *Akogun*, has Macbeth as an African tyrant. (Depending on the intonation, 'Akogun' can mean either 'he who goes out looking for battles' or 'he who teaches people how to fight'. The first meaning seems more appropriate for Macbeth). It played to audiences at London's Hackney Empire and other venues in London in 1997.

4 See Suzman (1996).

5 This interpretation of *Hamlet* is particularly associated with Yuri Lyubimov and the Taganka Theatre in Moscow. Lyubimov's production was first staged in 1972, with Hamlet played by folk singer and songwriter Vladimir Vysostki. The play opened with Vysostki playing a guitar and singing a Pasternak poem about Hamlet in the first person. The production itself had a series of 'cells' on stage, curtained off from each other to convey the idea that Elsinore was a prison. I wish to thank Jennifer Hargreaves of the BBC for inviting me to participate in a discussion on cross-cultural appropriations of *Hamlet* (African, Arab and Russian) in the spring of 1997 and for subsequently fishing out the details about the Lyubimov production.

6 *The Tempest* is particularly central to postcolonial interpretations. For a good account from a clearly postcolonial perspective, see Hulme (1992); A. and V. Vaughan provide a useful historical discussion of how the play became appropriated for postcolonial purposes (1991: 144–71). They also have a wide-ranging bibliography. For new perspectives on Othello, see Vaughan and Cartwright (1991); also Loomba and Orkin (1998).

7 All quotations are from the *Arden Shakespeare*, edited by John Russell Brown (1959).

8 See Hatlin (1980) for an interesting interpretation of this and of the implicit struggle between feudal and bourgeois concepts of value in the play.

9   Note how the July 1998 scandal about lobbyists at 10 Downing Street seriously embarrassed the UK government. These lobbyists are exemplary figures who capture the simultaneous expression of the cultural and the economic/political within a highly specialized area of public life. Crucially, however, their 'cultural' facility at networking is never supposed to be expressed as economically motivated because of the political domains in which they exercise their influence. The hypocrisy of this kind of imagined division does not bear any close examination.

10 The subtitle was 'Will World Cup Victory Heal the Wounds?' (*Guardian*, 15 July 1998).

Bibliography

Achebe, Chinua (1975). *Morning Yet on Creation Day: Essays*. Garden City, NY: Anchor Press.

Adorno, Theodor (1973). *Negative Dialectics*. New York: Seabury Press.

——(1978). *Minima Moralia: Reflections from a Damaged Life, 1951*. London: Verso.

Ahmad, Aijaz (1992). *In Theory: Classes, Nations, Literatures*. London: Verso.

——(1995). 'The Politics of Literary Postcoloniality'. *Race and Class* 36.3, 1–20.

Ahmed, Akbar S. (1992). *Postmodernism and Islam: Predicament and Promise*. London and New York: Routledge.

Amin, Shahid (1974). *Accumulation on a World Scale: A Critique of the Theory of Underdevelopment*. New York: Monthly Review Press.

——(1988). 'Gandhi as Mahatma', in *Selected Subaltern Studies*, ed. Guha and Spivak, 288–348.

Appadurai, Arjun (1986). *The Social Life of Things: Commodities in Cultural Perspective*. Cambridge: Cambridge University Press.

——(1994). 'Disjuncture and Difference in the Global Cultural Economy', in *Colonial Discourse and Postcolonial Theory*, ed. Williams and Chrisman, 305–23.

Appiah, Anthony Kwame (1992). *In My Father's House: Africa in the Philosophy of Culture*. Oxford: Oxford University Press.

Appignanesi, Lisa and Sara Maitland (1990). *The Rushdie File*. Syracuse, NY: Syracuse University Press.

Apter, Andrew (1992). *Black Critics and Kings: The Hermeneutics of Power in Yoruba Society*. Chicago: University of Chicago Press.

Arato, Andrew and Eike Gebhard (1997). *The Essential Frankfurt School Reader*. New York: Continuum.

Aravamudan, Srivanas (1989). ' "Being God's Postman is No Fun, Yaar": Salman Rushdie's *Satanic Verses*'. *Diacritics* 19.2, 3–20.

Armah, Ayi Kwei (1974). *Fragments*. Nairobi: East African Publishing House.

Ashcroft, Bill, Gareth Griffiths and Helen Tiffin, eds (1989). *The Empire Writes Back: Theory and Practice in Post-colonial Literatures*. London: Routledge.

——(1995). *The Post-colonial Studies Reader*. London: Routledge.

——(1998). *Key Concepts in Post-colonial Studies*. London and New York: Routledge.

Awoonor, Kofi (1972). *This Earth, My Brother*. London: Heinemann.

Barber, Karin (1991). *I could Speak until Tomorrow: Oríkì, Women, and the Past in a Yoruba Town*. Edinburgh: Edinburgh University Press.

——(1997). *Readings in African Popular Culture*. Bloomington: International African Institute in association with Indiana University Press.

——, John Collins and Alain Ricard (1997). *West African Popular Theatre*. Bloomington and Oxford: Indiana University Press and James Currey.

Barker, Francis, Peter Hulme and Margaret Iversen (1994). *Colonial Discourse, Postcolonial Theory*. Manchester and New York: Manchester University Press.

Bate, Jonathan (1989). *Shakespearean Constitutions: Politics, Theatre, Criticism, 1730–1830*. Oxford and New York: Clarendon Press and Oxford University Press.

Baudrillard, Jean (1983). *The Orders of Simulacra: Simulations*, trans. Paul Foss, Paul Patton and Philip Bleitchman. New York: Semiotext(e).

—— (1975). *The Mirror of Production*, trans. Mark Poster. St Louis: Telos Press.

Bayart, Jean-François (1993). *The State in Africa: The Politics of the Belly*. London: Longman.

Bayly, C. A. (1996). *Empire and Information: Intelligence Gathering and Social Communication in India, 1780–1870*. Cambridge: Cambridge University Press.

Beer, Gillian (1983). *Darwin's Plots: Evolutionary Narrative in Darwin, George Eliot and Nineteenth-Century Fiction*. London: Routledge & Kegan Paul.

Bell, Alexander (1973). *The Coming of Post-industrial Society*. New York: Basic Books.

Belsey, Catherine (1985). *The Subject of Tragedy: Identity and Difference in Renaissance Drama*. London: Methuen.

Bernal, Martin (1987). *Black Athena: The Afroasiatic Roots of Classical Civilization*. New Brunswick, NJ: Rutgers University Press.

Bhabha, Homi K. (1992). 'Postcolonial Criticism', in *Redrawing the Boundaries: The Transformation of English and American Literary Studies*, ed. S. Greenblatt and G. Dunn. New York: Modern Languages Association of America, 437–63.

——(1994). *The Location of Culture*. London: Routledge.

Bishop, Alan J. (1990). 'Western Mathematics: The Secret Weapon of Cultural Imperialism'. *Race and Class* 32.2, 51–65.

Borges, Jorge Luis (1983). *Labyrinths: Selected Stories and Other Writings*. New York: Modern Library.

Brantlinger, Patrick (1988). *Rule of Darkness: British Literature and Imperialism, 1830–1914*. Ithaca: Cornell University Press.

Cain, P. J. and A. G. Hopkins (1993a). *British Imperialism: Crisis and Deconstruction, 1914–1990*. London: Longman.
——(1993b). *British Imperialism: Innovation and Expansion, 1688–1914*. London: Longman.
Callinicos, Alex (1989). *Against Postmodernism: A Marxist Critique*. Cambridge: Polity Press.
Calvino, Italo (1978). *Invisible Cities*. New York: Harcourt Brace Jovanovich.
Carr, Edward Hallett (1962). *What is History?* New York: Knopf.
Cartelli, Thomas (1993). 'Prospero in Africa: *The Tempest* as Colonialist Text and Pretext', in *Shakespeare Reproduced*, ed. Howard and O'Connor, 99–115.
Chakrabarty, Dipesh (1992). 'Postcoloniality and the Artifice of History: Who Speaks for Indian Pasts'. *Representations* 37, 1–26.
Chatterjee, Partha (1989). 'The Nationalist Resolution of the Women's Question', in *Recasting Women*, ed. K. Sangari and S. Vaid. Delhi: Kali for Women, 233–53.
Childs, Peter and R. J. Patrick Williams (1997). *An Introductory Guide to Postcolonial Theory*. New York: Prentice-Hall.
Chinweizu (1975). *The West and the Rest of Us: White Predators, Black Slavers, and the African Elite*. New York: Random House.
——, Onwuchekwa Jemie and Ihechukwu Madubuike (1980). *Toward the Decolonization of African Literature*. Washington: Howard University Press.
Chrisman, Laura (1990). 'The Imperial Unconscious? Representations of Imperial Discourse'. *Critical Quarterly* 32.3, 38–58.
Clifford, James and George E. Marcus (1986). *Writing Culture: The Poetics and Politics of Ethnography*. Berkeley: University of California Press.
Cohen, Walter (1982). 'The Merchant of Venice and the Possibilities of Historical Criticism'. *ELH* 49, 765–79.
——(1993). 'Political Criticism of Shakespeare', in *Shakespeare Reproduced*, ed. Howard and O'Connor, 18–46.
Colman, George, Jnr (1787). *Inkle and Yarico: An Opera, in Three Acts*. London: G. G. J. and J. Robinson.
Connor, Steven (1997). *Postmodernist Culture: An Introduction to Theories of the Contemporary*. Oxford: Blackwell.
Cooper, Brenda (1998). *Magical Realism in West African Fiction: Seeing with a Third Eye*. London: Routledge.
Daniels, Anthony (1998). 'The Third World in Britain'. *Spectator* (London), 18 April.
Dawson, Christopher (1996). 'The Relevance of European History'. *History Today* 6.9, 606–15.
Dirlik, Arif (1994). 'The Postcolonial Aura: Third World Criticism in the Age of Global Capitalism'. *Critical Inquiry* 20.2, 328–56.
Dollimore, Jonathan and Alan Sinfield (1994). *Political Shakespeare: Essays in Cultural Materialism*. Manchester: Manchester University Press.

Doortmont, Michael (1994). 'Recapturing the Past: Samuel Johnson and One Construction of the History of the Yorubas'. Ph.D. diss., Erasmus University, Rotterdam.

Drakakis, John ed. (1985). *Alternative Shakespeares*. London: Methuen.

Drewal, Margaret (1992). *Yoruba Ritual: Performers, Play, Agency*. Bloomington: Indiana University Press.

Du Bois, W. E. B. (1997). 'The Souls of Black Folk', in *The Norton Anthology of African American Literature*, ed. Henry Louis Gates, Jnr and N. Y. McKay. New York: W. W. Norton and Co.

Eagleton, Terry (1990). *The Ideology of the Aesthetic*. Oxford: Blackwell.

——(1996). *Literary Theory: An Introduction*. Oxford: Blackwell.

——(1997). *The Illusions of Postmodernism*. Oxford: Blackwell.

Ekpo, Denis (1995). 'Towards a Post-Africanism: Contemporary African Thought and Postmodernism'. *Textual Practice* 9.1, 121–35.

Empson, William (1947). *Seven Types of Ambiguity*. London: Chatto and Windus.

Euripides (1963). *Medea and Other Plays*, trans. Philip Vellacott. Harmondsworth: Penguin.

Eze, Emmanuel (1997). 'The Colour of Reason: The Idea of "Race" in Kant's Anthropology', in *Postcolonial African Philosophy: A Critical Reader*, ed. Emmanuel Eze. Oxford: Blackwell, 103–40.

Fanon, Frantz (1961). *The Wretched of the Earth*, trans. Constance Farrington. Harmondsworth: Penguin, 1967.

——(1967). *Black Skin, White Masks*, trans. Charles Lam Markham. New York: Grove Press.

Farias, P. F. de Moraes and Karin Barber (1990). *Self-assertion and Brokerage: Early Cultural Nationalism in West Africa*. Birmingham: Centre of West African Studies.

Fish, Stanley Eugene (1989). *Doing What Comes Naturally: Change, Rhetoric, and the Practice of Theory in Literary and Legal Studies*. Durham, NC: Duke University Press.

Fishman, Joshua A., Charles Albert Ferguson and Jyotirindra Dasgupta (1968). *Language Problems of Developing Nations*. New York: Wiley.

Frank, Andre Gunder (1967). *Capitalism and Underdevelopment in Latin America: Historical Studies of Chile and Brazil*. New York: Monthly Review Press.

Gandhi, Leela (1998). *Postcolonial Theory: A Critical Introduction*. Edinburgh: Edinburgh University Press.

Geertz, Clifford (1983). *Local Knowledge: Further Essays in Interpretive Anthropology*. New York: Basic Books.

Ghosh, Amitav (1992). *In an Antique Land*. London: Granta.

Gilman, Sandra (1993). *Freud, Race, Gender*. Princeton: Princeton University Press.

Gilroy, Beryl (1996). *Inkle and Yarico*. Leeds: Peepal Tree.

Gobineau, Joseph Arthur, comte de (1853). *Essai sur l'inégalité des races humaines*, 4 vols. Paris: Firmin Didot.

Greenblatt, Stephen (1990). 'Marlowe, Marx, and Anti-Semitism', in *Learning to Curse: Essays in Early Modern Culture*. London: Routledge, 40–58.

Guha, Ranajit and Gayatri Chakravorty Spivak (1988). *Selected Subaltern Studies*. New York: Oxford University Press.

Gyan Prakash (1990). 'Writing Post-Orientalist Histories of the Third World: Perspectives from Indian Historiography'. *Comparative Studies in Society and History* 32.1, 383–408.

Hall, Stuart (1980). 'Race, Articulation and Societies Structured in Dominance', in *Sociological Theories: Race and Colonialism*. Paris: UNESCO Publishing.

——(1996). 'When was "the Postcolonial"? Thinking at the limit', in *The Post-colonial Question: Common Skies, Divided Horizons*, ed. Iain Chambers and Lidia Curti. London: Routledge, 242–60.

Harvey, David (1989). *The Condition of Postmodernity*. Oxford: Blackwell.

Harvey, Paul (1994). *The Oxford Companion to Classical Literature*. Oxford: Oxford University Press.

Hassan, Ihab (1985). 'The Culture of Postmodernism'. *Theory, Culture and Society* 2.3, 119–32.

Hatlin, Burton (1980). 'Feudal and Bourgeois Concepts of Value in *The Merchant of Venice*', in *Shakespeare: Contemporary Critical Approaches*, ed. Harry R. Garvin. London: Associated University Press, 91–105.

Hawkes, Terence (1985). 'Swisser-Swatter: Making a Man of English Letters', in *Alternative Shakespeares*, ed. Drakakis, 26–46.

——(1986). *That Shakespeherian Rag: Essays on a Critical Process*. London and New York: Methuen.

Heinemann, Margot (1994). 'How Brecht Read Shakespeare', in *Political Shakespeare*, ed. Dollimore and Sinfield, 226–54.

Hobsbawm, E. J. (1987). *The Age of Empire, 1875–1914*. New York: Pantheon Books.

Holderness, Graham (1985). *Shakespeare's History*. Dublin and New York: Gill and Macmillan, and St Martin's Press.

Holub, Robert C. (1995). 'Fragmentary Totalities and Totalized Fragments: On the Politics of Anti-systemic Thought', in *Postmodern Pluralism and Concepts of Totality*, ed. J. Hermand. New York: Peter Lang, 83–104.

hooks, bell (1994). *Teaching to Transgress: Education as the Practice of Freedom*. London: Routledge.

Horkheimer, Max and Theodor W. Adorno (1972). *Dialectic of Enlightenment*. New York: Seabury Press.

Hountondji, Paulin J. (1996). *African Philosophy: Myth and Reality*. Bloomington: Indiana University Press.

Howard, Jean E. and Marion F. O'Connor, eds (1987). *Shakespeare Reproduced: The Text in History and Ideology*. New York: Methuen.

Hulme, Peter (1992). *Colonial Encounters: Europe and the Native Caribbean, 1492–1797*. London: Routledge.

Hutcheon, Linda (1988). *A Poetics of Postmodernism: History, Theory, Fiction*. London: Routledge.
—— (1989). 'Circling the Downpost of Empire'. *Ariel* 20.4, 149–75. Reprinted in *The Post-colonial Studies Reader*, ed. Ashcroft, Griffiths and Tiffin, 130–5.
Hyam, Ronald (1990). *Empire and Sexuality: The British Experience*. Manchester: Manchester University Press.
James, C. L. R. (1993). *Beyond a Boundary*. London: Serpent's Tail.
—— and Anna Grimshaw (1992). *The C. L. R. James Reader*. Oxford: Blackwell.
——, Anna Grimshaw and Keith Hart (1993). *American Civilization*. Oxford: Blackwell.
Jameson, Frederic (1981). *The Political Unconscious: Narrative as a Socially Symbolic Act*. London: Methuen.
—— (1986). 'Third World Literature in the Era of Multinational Capitalism'. *Social Text*, 65–86.
—— (1990). *Late Marxism: Adorno, or, The Persistence of the Dialectic*. London and New York: Verso.
—— (1991). *Postmodernism, or, The Cultural Logic of Late Capitalism*. London: Verso.
JanMohamed, Abdul (1985). 'The Economy of Manichean Allegory: The Function of Racial Difference in Colonialist Literature'. *Critical Inquiry* 12.1, 59–87. Reprinted in *The Post-colonial Studies Reader*, ed. Ashcroft, Griffiths and Tiffin, 18–23.
—— and David Lloyd (1990). *The Nature and Context of Minority Discourse*. New York: Oxford University Press.
Jarvis, Simon (1998). *Adorno*. Cambridge: Polity Press.
Jay, Martin (1973). *The Dialectical Imagination: A history of the Frankfurt School and the Institute of Social Research, 1923–1950*. London: Heinemann.
—— (1984). *Marxism and Totality: The Adventures of a Concept from Lukács to Habermas*. Cambridge: Polity Press.
—— (1992). 'The Aesthetic Ideology as Ideology, or What Does it Mean to Aestheticize Politics'. *Cultural Critique* 21, 41–61.
Jencks, Charles (1980). *Late Modern Architecture*. London: Academy Editions.
Jenkins, Keith (1991). *Re-thinking History*. London: Routledge.
—— (1995). *On 'What is History?': From Carr and Elton to Rorty and White*. London: Routledge.
Jeyifo, Biodun (1990). 'For Chinua Achebe: The Resilience of Obierika', in *Chinua Achebe: A Celebration*, ed. Kirstin Holst Petersen and Anna Rutherford. Oxford and Plymouth, NH: Heinemann and Dangaroo, 51–70.
Johnson, the Revd Samuel (1920). *The History of the Yorubas: From the Earliest Times to the Beginning of the British Protectorate*. London: CMS.
Jones, Norman L. (1989). *God and the Moneylenders: Usury and Law in Early Modern England*. Oxford: Blackwell.

Kellner, Douglas (1995). *Media Culture: Cultural Studies, Identity and Politics between the Modern and the Postmodern.* London: Routledge.

Kennedy, Dane (1996). 'Imperial History and Postcolonial Theory'. *Journal of Imperial and Commonwealth History* 24.3, 345–63.

Kermode, Frank (1967). *The Sense of an Ending.* Oxford: Oxford University Press.

Kirk-Greene, A. H. M. (1991). 'His Eternity, His Eccentricity, or His Exemplarity?' *African Affairs* 90, 163–88.

Klein, Julie Thompson (1990). *Interdisciplinarity: History, Theory, Practice.* Detroit: Wayne State University Press.

Kristeva, Julia (1977). *About Chinese Women,* trans. Anita Barrows. London: Boyars.

LaCapra, Dominick (1985). *History and Criticism.* Ithaca: Cornell University Press.

Lauter, Paul (1991). *Canons and Contexts.* Oxford: Oxford University Press.

Laver, Ross and Paula Kaihla (1995). 'I Share My Husband with Seven Other Wives'. *Marie Claire* (November), 44–50.

Law, Robin (1976). 'Early Yoruba Historiography'. *History in Africa* 3, 69–89.

Lazarus, Neil (1987). 'Modernism and Modernity: T. W. Adorno and Contemporary South African Literature'. *Cultural Critique,* 131–56.

——(1990). *Resistance in Postcolonial African Fiction.* New Haven: Yale University Press.

——(1993). 'Disavowing Decolonization: Fanon, Nationalism, and the Problematic of Representation in Current Theories of Colonial Discourse'. *Research in African Literatures* 24.4, 69–98.

——(1999). *Nationalism and Cultural Practice in the Postcolonial World.* Cambridge: Cambridge University Press.

Loomba, Ania (1998). *Colonialism–Postcolonialism.* London: Routledge.

——and Martin Orkin, eds (1998). *Post-colonial Shakespeares.* London: Routledge.

Lyotard, Jean-François (1984). *The Postmodern Condition: A Report on Knowledge.* Manchester: Manchester University Press.

McClintock, Anne (1994). 'The Angel of Progress: Pitfalls of the Term "Postcolonial"', in *Colonial Discourse and Postcolonial Theory,* ed. Williams and Chrisman, 291–304.

——(1995). *Imperial Leather: Race, Gender and Sexuality in the Colonial Contest.* London: Routledge.

McHale, Brian (1987). *Postmodernist Fiction.* New York: Methuen.

MacKenzie, John M. (1995). *Orientalism: History, Theory, and the Arts.* Manchester and New York: Manchester University Press.

McLaren, Peter (1994). 'White Terror and Oppositional Agency: Towards a Critical Multiculturalism', in *Multiculturalism: A Critical Reader,* ed. D. T. Goldberg. Oxford: Blackwell, 45–74.

Mamdani, Mahmood (1996). *Citizen and Subject: Contemporary Africa and the Legacy of Late Colonialism.* Princeton: Princeton University Press.

Mani, Lata (1989). 'Contentious Traditions: The Debate on Sati in Colonial India', in *Recasting Women*, ed. K. Sangari and S. Vaid. Delhi: Kali for Women, 88–126.

Mann, Kristin (1985). *Marrying Well: Marriage, Status, and Social Change among the Educated Elite in Colonial Lagos*. Cambridge: Cambridge University Press.

Marechera, Dambudzo (1978). *House of Hunger: Short Stories*. London: Heinemann Educational.

Mazrui, Ali A. (1968). 'Some Sociopolitical Functions of English Literature in Africa', in *Language Problems in Developing Countries*, ed. Joshua A. Fishman, Charles Ferguson and Jyotirinda Das Gupta. New York: Wiley, 183–97.

Mbembe, Achille (1992a). 'The Banality of Power and the Aesthetics of Vulgarity in the Postcolony'. *Public Culture* 4.2, 1–30.

——(1992b). 'Prosaics of Servitude and Authoritarian Civilities'. *Public Culture* 5.1, 123–45.

——(1992c). 'Provisional Notes on the African Postcolony'. *Africa* 62, 3–37.

Mercer, Kobena (1992). '"1968": Periodizing Postmodern Politics and Identity', in *Cultural Studies*, ed. L. Grossberg, C. Nelson and P. Treichler. London: Routledge, 424–37.

Metscher, Thomas (1979). 'Literature and Art as Ideological Form'. *NLH* 11, 21–39.

Mintz, Sidney W. (1985). *Sweetness and Power: The Place of Sugar in Modern History*. New York and Harmondsworth: Penguin.

Mishra, V. and B. Hodge (1991). 'What is Post(-)colonialism?' *Textual Practice* 5.3, 399–415.

Mitchell, Timothy (1988). *Colonising Egypt*. Cambridge: Cambridge University Press.

Miyoshi, Masao (1993). 'A Borderless World? From Colonialism to Transnationalism and the Decline of the Nation-State'. *Critical Inquiry* 19, 726–51.

Mohanty, Chandra Talpade (1994). 'Under Western Eyes: Feminist Scholarship and Colonial Discourses', in *Colonial Discourse and Postcolonial Theory*, ed. Williams and Chrisman, 196–220.

Moody, A. D. (1964). *Shakespeare: The Merchant of Venice*. Edward Arnold.

Moore, Henrietta L. (1988). *Feminism and Anthropology*. Minneapolis: University of Minnesota Press.

Moore-Gilbert, Bart (1997). *Postcolonial Theory: Contexts, Practices, Politics*. London: Verso.

Morrison, Toni (1993). *The Bluest Eye*. New York: Knopf.

Morse, Ruth (1996). *The Medieval Medea*. Woodbridge: D. S. Brewer.

Mudimbe, V. Y. (1988). *The Invention of Africa: Gnosis, Philosophy, and the Order of Knowledge*. Bloomington: Indiana University Press.

Murphet, Julian (1998a). 'Identity and Difference in Anna Deveare Smith's Performance Art'. *Wasafiri* 27, 29–34.

——(1998b). 'Noir and the Racial Unconscious'. *Screen* 39.1, 22–35.

Nandy, Ashis (1983). *The Intimate Enemy: Loss and Recovery of Self under Colonialism*. Delhi and Oxford: Oxford University Press.

Natoli, Joseph (1997). *A Primer to Postmodernity*. Oxford: Blackwell.

Ndegwa, Stephen (1997). 'Citizenship and Ethnicity: An Examination of Two Transition Moments in Kenyan Politics'. *American Political Science Review* 91.3 (September), 599–616.

Nhlapo, Ronald Thandabantu (1998). 'Democratization and Women's Rights in the South African Constitution: The Challenge of African Customary Law', in *World Culture Report: Culture, Creativity and Markets*. Paris: UNESCO Publishing, 132–3.

Nnaemeka, Obioma (1997). *The Politics of (M)othering: Womanhood, Identity, and Resistance in African Literature*. London: Routledge.

Nzegwu, Nkiru (1996). 'Questions of Identity and Inheritance: A Critical Review of Kwame Anthony Appiah's *In My Father's House*'. *Hypatia* 11.1, 175–201.

Obeyesekere, Gananath (1992). *The Apotheosis of Captain Cook: European Mythmaking in the Pacific*. Princeton: Princeton University Press.

O'Hanlon, Rosalind (1988). 'Recovering the Subject: *Subaltern Studies* and Histories of Resistance in Colonial South Asia'. *Modern Asian Studies* 22.1, 189–224.

——and David Washbrook. (1992). 'After Orientalism: Culture, Criticism, and Politics in the Third World'. *Comparative Studies in Society and History* 34.1, 141–67.

Okri, Ben (1991). *The Famished Road*. London: Jonathan Cape.

——(1993). *Songs of Enchantment*. London: Vintage.

Olaniyan, Tejumola (1992). 'Narrativizing Postcoloniality: Responsibilities'. *Public Culture* 5.1, 47–55.

Oppong, Christine (1981). *Middle Class African Marriage: A Family Study of Ghanaian Senior Civil Servants*. Cambridge: Cambridge University Press.

Ortner, Sherry B. (1974). 'Is Female to Male what Nature is to Culture?', in *Woman, Culture, and Society*, ed. Renato Rosaldo, Michelle Zimbalist, Louise Lamphere and Joan Bamberger. Stanford: Stanford University Press.

——(1984). 'Theory in Anthropology since the Sixties'. *Comparative Studies in Society and History* 26.1, 126–66.

Oruka, Odera (1990). *Sage Philosophy: Indigenous Thinkers and Modern Debate on African Philosophy*. Leiden and New York: E. J. Brill.

Otieno, Wambui Waiyaki and Cora Ann Presley (1998). *Mau Mau's Daughter: A Life History*. Boulder: Lynne Rienner Publishers.

Palmer, Bryan D. (1990). *Descent into Discourse: The Reification of Language and the Writing of Social History*. Philadelphia: Temple University Press.

Parker, Patricia and Geoffrey H. Hartman, eds (1990). *Shakespeare and the Question of Theory*. New York: Methuen.

Parris, Matthew (1998). ' It's Good to be Needed'. *The Times*, 9 January.

Parry, Benita (1987). 'Problems in Current Theories of Colonial Discourse'. *Oxford Literary Review* 9.1, 2. Reprinted in *The Postcolonial Studies Reader*, ed. Ashcroft, Griffiths and Tiffin, 36–44.

—— (1994). 'Signs of Our Times'. *Third Text* 28, 5–45.

—— (1997). 'The Postcolonial: Conceptual Category or Chimera?' *Yearbook of English Studies* 27, 3–21.

Pateman, Carole (1988). *The Sexual Contract*. Cambridge: Polity Press.

Peel, J. D. Y. (1989). 'The Cultural Work of Yoruba Ethnogenesis', in *History and Ethnicity*, ed. Elizabeth Tonkin, Maryon McDonald and Malcolm Chapman. London: Routledge, 198–215.

Prakash, Gyan (1990). 'Writing Post-Orientalist Histories of the Third World: Perspectives from Indian Historiography'. *Comparative Studies in Society and History* 32.1, 383–408.

Pratt, Mary Louise (1992). *Imperial Eyes: Travel Writing and Transculturation*. London: Routledge.

Quayson, Ato (1997). *Strategic Transformations in Nigerian Writing: Orality and History in the Work of Rev. Samuel Johnson, Amos Tutuola, Wole Soyinka and Ben Okri*. Oxford and Bloomington: James Currey and Indiana University Press.

Rabinow, Paul (1989). *French Modern: Norms and Forms of the Social Environment*. Cambridge, MA: MIT Press.

Radhakrishnan, R. (1990). 'The Changing Subject and Politics of Theory'. *Differences* 2.2, 126–52.

Raja, Rao (1938). *Kanthapura*. London: George Allen & Unwin.

Rajan, Rajeswari Sunder (1997). 'The Third World Academic in Other Places: or, The Postcolonial Intellectual Revisited'. *Critical Inquiry* 23, 597–616.

Rattansi, Ali (1997). 'Postcolonialism and its Discontents'. *Economy and Society* 26.4, 480–500.

Rodney, Walter (1969). *How Europe Underdeveloped Africa*. Washington: Howard University Press.

Ropo, Sekoni (1997). 'Politics and Urban Folklore in Nigeria', in *Readings in African Popular Culture*, ed. Karin Barber. Bloomington and Oxford: Indiana University Press and James Currey, 142–5.

Rosaldo, Renato (1988). 'Doing Oral History'. *Social Analysis* 4, 89–99.

Rothschild, Joseph (1981). *Ethnopolitics: A Conceptual Framework*. New York: Columbia University Press.

Rouse, Roger (1991). 'Mexican Migration and the Social Space of Postmodernism'. *Diaspora* 1.1, 8–23.

Rushdie, Salman (1989). *The Satanic Verses*. New York: Viking.

Ryan, Kiernan (1995). *Shakespeare*. London: Harvester Wheatsheaf.

Sahlins, Marshall David (1995). *How 'Natives' Think: About Captain Cook, for Example*. Chicago: University of Chicago Press.

Said, Edward (1978). *Orientalism*. London: Chatto and Windus.

—— (1981). *Covering Islam: How the Media and the Experts Determine How We See the Rest of the World*. New York: Pantheon Books.

—— (1983). *The World, the Text, and the Critic*. Cambridge, MA: Harvard University Press.

—— (1993). *Culture and Imperialism*. London: Vintage.

—— (1997). *Covering Islam: How the Media and the Experts Determine How We See the Rest of the World*. London: Vintage.

San Juan, E. (1998). *Beyond Postcolonial Theory*. New York: St Martin's Press.

Sangari, Kunkum (1987). 'The Politics of the Possible'. *Cultural Critique* 7, 157–86. Reprinted in *The Postcolonial Studies Reader*, ed. Ashcroft, Griffiths and Tiffin, 143–50.

—— and Sudesh Vaid (1990). *Recasting Women: Essays in Indian Colonial History*. New Brunswick, NJ: Rutgers University Press.

Sardar, Ziauddin and Merryl Wyn Davies (1990). *Distorted Imagination: Lessons from the Rushdie Affair*. London and Kuala Lumpur: Grey Seal and Berita.

Saro-Wiwa, Ken (1985). *Sozaboy*. Port Harcourt: Saros International Publishers.

—— (1987). *Basi and Company: A Modern African Folktale*. Port Harcourt: Saros International Publishers.

Sekyi, Kobina (1974). *The Blinkards*. London: Heinemann.

Sekyi-Otu, Ato (1996). *Fanon's Dialectic of Experience*. Cambridge, MA: Harvard University Press.

Serequeberhan, Tsenay (1994). *The Hermeneutics of African Philosophy: Horizon and Discourse*. London: Routledge.

Shapiro, James S. (1996). *Shakespeare and the Jews*. New York: Columbia University Press.

Shohat, Ella (1993). 'Notes on the Postcolonial'. *Social Text* 31/2, 99–113.

Sinfield, Alan (1994). 'Give an Account of Shakespeare and Education, showing Why you Think they are Effective and What you have Appreciated about Them. Support your Comments with Precise References', in *Political Shakespeare*, ed. Dollimore and Sinfield, 182–205.

Sinha, Mrinalini (1995). *Colonial Masculinity: The 'Manly Englishman' and the 'Effeminate Bengali' in the Late Nineteenth Century*. Manchester: Manchester University Press.

Skinner, Quentin (1985). *The Return of Grand Theory in the Human Sciences*. Cambridge: Cambridge University Press.

Slemon, Stephen (1994). 'The Scramble for Post-colonialism', in *The Postcolonial Studies Reader*, ed. Ashcroft, Griffiths and Tiffin, 45–52.

—— (1995). 'Magic Realism as Postcolonial Discourse', in *Magic Realism: Theory, History, Community*, ed. Lois Parkinson Zamora and Wendy B. Faris. Durham, NC: Duke University Press.

Sombart, W. (1967). *Luxury in Capitalism*. Ann Arbor: University of Michigan Press.

Soyinka, Wole (1976). *Myth, Literature and the African World*. Cambridge: Cambridge University Press.

Spivak, Gayatri (1981). 'French Feminism in an International Frame'. *Yale French Studies* 62, 154–84.

——(1985). 'Three Women's Texts and a Critique of Imperialism'. *Critical Inquiry* 12.1, 243–61. Reprinted in *The Postcolonial Studies Reader*, ed. Ashcroft, Griffiths and Tiffin, 269–72.

——(1987). *In Other Worlds: Essays in Cultural Politics*. New York: Methuen.

——(1988). 'Can the Subaltern Speak', in *Colonial Discourse and Post-colonial Theory*, ed. Williams and Chrisman, 66–111.

——(1993). *Outside in the Teaching Machine*. New York: Routledge.

——, Donna Landry and Gerald M. MacLean (1996). *The Spivak Reader: Selected Works of Gayatri Chakravorty Spivak*. New York: Routledge.

Stam, Robert and Ella Shohat (1994). 'Contested Histories: Eurocentrism, Multiculturalism, and the Media', in *Multiculturalism: A Critical Reader*, ed. David Theo Goldberg. Oxford: Blackwell.

Stoler, Ann Laura (1995). *Race and the Education of Desire: Foucault's History of Sexuality and the Colonial Order of Things*. Durham, NC: Duke University Press.

Strathern, Marilyn (1991). *Partial Connections*. Savage, MD: Rowman & Littlefield Publishers.

Stratton, Florence (1994). *Contemporary African Literature and the Politics of Gender*. London: Routledge.

Suzman, Janet (1996). 'Othello in Africa' and 'Africa in Othello'. *The Tanner Lectures on Human Values*, No. 17. Salt Lake City: University of Utah Press.

Tharu, Susie J. and K. Lalita (1991). *Women Writing in India: 600 B.C. to the Present*. London: Pandora.

Thomas, Nicholas (1994). *Colonialism's Culture: Anthropology, Travel and Government*. Cambridge: Polity Press.

Tiffin, Helen (1988). 'Post-colonialism, Post-modernism and the Rehabilitation of Post-colonial History'. *Journal of Commonwealth Literature* 23.1, 169–81.

Tosh, John (1991). *The Pursuit of History: Aims, Methods, and New Directions in the Study of Modern History*. London and New York: Longman.

Vail, Leroy and Landeg White (1991). *Power and the Praise Poem: Southern African Voices in History*. Charlottesville and London: University of Virginia Press and James Currey.

Van Onselen, Charles (1996). *The Seed is Mine: The life of Kas Maine, a South African Sharecropper, 1894–1985*. Oxford: James Currey.

Varadharajan, Asha (1995). *Exotic Parodies: Subjectivity in Adorno, Said and Spivak*. Minneapolis: University of Minnesota Press.

Vaughan, Alden T. and Virginia Mason Vaughan (1991). *Shakespeare's Caliban: A Cultural History*. Cambridge: Cambridge University Press.

Vaughan, Virginia Mason and Kent Cartwright (1991). *Othello: New Perspectives*. London: Associated University Presses.

——and Alden T. Vaughan (1998). *Critical Essays on Shakespeare's The Tempest*. London: Prentice-Hall.

Veeser, Aram (1989). *The New Historicism*. London: Routledge.

Viswanathan, Gauri (1990). *Masks of Conquest: Literary Studies and British Rule in India*. London: Faber.

Visweswaran, Kamala (1994). *Fictions of Feminist Ethnography.* Minneapolis: University of Minnesota Press.

Wa Thiongo, Ngugi (1986). *Decolonizing the Mind.* London: James Currey.

Watson, Ruth (1998). 'The Cloth of Field of Gold: Material Culture and Civic Power in Colonial Ibadan, 1900–1936'. *Journal of Historical Sociology* 11.4.

White, Hayden V. (1973). *Metahistory: The Historical Imagination in Nineteenth-Century Europe.* Baltimore: Johns Hopkins University Press.

—— (1978). 'The Irrational and the Problem of Historical Knowledge in the Enlightenment', in *Tropics of Discourse.* Baltimore: Johns Hopkins University Press, 135–49.

Wilkinson, Jane (1992). *Talking With African Writers.* London: Heinemann.

Williams, Patrick and Laura Chrisman (1994). *Colonial Discourse and Post-colonial Theory: A Reader.* London: Harvester Wheatsheaf.

Williams, Raymond (1977). *Marxism and Literature.* Oxford: Oxford University Press.

Wright, Gwendolyn (1991). *The Politics of Design in French Colonial Urbanism.* Chicago: University of Chicago Press.

Young, Robert (1990). *White Mythologies: Writing History and the West.* London: Routledge.

—— (1995a). *Colonial Desire: Hybridity in Theory, Culture and Race.* London: Routledge.

—— (1995b). 'Foucault on Race and Colonialism'. *New Formations* 25, 57–65.

Zizek, Slavoj (1991). *Looking Awry: An Introduction to Jacques Lacan through Popular Culture.* Cambridge, MA: MIT Press.

—— (1997). 'Multiculturalism, or, The Cultural Logic of Multinational Capitalism'. *New Left Review*, 22.5, 29–51.

Index

Printed in Great Britain
by Amazon